CARLOS FUENTES

CARLOS FUENTES

Wendy B. Faris

FREDERICK UNGAR PUBLISHING CO.
NEW YORK

Portions of this work have appeared in *Review* 29
(May/August 1981, Center for Inter-American Relations,
New York City); *Latin American Literary Review,* Volume
10, No. 19, Fall/Winter 1981; and *Comparative Literature
Studies,* Vol. 19, No. 2, Summer, 1982, published by
University of Illinois Press, © 1982 by the Board of Trustees
of the University of Illinois; *World Literature Today,* Carlos
Fuentes Issue, Fall, 1983.

Library of Congress Cataloging in Publication Data

Faris, Wendy B.
    Carlos Fuentes.

    (Literature and life series)
    Bibliography: p.
    Includes index.
    1. Fuentes, Carlos—Criticism and interpretation.
I. Title.   II. Series.
PQ7297.F793Z64   1982   863   82–40281
ISBN 0–8044–2193–5

For
D. E. F.
and
L. P. Z.

Acknowledgments

Many thanks to the following friends, relatives, colleagues, and strangers for help and encouragement of all kinds: Robert and Nancy Bush, Joaquín Diez Canedo, David Faris, Avrom Fleishman, Jean Franco, Carlos Fuentes, Juan Loveluck, Patricia Merivale, Stephen Rabe, Richard Reeve, Gustavo Sainz, Jaime García Terrés, Janet and Steven Walker, Shirley Williams, Philip Winsor, Michael Wood, and Lois Zamora. I am grateful to the National Endowment for the Humanities for a Summer Stipend which permitted me to work on this project, and to support from the Colgate University Faculty Research Council.

Contents

Preface

In this introduction to the writings of Carlos Fuentes, I have concentrated primarily on close analysis of individual works. For me, the particular strength of Fuentes's texts lies in their complex conceptual structure and the brilliant images that reinforce their form. The mirror images in *The Death of Artemio Cruz,* for example, "reflect" the mirrorlike structure of the narrative; the treatment of eyes in *Where the Air is Clear* underscores that novel's central alternation between visible and invisible worlds. My primary aim, then, has been to reveal how structures and images produce compelling ensembles. To this end, I have provided essentially self-contained analyses of individual works so that the reader may consult sections of this study individually.

Even so, throughout these analyses I indicate a number of elements that characterize Fuentes's work as a whole or particular areas of concern within it. Beyond this general sense of continuity, my principal *fil conducteur* is the idea of the "multivocal text" as it reflects a many-layered country and a complex contemporary world. By this I mean that Fuentes's writings show a striking capacity to absorb, transform, and transmit multiple voices. This general capacity varies with the particular ideological structure and imagery of the individual works. I have focused on this aspect of Fuentes's texts because it is central to them and also because it may be initially confusing to the reader. I investigate relevant multivocal techniques as I analyze the individual works and then take up the implications of these techniques in the final chapter.

In my discussions of Fuentes's works, I stress analysis rather than assessment of value. My own preference for *Where the Air is Clear* and *The Death of Artemio Cruz* is implicit in the amount of space I devote to them. I believe that they are still the most widely read of Fuentes's novels, particularly in this country, and that they have had a significant influence on other Latin American writers.

Finally, Fuentes is a perceptive critic of his own work and of the work of other writers. That is why I refer frequently to his criticism and interviews. They are unusually helpful in understanding his texts.

Note on translations: I have quoted from English translations when they exist, since these are most accessible to English-speaking readers. In some cases (most notably in *A Change of Skin*), the translations differ from the original Spanish; but in all cases I have checked the English version against the Spanish to assure similarity in meaning. All other translations are mine.

Chronology

1928   Born on November 11 in Panama City, son of Rafael Fuentes Boettiger and Berta Macías Rivas.

1929–34   Lives in Panama City, Quito, Montevideo, and Rio de Janeiro, where his father occupies various diplomatic posts.

1934–40   Lives in Washington, D.C., where his father serves as Counselor of the Mexican Embassy. Attends the Henry D. Cooke public school there. Summer trips to Mexico.

1941–43   Lives in Santiago and Buenos Aires with his family. First articles and short stories published in the *Boletín del Instituto Nacional de Chile*.

1944   Returns to Mexico, where his father serves as director of protocol in the Ministry of Foreign Affairs.

1946   Graduates from the Colegio México (high school) in Mexico City.

1947–49   Attends the Colegio Francés Morelos (French preparatory school). Short stories published in the reviews *Mañana* and *Ideas de México*.

1950   Attends the Institute for International Studies in Geneva.

1951   Serves as Press Secretary for the United Nations Information Center in Mexico City. Enters the law school of the National University of Mexico (UNAM).

1953   Helps edit the *Universidad de México* journal. Serves as Secretary for Cultural Affairs at the National University.

1954   Publishes his first book, *Los días enmascarados (The Masked Days)*, a collection of short stories. Begins to contribute columns on literature, the other arts, and politics to newspapers and journals in Mexico and abroad. Serves as Assistant Press Secretary at the Ministry of Foreign Affairs.

1956   Founds and edits the *Revista Mexicana de Literatura* with the writer Emmanuel Carballo. Fellow at the Centro Mexicano de Escritores (working on *Where the Air is Clear*).

1957   Head of the Department of Cultural Relations at the Ministry of Foreign Affairs.

1958   Publishes his first novel, *Where the Air is Clear.*

1959   Publishes *The Good Conscience* (novel). Marries the actress Rita Macedo. Resigns from the diplomatic service. Travels to Cuba immediately following the success of the Cuban revolution. Collaborates with Víctor Flores Olea, Enrique González Pedrero, and others in founding *El Espectador* in Mexico.

1960   Serves on the jury for the Casa de las Américas literary competition in Havana.

1961   Travels to Czechoslovakia and Holland, where his father is the Mexican ambassador.

Travels to Cuba as a delegate to the Congress for Solidarity with Cuba.

1962   Publishes *The Death of Artemio Cruz* (novel) and *Aura* (novella). Daughter Cecilia born.

1963   Participates in the Conference of Unaligned Countries in Belgrade.

1964   Publishes *Cantar de ciegos* (*Songs of the Blind;* short stories).

1965–66   Helps found the Siglo XXI publishing house. Begins work on a novel called *Renaissance*— eventually *Terra Nostra*. Lives in Paris.

1967   Publishes *A Change of Skin* (novel) and receives the Biblioteca Breve prize for it from the publisher Seix Barral in Barcelona. The novel is subsequently banned from publication in Spain. Publishes *Holy Place* (novel). Serves on the jury of the Venice Film Festival.

1968   Lives in London and Paris. Publishes *París, la revolución de mayo* (*Paris, the May Revolution;* essay) and *Líneas para Adami* (*Lines for Adami;* essay). Visits Czechoslovakia with Julio Cortázar and Gabriel García Márquez. Collaborates with François Reichenbach on the film *México, México*.

1969   Moves back to Mexico. Publishes *Cumpleaños* (*Birthday;* novella), *The World of José Luis Cuevas* (essay), and *La nueva novela hispanoamericana* (*The New Hispanic American Novel;* essay). Divorced from Rita Macedo.

1970   Publishes *Casa con dos puertas* (*House with Two Doors;* essays), *El Tuerto es rey* (*The One-Eyed Man is King;* play), and *Todos los gatos son pardos* (*All Cats are Gray;* play).

	Performances of *The One-Eyed Man is King* in Vienna and Avignon.
1971	Publishes *Tiempo mexicano* (*Mexican Time;* essays). Father dies. Performances of *The One-Eyed Man is King* in Paris, Barcelona, and Brussels. Publishes his two plays in a volume entitled *Los reinos originarios* (*The First Kingdoms*).
1972	Lives in Paris. Elected to the Colegio Nacional (National College) in Mexico City. Covers the Democratic Convention in Miami for Mexican television. Marries journalist Sylvia Lemus.
1973	Speaks at the memorial observance in honor of Pablo Neruda in New York. Birth of son Carlos Rafael.
1974	Fellow at the Woodrow Wilson International Center for Scholars in Washington, D.C. (working on *Terra Nostra*). Addresses the P.E.N. Club in New York. Birth of daughter Natascha.
1975	Publishes *Terra Nostra* (novel), and *Don Quixote or the Critique of Reading* (essay). Serves as Mexican ambassador to France (until 1977). Receives the Javier Villarutia prize in Mexico City for *Terra Nostra.* Delegate to the Conference on Science and Development in Yugoslavia.
1976	Publishes *Cervantes o la crítica de la lectura* (*Cervantes or the Critique of Reading;* essay). Head of the Mexican delegation to the North-South Conference on International Economic Development.
1977	Receives the Rómulo Gallegos award in Caracas for *Terra Nostra.* Resigns ambas-

sadorial post. Lectures at the Colegio Nacional in Mexico City, at Barnard College,
and at Cambridge University. Member of the
Cannes Film Festival jury.

1978   Lives in Princeton. Publishes *The Hydra
Head* (novel). Teaches at the University of
Pennsylvania and Columbia University. Lec-
tures at Princeton.

1980   Publishes *Distant Relations* (novel). Receives
the Alfonso Reyes prize in Mexico City for
the corpus of his work. Publishes *Burnt
Water* (short stories).

CARLOS FUENTES

Biographical Introduction

Carlos Fuentes was born in 1928 in Panama City into a Mexican family that he characterizes as coming from "typical petit bourgeois stock."[1] His great grandfather on his father's side was a coffee planter, his grandfather a banker. His mother's father was a merchant in Mazatlán, her mother a school inspector. Fuentes's own father was a diplomat, so that the family traveled frequently and lived abroad a great deal. By the time Fuentes was four, the family was living in Washington, D.C., where Fuentes attended an American school.[2]

Interestingly, a photograph taken in Washington in 1934 shows Fuentes in the most recognizably—even os-tentatiously—Mexican costume, complete with fancy gold braid, a serape, and a sombrero.[3] One wonders whether he was about to set off for some diplomatic children's party where he would "represent" Mexico. In any case, Fuentes confronted early the problems of Mexican identity—what it meant to be Mexican—in an international context. During the same years back in Mexico, writers and artists were facing similar problems, debating the relative merits of "Mexicanism" and "internationalism" in a postrevolu-tionary resurgence of national consciousness. Fuentes often illustrates the problematic force of his Mexican heri-tage by recounting a seminal experience that made him wish to affirm his identity as a writer in Spanish. As a child in Washington, Fuentes had many friends until President

Cárdenas nationalized the oil companies in Mexico. Since the majority of these companies were American, the reaction in the United States was naturally hostile. And so, according to Fuentes, he was instantly an outcast at school.[4]

In addition to his stay in Washington, Fuentes lived in Chile, Argentina, and Switzerland during his youth. He claims that since childhood "writing was my vocation" and remembers publishing fantastical short stories in the literary magazine of the Grange School in Chile.[5] A few years later in Argentina, Fuentes apparently refused to attend what he regarded as the fascistically oriented schools of the military regime there and contentedly educated himself through books and movies, both to remain consuming interests for him.[6] After graduating from high school in Mexico City, Fuentes studied law at the National University and the Institute for International Studies in Geneva. While he was studying international law in Geneva, from 1950 to 1952, he was a member of the Mexican delegation to the International Labor Organization. He also perfected his French, which he has used throughout his life to become increasingly familiar with French literature and criticism. On his return to Mexico, Fuentes worked in various administrative and editorial positions at the National University and served for a time as head of the Department of Cultural Relations at the Ministry of Foreign Affairs.

During this period of preparation for his future career as a diplomat, Fuentes was active in the literary world as well. Among other things, he served on the editorial boards for a number of publishing houses and edited the journal of the National University. With another writer, Emmanuel Carballo, Fuentes started the *Revista Mexicana de Literatura (Mexican Review of Literature)*. The review presented new developments in world literature at the same time that it encouraged Mexican writers. In this way, Fuentes hoped to bridge the gap between those who held, in loyalty to postrevolutionary feelings of cultural nationalism, that Mexican literature must reflect primarily Mexican realities, and those who preferred to look principally to Europe for inspiration. The journal would show that "a culture can be profitably national only when it is generously universal."[7]

In 1954, Fuentes published his first book, a collection of short stories called *Los días enmascarados (The Masked Days)*. He claims to have written it quickly in response to the recent establishment of a publishing house called Los Presentes (Writers Now) that was receptive to young authors. According to Fuentes, "All those of us with an itch started to write like mad for the publishing house."[8] This first collection includes the marvelous story "Chac Mool," which recounts the modern adventures of an Aztec rain god. In dealing with ancient Mexican mythology, the story responded to the postrevolutionary interest in indigenous Mexican culture that Fuentes encountered on his return from abroad. Another instance of this interest is the influential essay *The Labyrinth of Solitude* (1950) by the Mexican poet Octavio Paz. Paz provides a wide-ranging psychological investigation of Mexican culture. As we shall see in discussing *Where the Air is Clear* and *The Death of Artemio Cruz,* Paz's scrutiny of the national character has led Fuentes to attempt similar definitions in his fiction. For both Paz and Fuentes, familiarity with other cultures enhances their appreciation of the diversity within Mexican society.

About this time, Fuentes gave up his career as a diplomat to write full time. He continued his interest in politics, developing a critique of Latin American problems from a socialist viewpoint. As a result, he began to write articles on culture and politics for several left-wing papers, including *Política (Politics)* and *Siempre (Always)*. Marxian socialism was particularly attractive to many Mexican artists and intellectuals during Fuentes's youth. It proposed to implement the goals of the Revolution that

seemed to have been forgotten by the increasingly prosper-
ous leaders of the country. Some of Fuentes's political
pieces have been collected in *Tiempo mexicano (Mexican
Time,* 1971); articles on art and literature appear in *Casa
con dos puertas (House with Two Doors,* 1970). Fuentes
continues to support himself by his writing. He has published in *The New York Times, The New York Review of
Books, The London Times, Les Temps Modernes,* and
countless other periodicals throughout the world.

The two novels Fuentes published next reflect his
social and artistic concerns. *Where the Air is Clear* (1958)
deals with the social, political, and cultural problems of
Mexico from a loosely Marxist perspective. The book was
widely read, became controversial, and established
Fuentes as the leading young novelist in Mexico. It responded in theme to Mexico's desire for self-knowledge,
because it is a critical portrait of Mexico City that juxtaposes modern figures and ancient traditions. It responded in technique to the country's desire to belong to the
world community because, as we shall see, it incorporates
a number of stylistic innovations from European and
American literature. Fuentes's fiction will continue to
unite the innovative forms and techniques of modernism
to the Mexican tradition of social criticism. *The Good
Conscience* (1959) is a portrait of a single bourgeois family
in the provincial town of Guanajuato, to the west of Mexico City. It focuses on the struggles of the family's eldest
son, who questions the values and the way of life he has
been taught.

Where the Air is Clear points towards Fuentes's future directions as a writer to a greater extent than does
The Good Conscience because of its innovative techniques.
These techniques are more fully developed in his next
book, *The Death of Artemio Cruz* (1962). That novel treats
the Mexican Revolution and its betrayal in modern Mexican society through the memories of Cruz as he lies dying.
It is Fuentes's most successful novel and has been trans-

lated into fifteen languages. Fuentes began *The Death of Artemio Cruz* on a visit to Cuba, just after the revolution there. It continues his criticism of Mexican bourgeois society from a socialist viewpoint.

Fuentes's political views have caused the U.S. State Department to deny him a visa on several occasions. The first time, in 1962, Fuentes was to have participated in a television debate about U.S. policy in Latin America. Since then, however, Fuentes has visited this country many times and has written articles for large American magazines and newspapers, including *Holiday, Show, The Nation, The Atlantic,* and *The New York Times.* In 1963, he contributed a long essay on U.S.–Latin American relations to a volume published in New York called *Whither Latin America?* Recently he gave a series of lectures at the University of Texas at Austin, which have been published as *Don Quixote, or the Critique of Reading* (1975).

Fuentes believes that revolutionary social ideas can and should develop in conjunction with a revolutionary form of expression.[9] But when this belief is put into practice, it often presents a dilemma to a socialist author: just who are his readers? Technically innovative books like *Where the Air is Clear* or *The Death of Artemio Cruz* are too difficult to reach a mass public, and the revolutionary writer is left with an élite audience. The answer of social realism, which subordinates literary form to social content, does not tempt Fuentes, for it jars with his innovative sense of style. Recently, in an article on Czechoslovakia, he repeats a statement from a critic in Prague: "Socialist realism consists of writing praise of the government and of the party in such a way that even the government and the party can understand it."[10] Fuentes seems to have resolved the question of social relevance to his own satisfaction; in speaking of his novel *A Change of Skin* (1967), Fuentes says:

I don't care if two people read the novel. I think things seep down. I am part of a very élitist culture, the culture of Spain and Latin America. . . . But let's hope that the élite in Latin America will go on working in this sense and not just go on accepting that they are élites and crossing their arms. . . . I would be a demagogue and an idiot if I thought I were writing for the people![11]

On the other hand, he has said that he can't go along with Mallarmé's divorce of literature from society: "I'm equidistant from Mallarmé and Joseph Stalin."[12]

With his novella *Aura,* a psychological fantasy published in the same year as *The Death of Artemio Cruz* (1962), Fuentes begins to turn away slightly from his earlier concentration on social issues toward a more "magical realism." Magical realism is perhaps the most important development in recent Latin American literature. It has grown out of several literary traditions, from the 1940s on, in the works of Alejo Carpentier, Julio Cortázar, Gabriel García Márquez, and others, including Fuentes. The psychological fantasies of Edgar Allen Poe and his Latin American descendants, Horacio Quiroga and Jorge Luis Borges, combine with the strange and dreamlike images of European surrealism and the marvels reported by early travelers to the new world. Rather than creating fantastic domains and events "out of this world," this mode underlines what is marvelous and surprising in the everyday world by describing it in magical images and sequences of events.[13]

Fuentes's next book, a collection of short stories, *Cantar de ciegos (Songs of the Blind;* 1964), is different again. It concentrates on the secret and often bizarre lives of individuals, in a more realistic vein. In the next several years, Fuentes lived primarily in Paris, though he returned frequently to a rambling colonial house in the San Angel district of Mexico City. During this period, Fuentes expressed the idea that enclosure in a "cultural ghetto" weakens writers and that often a literature surges forward thanks to its emigrés. He believes this is the case for Latin

American literature now. The two most important Latin American writers, according to Fuentes—his compatriot Octavio Paz and the Argentine novelist Julio Cortázar—often live abroad. Their voluntary exile serves the same regenerative purpose as that of Henry James and of the writers in the generation of Hemingway and Fitzgerald.[14] During the mid- and late-1960s, a number of increasingly successful Latin American writers lived in Paris, or made extended visits there: Cortázar, Paz, García Márquez, Carpentier, Mario Vargas Llosa, and José Donoso, among others. The journal *Mundo Nuevo,* edited by the Uruguayan critic Emir Rodríguez Monegal, served as one focal point for these writers, and several portions of their novels originally appeared there.

Fuentes claims he is able to work well in Paris, where he wrote much of his next two novels, *A Change of Skin* and *Holy Place,* both published in 1967. *A Change of Skin* juxtaposes the activities of four people as they drive from Mexico City to Veracruz with their memories of New York, Nazi Germany, and Greece. The book won the prestigious Biblioteca Breve prize awarded by Seix Barral in Barcelona. Rather ironically, publication was prohibited in Spain because the book was judged to be blasphemous and obscene. The action of the Spanish censor could only confirm Fuentes and other novelists in their criticism of right-wing regimes. *Holy Place* narrates the passion of a young man for his mother, a famous actress. It is shorter than *A Change of Skin* and narrower in focus, but equally intense.

In both *A Change of Skin* and *Holy Place,* Fuentes uses "cinematic" techniques of montage—juxtaposition of seemingly disconnected scenes—and flashback. Both contain frequent references to actual movies and movie personalities—a continuing interest for Fuentes. He reviewed films regularly for the journal of the National University in Mexico in 1953 and 1954, and collaborated in making a number of movies himself: a film version of Juan Rulfo's

novel, *Pedro Páramo* (1966); a western called *Tiempo de
morir* (*Time to Die;* with García Márquez).[15] In the mid-
1960s, he participated in producing film versions of two of
his own short stories from *Songs of the Blind*—"The Two
Helens" and "A Pure Soul."

Movies and other popular art forms, particularly the
exaggerated styles of "pop art" and camp, interest Fuentes
because they correspond to the world as it has "become
violent, expressionist, and baroque."[16] But as usual,
Fuentes suggests a Mexican parallel to what are often
considered primarily foreign trends:

Mexico, of course, has a *pop art* before its time. I mean, a
celebration of objects that belong to everyday life, of absurd
objects. I think that even the art of Diego Rivera is nothing other
than *pop art.* It's Mexican history told by Terry and the Pirates,
with the little balloons coming out of the characters' mouths and
everything.

In the same interview, Fuentes expands on this idea that
Mexico has developed its own versions of international
movements before their times:

There's also an existentialism *avant la lettre,* and a very obvious
one. Mexico is a country of the moment. Tomorrow is completely unlikely, dangerous: you can get killed in a bar, on a street
corner, because you gave someone a dirty look, because you ate
a taco.[17]

At about this time, Fuentes traced his own intellectual biography for a volume on contemporary Mexican writers.[18] In relation to his novel *A Change of Skin,* he
mentions the "personal stimulus" of Cortázar, Vargas
Llosa, and Carpentier, and the Mexican painter José Luis
Cuevas. Earlier, in Mexico, the universalizing spirit of
Alfonso Reyes and the innovative prose in the essays of
Salvador Novo were important to him. He values the sense
of continuing the modern narrative tradition in Mexico
begun by Agustín Yáñez, José Revueltas, and Juan Rulfo.

Octavio Paz, in addition to leading Fuentes toward a definition of the Mexican character with relation to its past,
encouraged Fuentes's childhood enthusiasm for gothic
fiction and for "the beauty of the horrible" in the late
Romantics and the surrealists. Fuentes's continued contact with the Spanish surrealist film-maker Luis Buñuel
kept him in touch with a dissenting sense of the sacred.
Fuentes maintains that his most important literary influ-
ences include first of all Cervantes, then Dante, the Spanish picaresque novel, Balzac, Joyce, Faulkner, T. S. Eliot,
and D. H. Lawrence.

In the next several years, Fuentes treated a variety of
topics in a number of different genres; all of these publications were quite brief. In retrospect, one can imagine him
preparing his next—and longest—novel, *Terra Nostra.*
Fuentes was in Paris during the student uprisings in 1968.
Out of this experience he published a photographic essay,
París, la revolución de mayo (Paris, The May Revolution,
1968), which described the student movement sympatheti-
cally. In that same year he wrote an impressionistic introduction to the work of the Italian painter Adami for the
Venice Biennial—*Righe per Adami (Lines for Adami).* The
next year he did another, larger catalogue for an exhibition of works by José Luis Cuevas, *El mundo de José Luis
Cuevas (The World of José Luis Cuevas,* 1969). Cuevas's
work often resembles Fuentes's own in its combination of
formal innovation and social criticism.[19]

Fuentes moved back to Mexico in 1969 and published
his now well-known essay on Latin American literature,
*La nueva novela hispanoamericana (The New American
Novel).* In it he deals with the social and linguistic factors
that constitute the Latin American novel's "coming-of-
age." *The New Hispanic American Novel* also marks the
beginning of Fuentes's strong interest in French critical
thought, with its theoretical investigations of linguistic
structures in literary texts. The French *nouveau roman,* on
the other hand, has not influenced Fuentes greatly. The

minute objectivist descriptions of Robbe-Grillet, for example, may have seemed unsuited to the new world Fuentes was attempting to portray. His work is more lush, baroque—even surrealistic—than that of the *nouveau romanciers.* Fuentes's second novella, *Cumpleaños (Birthday),* appeared that same year. Like *Aura* and *Distant Relations,* it deals with medieval and Renaissance ideas of parallel lives and reincarnations, ghosts, and magic spells.

In 1970, Fuentes published two plays, *El tuerto es rey (The One-Eyed Man is King)* and *Todos los gatos son pardos (All Cats are Gray),* as well as his collection of literary essays, *Casa con dos puertas (House with Two Doors). The One-Eyed Man is King* is a dialogue between a blind woman and her blind manservant as they wait for the arrival of the woman's husband—deceiving each other continually. The second play dramatizes the Spanish conquest, centering on the figure of Marina, La Malinche, who served as Cortés's interpreter. In subject matter, then, it anticipates parts of *Terra Nostra.*

In the political sphere, Fuentes joined with Octavio Paz and others in an attempt to start a new political organization to challenge the monopoly of the Partido Revolucionario Institucional, the single official political party. As a response to the Tlatelolco massacre of 1968, they wished to develop additional channels of communication that would lead toward a less centralized political structure. Such a structure would be more directly responsive to a broader spectrum of the population than the current system. Other reforms they favored included the nationalization of basic industries, control over foreign investments, union democracy, and an end to Mexico's dependency on the U.S. At about this time, Fuentes and a number of other writers withdrew from the editorial board of the journal *Política.* They argued that the journal was no longer open to free discussion among different leftist viewpoints, but simply required adhesion to an intransigent party line.[20]

The creation of more responsive democratic governmental structures also formed part of President Luis
Echeverría's program.[21] Fuentes felt that with Echeverría
as president, for the first time since Cárdenas (in the
1930s) he agreed with government policy and might see
some of his own ideas put into action. This is why he
served as ambassador to France from 1975 to 1977 and
wrote a number of articles supporting Echeverría's pro-
grams. When the former president Díaz Ordaz, whom he
held responsible for the Tlatelolco violence became ambassador to Spain, Fuentes resigned his own diplomatic
post. Fuentes now consistently supports the idea of constructive reforms. He believes that violent action can only
generate repressive measures and annihilate centers of
fruitful discussion such as the universities. The volume of
political essays that Fuentes published just after
Echeverría came to office, *Tiempo mexicano* (1971), has
gone through a number of printings.

Throughout the 1970s, Fuentes continued to be active in the national and international literary worlds. In
1972, he was elected to the prestigious Colegio Nacional
(National College) of Mexico. Abroad, he participated in
a celebration honoring Pablo Neruda in New York in
1973 and addressed the P.E.N. Club there in 1974. In 1974
Fuentes was a fellow at the Woodrow Wilson Center for
Scholars, where he finished *Terra Nostra.* Commentators
often point out that Fuentes has always been rather a
literary lion—articulate, engaging, polemical, and, above
all, visible. The image is slightly disturbing, but it does
concur with his philosophy of commitment, his rejection
of the ivory tower. Though he lives very comfortably,
Fuentes conceptually affirms his opposition to the capitalist system by owning no major property other than books
and paintings.[22]

In his most recent work, Fuentes often turns toward
Europe to investigate the new world's literary and emotional origins overseas from a Latin American perspective.

Though a concern for social reform is less central in this later work, it never entirely disappears from the surface of the text. *Terra Nostra* (1975) ranges widely between the Roman Empire and Paris at the end of the twentieth century, but concentrates primarily on the Spain of Philip II. Bizarre and mysterious events in his hermetic Escorial are disturbed by the discovery and exploration of the new world. Fuentes's next long essay, *Cervantes o la crítica de la lectura* (*Cervantes or the Critique of Reading*, 1975), forms a parallel with *Terra Nostra.* It discusses a number of early Spanish texts, but focuses primarily on *Don Quixote.* Fuentes investigates how Cervantes's innovations in that novel revolutionize the act of reading and constitute the beginnings of modern fiction. Fuentes continues here in the French critical idiom that he adopted several years earlier in *The New Hispanic American Novel.* After finishing *Terra Nostra,* Fuentes says he took a rest and wrote "nothing" while he was ambassador to France.[23] Following that, he achieved a complete change of pace with *The Hydra Head* (1978), an international spy thriller set in Mexico City.

Following this brief excursion (he wrote *The Hydra Head* very quickly), Fuentes returned to his investigation of the European scene. *Distant Relations* (1980) concerns the adventures of a young Mexican boy and his father in France, filtered through the perceptions of their aging French host. It is both a search for lost origins and a quest for rejuvenation. Fuentes employs a fantastical mode to establish mysterious connections between the young and the old, the living and the dead. Unresolved questions of time and identity resonate throughout the text.

At this time, Fuentes lives in Princeton, perhaps because, as he has said, the east coast of the U.S. contains the largest concentration of brilliant minds, resources, libraries, and great universities in the world.[24] From that base, he travels a great deal, as he always has, lecturing on his own work and on other Latin American writers. He continues to contribute literary and political essays and stories to journals in Mexico and throughout the world. A collection of old and new stories was published with the title *Burnt Water* in 1980.

In a regular column for *Vuelta,* Fuentes reviews books, films, and exhibitions. He also expresses his political opinions—criticism of the two superpowers, of the U.S. presence in Mexico and the rest of the world, of Mexico's one-party system, its unequal income distribution, its lack of significant agrarian reform. He persistently reiterates his dislike of all systems that deny individual freedoms, whether on the left or the right, and wishes for a multi- rather than a bipolar power structure in the world.

Fuentes's combination of political and literary activity supports his view of man: molded by history, yet at the same time morally responsible for individual actions; situated *in* time, yet responsive to eternal values. For him there is "no such thing as an abstract general human nature." Human nature "is defined socially, economically, historically."[25] Quite early in his career, Fuentes defined the mode he uses to express this view as "symbolic realism": "a realism that can only be comprehensible and totalizing through symbols." This mode was a response to the necessity of going beyond the realistic or naturalistic thesis novel and at the same time surmounting the artificial practice of art for art's sake.[26] Richard Reeve has described Fuentes as *"un ser combativo"*—"a fighting man."[27] Fuentes's decisive, enthusiastic—even combative—personal style shows through transcripts of interviews as it does in his published work: he often repeats a phrase for emphasis or answers "no, no, no," or "yes, yes, yes" to a question, and characterizes himself as inhabited by a given number of "resident obsessions."[28] Finally, perhaps the most brilliant, succinct definition of Fuentes's work comes from his old friend Octavio Paz. In his introductory remarks before Fuentes's inaugural address at the

Colegio Nacional, Paz maintains that it is above all a questioning spirit that unites the Fuentes he met twenty years ago with the Fuentes he knows today. The constants of Fuentes's work are the extremes Paz calls "eroticism and politics": Fuentes asks, "How are erotic and social ties made, unmade, and remade?" He shows us "the bedroom and the public square, the couple and the crowd, the young girl in love in her room, and the tyrant caught in his den," for his is a double fascination, a concern with "desire and power, love and revolution."[29]

1

Early Novels: Ancestral Presences, Modern Quests

Fuentes has characterized his early novels as particularly concerned with the theme of freedom: "In *Where the Air is Clear* it is confronted as historical and social necessity. In *The Good Conscience* it appears as a failure of individual rebellion. In *The Death of Artemio Cruz* it is at once chance, free will, and necessity."[1] This preoccupation with freedom is the youthful center of Fuentes's perennial investigation of national identity, a concern he shares with other Latin American writers of this century. In 1966, Fuentes asked himself if any country—except Russia and Spain—had worried as much as Mexico over questions of national identity and recognized that "the theme of the country, the culture, and the society in which I work . . . has been the most powerful external impulse" of his writing.[2] All three of Fuentes's first novels are quests for identity—*Where the Air is Clear* of a city and a country, *The Good Conscience* of an individual, and *The Death of Artemio Cruz* of a man and his country.

Within this national quest, certainly in *Where the Air is Clear*, and to a lesser extent in *The Death of Artemio Cruz*, perhaps the most striking element is the presence of ancestral voices, of indigenous mythologies. One reason myths attract Fuentes is that they seem to play tricks with time. For him, as for Octavio Paz, "myth is a past which is future, ready to realize itself in the present."[3] Emir Rodríguez Monegal has characterized Fuentes as above all a creator of myths.[4] A creator and a perpetuator. Fuentes often builds modern versions of ancient patterns: contemporary rituals of sacrifice, unknown or displaced fathers, devouring mothers—or aunts, battles between male and female principles. The "mythic" pattern in *The Good Conscience* is of more recent origin, largely literary, and concerns the growth of a sensitive individual in conventional society.

In the narrative, these ancestral presences link us with the past, and with the universe. Modern life and literature are rejuvenated, in a sense, through contact with an original, a fresh time, which is also very old. As we shall see, indigenous mythology represents a partial defense against "pentotal"—the full-speed-ahead homogenization of twentieth-century culture. Yet it is also a frightening presence, for we do not always control it. Perhaps because history has not fulfilled the utopian potential of the New World, the destructive figure of Huizilopochtli predominates over the benevolent figure of Quetzalcóatl in Fuentes's portraits of modern Mexico.[5] Furthermore, nostalgia can be a trap, and as Lanin Gyurko has pointed out, Fuentes portrays "both the resurgence and the demythification of the Gods."[6]

In these early novels, then, and throughout his life, Fuentes works within the universal time of myth, the linear time of history—which often turns out to resemble the cyclical time of myth—and the subjective time of individual thought. Though those three times coexist in all three early novels, the mythic mode predominates in *Where the Air is Clear,* the historical in *The Death of Artemio Cruz,* and the subjective in *The Good Conscience.* So that taken all together, the texts constitute an extended meditation on the relationships between eternal, historical, and individual times, a subject that prefigures much of Fuentes's later work as well.

The Development of a Collective Voice: *Where the Air is Clear*

The Cuban writer Alejo Carpentier has said that modern Latin American novelists "must establish the geography of our cities as Joyce established Dublin's."[1] Fuentes first attempts this task with his portrait of Mexico City in *Where the Air is Clear,* a compelling conceptual design that contains a succession of striking vignettes and images. With this book, Fuentes moves away from the traditional novel of the land and toward the recent wave of urban novels in Latin America.[2] At the same time, he creates a celebration of the mestizo, born from the union of Spaniard and Indian. For this reason the novel is built around the dualities that structure urban society in Mexico. The most important of these is the interaction of visible and invisible realms. Contact between these realms may occur through the union of contrasting characters, through memory, through mythological resonances in the modern city. Physical proximity and fortuitous yet significant encounters suggest the ideal of a communal existence that would encompass conflicting forces in the city.

In Mexico, Agustín Yáñez's great novel about the coming of the Revolution, *The Edge of the Storm,* is an important precursor of *Where the Air is Clear;* it is a similar collective portrait, though of a smaller town.[3] Fuentes's novel resembles another product of the Revolution as well: the frescoes of Diego Rivera. Both Fuentes and Rivera work a broad spectrum of figures into a given space and transmit a sense of energy through action and style. In Rivera's mural, "Chapultepec Park," for example, as in *Where the Air is Clear,* from a central group of figures the eye extends outward in all directions to a sea of individuals representing aspects of life in the capital and movements in Mexican history. Since Fuentes's narrative

moves freely between past and present, one might imagine
a flattened out time frame where different sequences are
spread side by side like figures in a painting.[4]

The pattern of events in *Where the Air is Clear* resembles the rotation of an ancient "wheel of fortune." Some
figures rise as others fall. As Norma Robles says to Pimpinela de Ovanda, "Maybe you didn't know that my husband's parents were peons on your uncle's hacienda. Yes:
and now you, all of you, are Federico's peons! Ja! What
flip-flops, sweetheart."[5] Starting from peasant origins,
Federico Robles makes his way to the head of a powerful
financial empire, which he has created in the wake of the
Revolution. Then, having negated his mestizo past by
marrying green-eyed Norma Larragoiti, Robles takes as
his mistress the blind mestizo woman Hortensia Chacón,
with whom he finds love and happiness. Finally, Norma
accidentally burns to death in the Robles mansion. The
fire begins when Federico rushes downstairs from her bedroom after she refuses to give him her jewels to sell; he
needs them because his financial empire is in ruins. Federico loses everything and returns to his origins; he goes to
live with Hortensia and their son on a farm in the north
of Mexico. Robles's "fall" turns out to be an uplifting
experience in the end. But his story is really the only one
with a "happy" ending. And we do not actually see this
conclusion; we only hear about it secondhand.

The writer Rodrigo Pola seems fixed to the opposite
side of the social wheel from Robles. Their sharing of
Norma (married to Robles, loved by Pola) serves to underline their parallel yet contrasting movements. Pola
changes from an aspiring poet to a successful screen
writer. So that artistically, Pola experiences a rise that is
really a fall, unlike Robles, whose fall is really a rise.

Moving between these lives, serving as a kind of fluid
adhesive, is Ixca Cienfuegos. He is often described as a
misty, insubstantial presence because he represents the
ubiquitous spirit of the city: "Ixca Cienfuegos . . . the one

and only. Like God, he's everywhere, but no one ever sees him" (22). Manuel Durán compares Ixca to the all-seeing figure of Tiresias in *The Wasteland*—another portrait of a modern city with ancient resonances.[6] Together with his mother, Teódula Moctezuma, Ixca symbolizes the persistence of mysterious Aztec forces in Mexico. His first name means "to roast" in Nahuatl, language of the Aztecs, his last name "a hundred fires" in Spanish.[7] Both recall the burning of sacrificed victims to the gods.

A whole range of briefer portraits surrounds the central figures of Fuentes's verbal fresco. These minor characters suffer unseen throughout the city. Gabriel, a migrant worker, for example, whose brother sometimes serves as a waiter at parties the rich characters attend, comes back from the United States with a blender for his mother, only to find that the family shack lacks electricity. So they use the blender as a flower vase. Later, Gabriel is senselessly killed by a local hood.

Moving even farther out to the periphery of the fresco, Fuentes includes a series of short vignettes that portray people who, because they appear only once, represent even more clearly the anonymous suffering masses. In one scene, an old man takes his nephew for a bus ride along the Paseo de la Reforma, past the grand palaces built in the prerevolutionary era of Porfirio Díaz. Now, however, a "chill plain of steel and concrete hemmed in those lovely, barren islands of the past." The old man tells his nephew, "We have maimed this city forever, my son. Once it was the City of Palaces! Here, there, pay attention to what I am telling you and stop licking that ice cream" (121). But the nephew licks away contentedly, craning his neck eagerly to see the tops of the newest skyscrapers.

The large number of characters in *Where the Air is Clear* and the rapidity with which the narration moves between them center the reader's attention on the city itself as chief protagonist of the novel. Individuals are dwarfed by the collective picture. Early on, for example, we feel as if individual lives are "cheap," so to speak, in this narrative space; no sooner have we met the taxi-driver Juan Morales than we hear almost immediately of his death, and only secondhand at that. Fuentes presents the same idea in a different way when Ixca is having dinner with Federico and Norma Robles: Robles's "words stopped only when he raised his wine glass. Then Norma would mechanically carry out her assignment and say to Cienfuegos, 'And have you read "Town Tattletale"? The Hindu ballet is coming to Bellas Artes soon . . . last Sunday, at the Jockey . . .' and when her husband's rose-tinted glass touched the white cloth again, her mouth would close" (238–39). The woman is absorbed by her social role.[8] People frequently act like automatons because a system larger than they overpowers them, just as the city often overpowers its inhabitants. The system is not a co-herent and fulfilling system of belief; rather it is one of a number of strategies for survival or domination.

Just as the city is divided into different neighbor-hoods, the characters in *Where the Air is Clear* are ar-ranged in different groups that appear in quick succession.[9] And just as Fuentes creates vignettes of in-dividuals that typify a particular situation, so he evokes the mood of a particular group through a snatch of con-versation, a motion, an object—even a name. The harsh and seedy end of Gladys García's night as a call girl in a cabaret comes out in a quick word and an act: " 'Morn-ing!' The floor-sweeper goosed her and Gladys breathed cold morning" (5). The name Gladys—anglicized, prob-ably thought elegant by her family—indicates the desire for a better—a more American—life. García, the com-monest of surnames, cuts off the striving and pretension of the "Gladys." True to her name, when Gladys sees a group of rich socialites on the sidewalk, she gawks at them enviously for they look like gringos to her, and she imme-diately buys a cigarette holder in imitation of theirs.

The rising bourgeois, the declining aristocracy, the

intellectuals, the foreigners meet at a party given by a man called Bobó, whose occupation seems to be organizing parties. His name (without the accent) means stupid in Spanish; the accent adds Francophile affectation to vapidity. One of Bobó's guests, Federico Robles, inhabits the world of high finance. The vignette that characterizes this world begins and ends with Robles pushing a button to command "the electric voice of his secretary," as "his thumb stroked his silk tie" (14). Robles stands high above the city in his office, protected from contact with "The People" and their problems.

These different milieux evoked one after the other reveal the richness and confusion of the city. In moving from one to the other, we experience the disconcerting clashes and shifts that characterize Mexican society. Interconnecting scenes in the text are a structural analogue for contact between classes in society. Robles initially avoids such contacts by sticking to his own protected niche:

Robles liked to lean out his window and smell the flea circus hopping below without being bitten by all the necessary nobodies and all the nonentity weavers of life who passed oblivious to skyscrapers and to Federico Robles. Two worlds: clouds and excrement. Encased in glass, isolated, privileged, he always traveled from his colonial-style home, grill-windowed, the entrance spumy with meringue stonework, to his auto, from his auto to the iron and nickel elevator, from the elevator to the great window and the leather chairs; and just by touching a button, he could reverse the trajectory. (41)

Near the midpoint of the novel, Fuentes calls attention to different social zones in the city. Pola stands in a square between the unfashionable sections where he has grown up and the fashionable sections he now visits: He "was aware of the middle ground, planted between two worlds, both of which refused him. . . . He stood between two lands in a city of physically invisible but spiritually high and barbed frontiers. Had the city itself created those barriers, or were they the work of its inhabitants?" (199). This is not a rhetorical question. Fuentes balances the narrative between individual choice and collective inertia. Ideally, man is responsible for his life, but in many cases, circumstances weigh too heavily for him to act.

Fuentes evokes the physical presence of Mexico City in single images throughout the novel, but more importantly, through poetic descriptions that pile series of images one upon the other. They correspond on the linguistic level to the diverse districts in the city and the many characters in the novel. Different units jostle each other in the urban literary space. Pola, on his walk, sees the surrounding world of all the city's trades and lives: "a small cheap family restaurant, vegetable stores, hardware, shoe, tortilla shops, a bar, flophouses, a hospital for dolls and religious statuettes . . ." (199).

Fuentes includes many references to neon lights in Mexico City. They are important because they are so insistently modern, so visually demanding—a sign of twentieth-century urban development, which has hit Mexico with its full strength already collected. Generally, the lights simply exist, towering above the inhabitants. Once, though, Rodrigo Pola seems to adopt their strength for himself. When at long last he feels in control of the modern world, he expresses his delighted sense of power as the ability to write across the sky—in neon perhaps?—possibly in anticipation of his name on a movie marquee: "Rodrigo opened his eyes and felt like writing the words 'The End' across the rose heavens" (259). But even the neon lights flicker; they undergo moments of relative brilliance and weakness, measuring the rhythm of the city. As Gladys García emerges from her cabaret, the statue of Charles IV holds court over a whole range of neon signs. Later on, in the popular Plaza Garibaldi "dancing neon tubes displaced the sky" (158; in Spanish, "shot at the sky"). Near Christmastime "an endless chain of advertisements and electric lights . . . tied Insurgentes [the main artery of the city] together in one long glitter" (356). At another point, however, Cienfuegos and his friend Manuel Zamacona enter a café "faintly illuminated by the dying green light of neon tubes" (292). And earlier, Rodrigo Pola notices that just before a rainstorm when the sky was "trembling with dry lightning," "electric sky signs were made dark by intermittent sky flashes" (198). At times like these, we sense that the city's pulse has slowed; it seems tired of its own brashness.

MYTH AND NATIONAL IDENTITY

This last image suggests that Fuentes uses neon to characterize not only the modern city, but also the contrast between ancient and modern ways of life; the ancient powers of the earth worshipped as the Aztec gods of fire and rain contend with modern inventions. Significantly, just before these natural sky flashes, Ixca stands in the center of the cathedral square and "searche[s] the sky for one star sign," some message from the natural world (198). This is the culmination of a mysterious scene where Ixca symbolically reenacts the ancient rite of human sacrifice. He attempts to bring a small boy home with him, but the boy becomes frightened, bites Ixca's hand (drawing blood), and runs away. Ixca "looked down and shook his bitten hand over the soft earth until one drop of blood fell, turning to a dry color when it touched the dust" (197). The ancient Aztecs believed in the power of human blood to feed the earth and assure that life would continue. Reaffirming this symbolic sacrifice where his blood drips into the earth, Ixca tastes his own blood, his head swims, and "blood whirled in his ears like two breaths, united by an hour of terror: the breath of a man, the breath of a ghost, one standing in front of the other, and both invisible" (197). He feels the touch of mysterious ancestral presences, and for a moment seems to become invisible and double—transported back into an ancient ceremony where he is both witness and victim.

Immediately preceding this symbolic sacrifice, where Ixca feels inhabited by an earlier Aztec self, he experiences a similar double vision of the ancient city of Tenochtitlán behind the colonial architecture of the Zócalo.[10] He sees "a corner where stone broke into shapes of flaming shafts and red skulls and still butterflies: a wall of snakes beneath the twin roofs of rain and fire" (197). Ixca's vision of an Aztec temple in the Zócalo is analogous to Fuentes's text itself as a continual conflation of ancient and modern Mexico, "a night when pieces of moon may be gathered up, all the broken fragments of origin" (197). As Joseph Sommers has pointed out, Fuentes's frequent use of ancient images translates into fictional terms Octavio Paz's idea that Mexico's pre-Columbian culture has never really been conquered.[11]

Images or concepts that juxtapose ancient and modern culture recur with haunting frequency throughout *Where the Air is Clear*. The title itself prefigures such resonances, for it refers to the region of Mexico City in the sixteenth century.[12] In a sense, the descriptions of Ixca's airy substance make him an incarnation of the title, representing the very atmosphere of the town: "He became, in his stone-eagle, air-serpent eyes, the city itself, its voices, sounds, memories, presentiments, the vast and anonymous city" (361–62). More importantly, however, the title is ironic, for already by 1950 the mountains around Mexico City were frequently obscured by smog. Appropriately then, references to dust and haze fill *Where the Air is Clear*. The title also serves as a linguistic foreshadowing of the many ways in which the past obtrudes into the present throughout the novel. To continue the comparison of *Where the Air is Clear* with a fresco, one might imagine that Fuentes's canvas has been painted on before. Old

patterns show through the new; the text resembles a palimpsest.

We have already seen how—except when a storm
threatens—city neon usurps the ancient sky. Similarly,
Norma Robles sunning herself by her pool, and the hordes
of people on the beaches at Acapulco, represent the
degenerated modern version of ancient Aztec sun worship. Speaking to his mother, Ixca says that "today's sun
isn't our sun, Teódula; it's a sun . . . to bake skin anointed
with synthetic oil." This is Ixca's negative response to
Teódula, who has just told him that "men don't make life,
but the earth under their feet makes it . . . always beneath
the land in hidden places our feet can't stomp, there everything goes on the same, and the same voices can be heard
as in the beginning" (269). They are both right. Even
though the synthetically oiled Norma has cotton pads
over her eyes to protect them from the sun, the sun god's
power still reaches her: "Sun came through the pads,
through the eyelids, and glowed inside her eyes like two
diffuse egg yolks. Sun: her first memory, she wanted to be
the sun, felt a seed of sun burning in her breast and repeated, in the heat of the sun, her name, once, twice, over and
over" (90). We sense that the sun is somehow tied to
Norma's identity because it causes her to repeat her name.
Indeed, this paragraph introduces a section that recounts
Norma's past, as if the sun had revived her memory. The
rain god appears as well: Ixca says, "I see true proofs, sun
and rain, of higher power" (206; in the original Spanish
"Sun" and "Rain" are capitalized). But the deity is similarly diminished, for the rain that falls now is "city rain,
contaminated with stenches, that never reaches soil" (9).
Even so, the land still seems to elicit love and sacrifices
(188–89).

This concept of sacrifice is central to the novel.
Fuentes himself wonders if perhaps Moctezuma's true revenge is that the outraged Mexican soil demands continual sacrifices of human lives to maintain cosmic order.[13]

Here as elsewhere in Fuentes's work the theme often serves as a warning not to ignore or repress past history. But the issue is more complicated than this. *Where the Air is Clear* has been compared to D. H. Lawrence's novel *The Plumed Serpent*.[14] There Lawrence proposes the ancient way of life, symbolized by the benevolent god Quetzalcóatl —the plumed serpent—as a valid alternative to modern alienation and neurosis. Fuentes, on the other hand, while advocating consciousness of the past, investigates the problems involved in such a view.

He centers his investigation in the figures of Ixca Cienfuegos and his mother Teódula Moctezuma. (Her name, of course, recalls the last Aztec emperor who was killed in the Spanish conquest of Tenochtitlán and whose ghost may await revenge.) Teódula "represents the nocturnal horror of Mexican sacrifices." She is thus "a genuine Aztec sorceress."[15] Fuentes calls her "Tonantzín"—a popular name meaning "our mother," which refers to the protective face of Coatlicue, the Aztec goddess of creation and destruction. Ixca is her loyal son, Huizilopochtli, God of War. As I have said, Ixca and Teódula represent a permanent mythic substratum in the modern city. But they are not passive observers; they wish to reactivate the ancient Aztec rituals, and that's where the problems begin. Teódula keeps dead family members under her floor boards and believes that for her ancestors to remain contented and for her life to continue, Ixca must sacrifice a human life to the gods, for "our gods walk abroad, invisible but alive. You'll see, you'll see. They always win. They take our sacrificed blood, our killed heroes, our deaths fallen across a land of song and color" (270). At dawn, after Norma has burned to death, Teódula points to the sun, rising again because of the rejuvenating sacrifice. We encounter Teódula briefly in the novel, and always alone with Ixca, who never contradicts her religious pronouncements. In comparison to the other characters, particularly the socialites, she retains a certain dignity. But when we realize that Ixca has been searching for a victim in order to put his mother's beliefs into practice, both mother and son seem more ominous than before.

Near the end of the novel, Ixca momentarily revolts against Teódula's domination and makes us realize how obedient to her wishes he has been thus far. Ixca is finally exhausted by his attempts to conform to ancient patterns and cries out, "You don't know my mother, Rodrigo . . . my mother is stone, serpents" (361). Perhaps Teódula has usurped the place of an idol, demanding rather than offering sacrifices. She remembers once in her youth wanting to make herself a snakeskin skirt for fiestas, presumably in imitation of the snakes worn by Coatlicue.[16]

Some time before the Robles fire, Ixca is talking to Rodrigo Pola and seems to suggest that Rodrigo should sacrifice himself because "the world isn't just given to us. . . . We have to recreate it. . . . Daily sacrifice is needed, daily feeding so that the sun will give light, and in turn feed us." As he tries to convince Rodrigo that "you want this sacrifice," his face becomes like the image of an idol with "shining carved teeth," and "straight drawn lips" (203). In a sense, here, as in Norma's case, Ixca obtains a sacrificial victim after all, if not a willing believer in the ancient order. For Rodrigo sacrifices his old ideals—indeed his old self, and thus symbolically he dies.

Ixca and Teódula do inadvertently obtain three other "sacrificial victims" on September 16, 1951, for we see three people die, two of them senselessly gunned down in bars. Like Federico Robles, these victims all fall on Independence Day. They link the mythic presences lurking behind the city to the quest for national identity. This subject motivates an essaylike discussion at the center of the novel. In the figures of Ixca, who advocates a return to the indigenous past, of Robles, who wishes to forget the past and move toward a progressive future, and of the intellectual Zamacona, who pleads for some kind of compromise, Fuentes mirrors a significant phase of Mexican intellectual history.[17] The discussions draw on the ideas of Octavio Paz and other essayists of the postrevolutionary period, such as Samuel Ramos and Leopoldo Zea. Indeed, Paz's *The Labyrinth of Solitude* serves as a kind of pre-text for *Where the Air is Clear,* a continual presence behind the work.

Zamacona claims that Mexicans don't feel part of any nourishing rational system. Ixca, on the other hand, attempts to cling to an ancient system. He believes that salvation depends on "Mexico's people . . . who live with their teeth biting into the aboriginal breast" (299). While this may be true, those people must evolve and get beyond Ixca's idea that "what Mexico is, is fixed forever, incapable of evolution. Mother stone cannot be shifted" (102). Ixca, like Mexico itself perhaps, remains attached to an earth mother who demands sacrifices, in an uneasy dependence on the past. Zamacona argues against Ixca, maintaining that "origin is creation. Mexico must find her origin by looking ahead, not behind. We have to create our beginning and our originality" (44–45). Zamacona rejects the idea that spiritual and material progress must be separate, so that to affirm the spiritual origins of its culture, Mexico must renounce material progress. Perhaps because of this belief, to triumph spiritually, Mexican heroes had to be failures in the material world (47). Ironically, Zamacona's own death, like Robles's fall from power, makes him a traditional Mexican hero. In Zamacona's thought, a fatalistic view of Mexico haunts his notions of existential responsibility. On the one hand, "one isn't sure whether this land, instead of demanding vengeance for every drop of blood that stained it, doesn't demand the blood itself" (300). On the other hand, "It isn't enough to testify to the misery; . . . responsibility must be placed. . . . For every Mexican who dies in vain, sacrificed, there is another Mexican who is guilty" (300).

At this point, Robles, who has been listening to Ixca and Zamacona's discussion, becomes an illustration of

Zamacona's last idea: He remembers sacrificing a labor leader to his personal god of ambition. This leader, Feliciano, fell dead "among the weeds," and in the next scene, Robles oversees the construction of his new house —decorated with reliefs of Ceres (304). Robles's adoption of the classical goddess of cereals underlines (besides his pretension) his betrayal of a countryman who dies in the Mexican grasses. Zamacona's words move Robles *now* because he has been divested of his former godlike status. Before his bankruptcy, "Robles was the inscrutable, the enemy, the master of the new world before which Norma and Rodrigo knelt" (281). The day after the discussion— Independence Day—Robles assumes full status as a Mexican through a combination of individual responsibility and collective identity: "It was I, I am your murderer. Froilán Reyero, Feliciano Sánchez, two names that were a way of naming all the anonymous dead, enslaved, starving; and at this moment Robles felt the sadness and desolation of every Mexican life" (310; here, as elsewhere, the translation abbreviates). Robles's present view over the city recalls his earlier survey of the same domain as a conquerer. Soon he will walk among the "weavers of life" he formerly looked down on.

A small but persistent reminder of the novel's concern to define what is truly Mexican appears in the form of objects that—like the folkloric costumes we will encounter in *The Death of Artemio Cruz*—trivialize ancient symbols: "Tired corn mortars converted into ash trays stood on the low tables, pieces of an Indian kitchen, little clay figures. In the actual kitchen, Rodrigo reflected, they probably used pressure cookers and liquidizers" (258). The mortars have collapsed because their true function has been taken away. As we shall see, Fuentes suggests that ancient traditions often fascinate because they remain partially hidden. Their discovery requires an effort; their potency should be protected from overuse. Just as disturbing as the complete neglect of traditional culture is the commercialization of what should be strange and mysterious powers. Fuentes rarely names indigenous deities in his texts, as if to save their power from diffusion: "What is hidden is more exciting."[18]

MEMORY AND PERSONAL IDENTITY

In this search for a national identity in the mythical and the historical past, as well as in the quest for personal identity that accompanies it, memory plays an important role. It offsets the alienation of a city dweller like Robles from his personal and social origins. Through memory, Robles becomes a full member of the community. The process begins as, prompted by Zamacona's words, he first remembers Feliciano Sanchez's murder. The image of "voices turned together like snakes" that "spoke to him of a name forgotten long ago" recalls ancient Aztec sculpture and thus suggests the collective nature of his individual experience.

Robles is described as a "silent old man" here because he has finally begun to remember his past and to assume responsibility for his actions. This is why "his was now the common being accepted by all," and he can participate spontaneously in Gabriel's funeral as he never could have before. He has come a long way from the Robles who, when Ixca initially calls on him to remember his past, says "all that has to be forgotten" if they are to "raise the nation to greatness" (72).

Fuentes speaks frequently about Mexican society as one which has experienced defeat. He believes this is one reason why Faulkner has influenced him—and so many other Latin American writers—to such an extent. They feel close to him because "he is the only novelist of defeat in a country that basically has been a nation of optimism and success."[19] Fuentes maintains that a tradition of defeats may eventually constitute a source of good diplomacy. Instead of dominating from a secure position by brute force, less powerful countries seek to understand other cultures so as to predict how they will react in given situations.[20] Like Manuel Zamacona, Fuentes suggests that "Mexico's defeat . . . led us to truth, to honor, the correct limits of a man of culture and good will. . . . Good may not be identified with victory, nor evil with defeat" (47). Robles's case illustrates this pattern; his defeat is in many ways a triumph; he no longer dominates "from a secure position by brute force." Furthermore, in moving from the parasitic bourgeoisie of high finance to the productive rural bourgeoisie, Robles represents a progressive force in Mexico's development,[21] an affirmation of the Zapatistas' agrarian ideal.

Ixca Cienfuegos, in addition to recalling the collective past, also serves to elicit personal memories from individual characters. Several people resist Ixca's efforts, but the power of the past overcomes the resistance. Pimpinela de Ovando refuses to tell him her story, but the next section transcribes her memories so that fictionally, at least, Ixca succeeds. Similarly, just before Rosenda Pola's monologue of memories pours out, she says, "No, I won't tell you anything" (175). Her thoughts lack quotation marks; the memories exist primarily for herself. In any case, digging back through memory may be painful, but it represents a source of strength, of knowledge, of self-affirmation—an existential choice. Ixca sums up this idea when he says to Rodrigo, "Choose . . . and remember." The phrase looks forward to Artemio Cruz, who waits too long and can choose through memory only as he dies.

Even *before* his fall, Robles gains special stature from his memories:

Robles was silent, his eyes stared into Ixca's, he forgot his hands, his body, let his arms fall and let the heavy curtains inside his eyes slowly rise and reveal the inner pupil of memory, liquid, pinpoint. Ixca Cienfuegos did not allow one muscle to twitch.

Like an eloquent idol, rigid, silent, he invited Robles to open, not his lips, but his life, the slit-eyes to spread the curtain more and permit a revelation, always a memory, that would ripen and become the fruit of all the days memory could not bring back. And now Robles' eyes were fugitive with light, trembling, like turquoise wings aflame in darkness. (81)

The Robles that emerges from this brilliant description is a different idol from the one Rodrigo and Norma mistakenly worship. The visual attractiveness of the final image tends to enhance Robles in our minds' eye; it also lends him the glamour and dignity of ancient art encrusted with real turquoise and suggests a latent continuity with the distant past.

HOMAGE TO THE MESTIZO: DUALITIES

The morning of Independence Day, after his bankruptcy, Robles's "razor moved and the dark face beneath the white mask of lather appeared" (306). The path cut by the razor reveals Robles's identity as a "brown" man, a mestizo. It heralds his identification with the Mexican people at Gabriel's funeral, marking a clear change from the earlier Robles whose Indian origin was "so carefully disguised by cashmere and cologne" (88). (It also prefigures his use of a plow.) When Robles affirms his love for Hortensia Chacón, he assumes his full status as a mestizo. Dignified yet lyrical prose celebrates their union as Independence Day ends:

Hortensia's delicate Indian features smiled faintly. Dark lenses hid her eyes. Blood pulsed in the pads of her fingers, lightly resting on Federico's. They sat with life between their fingers and without speaking, man and woman, both brown skinned. . . . A common sweetness anticipated a recognition. . . . With suffocated steps, night descended upon the sixteenth of September, 1951. (342–43)

This homage to the mestizo and his Indian past redresses the historical imbalance that had long favored the Spanish conquerors. Dark hair and dark eyes shot with gleams of ancient turquoise replace light skin and green eyes.[22]

Celebration of brown people, of mestizos, further defines the Mexican national character. In support of this definition, a number of dualities in the conceptual structure of the novel reflect the double nature of the mestizo race. We have already touched on the ancient mythical resonances in the modern city. They constitute the principal heritage of mestizo culture. Another central dichotomy, related through the union of Robles and Hortensia to the idea of the mestizo is the division between visible and invisible worlds. Of course the mestizo was never literally invisible in Mexico, but appreciation of his race and culture tended to disappear under the veneer of old Spanish colonial and recent North American domination. As Rodrigo stands at one point between two physical areas of the city, so here, as Robles gets up from Hortensia's bed, he spans two separate emotional and social spaces: "A world trimmed in chrome and neon crossed behind his eyes; behind him lay another world, flat and rosy, full of songs and names and tree colors and furious horses; and he stood planted in the center of each of these worlds" (224). Positive images favor the heretofore invisible indigenous world that Robles shares with Hortensia over the public world he dominates with Norma. Songs and tree colors overpower chrome and neon. But not forever; both worlds belong to the city.

To illustrate the duality between seen and unseen, the highly visible marriage of Federico and Norma Robles splits into two sets of lovers that are hidden from public view: Robles and Hortensia, and—briefly but significantly —Ixca and Norma. Both pairs experience intense sexual passion, a force that Fuentes frequently shows flowing underneath and counter to accepted social patterns. Robles reflects that "to go to bed with Norma was not dangerous. With Hortensia, to make love was a somersault in the air, you never knew what veil was tearing or what fire-glass burned your tongue" (123). With Norma, "the ceremony was always as precise as the four quarters of a watch dial. With Hortensia, it was time, the unmeasured hours" (124). Robles's secret visits to Hortensia's small, dark room contrast markedly with his and Norma's life in their large mansion with its yellow stained glass. Norma is polished to a glossy elegance, as if she wore a "diamond mask," and is consciously sun-tanned; Hortensia is earthy, naturally brown, and if she shines, it is with the incandescence of the stars: "She was all this: silence and power, the direct quiet power which is the consummation of individual actions that lie below the exterior and daily pomp forms of power. Earth, sap, air" (223).

Similarly, the longest encounter between Norma and Ixca takes place in the natural world (on the beach), away from the chrome and neon of the city. Like that of Robles and Hortensia, their coupling is wordless and abolishes ordinary time: "Their bodies bound together on a wet beach, his spume and salt exciting her dry[ness] and sun, stopping time and the future" (248). As if to emphasize their temporary alliance with sea and sand, above them, "Federico Robles's house stood out against the sky like an enormous yellow peach made of tinted plaster" (250). They are alone, beyond social demands, and we sense that Ixca is almost humanized. This is particularly true when the two meet for the first time in the Robles mansion: Ixca's eyes shine, and a highly charged current of sexuality runs through his body toward Norma. He is nearly drawn out of his eternal role as attendant spirit of the city into a man of flesh and blood. But not quite.

In addition to these movements between visible and invisible worlds, a character may reveal a dialectical mode of thought by undercutting his own words or actions, thus indicating his awareness of an opposing point of view. We have seen, for example, how Zamacona provides contrast-

ing views of Mexican society. Similarly, in the midst of a
heated discussion about the Revolution, he suddenly sees
for a moment how ridiculous all his theorizing is and stops
himself with a curse and a burst of laughter (292). In a
sense, this ironic, dualistic stance is a luxury, though.
Gladys García or Gabriel "the Wetback" have neither the
leisure nor the education to see beyond one way of being.
Yet this dualistic vision is also a source of strength since
it enables those that do possess it to deal with contradictions in life.

Sometimes the ironic vision belongs not to the character himself but to the language that describes him.
Fuentes may undercut an idea with an internal contradiction or a critical image. Robles, for example, claims that
after having fought and suffered so much in the Revolution, "now our ambition could grab what it cared to. Yes,
but always working for the good of the nation" (86). He
seems not to see the implied contradiction between personal and national interest. Some of his points regarding
economic development are valid, but his image of great
social progress since the Revolution destroys itself: "Girls
who would be cooks and maids are now typists" (87). Are
"men and women who do not want to lose their jobs, their
installment-plan furniture, their little cars, for anything in
the world" a satisfactory result of the Revolution?

One set of images in particular supports the ideological structure of duality. Images of eyes recur over and over
in *Where the Air is Clear,* and they undergo a fascinating
variety of changes. Eyes are primarily a sign of vision and
understanding; Fuentes often draws attention to a character's eyes during a significant experience. Furthermore,
the very idea of seeing participates in the oscillation between visible and invisible in *Where the Air is Clear.* Eyes
seem to be most powerful however, when their force is
turned inward, so that blindness often signals unusual
insight. Hortensia (who is blind) sees with the mind's eye
beyond the world of appearances to "the world which at

last will be Federico's and mine. . . . Not yet, for Federico
is not yet what in reality he is, but what life has made him.
Like me. But behind, *Señor*, behind there is the true face"
(279). At one point Teódula's eyes resemble Hortensia's:
"Her eyes narrowed to two black nails hidden in her flesh,
tense in their expectation of the rebirth of a lost world"
(268). Both women look beyond the visible world, Teódula primarily backward, Hortensia both backward and forward. Interestingly, the same image of eyes in fingertips
describes the sensual passion of Robles's first sexual encounter with Mercedes Zamacona and also the way Hortensia later finds her way to his side. Insight into the
invisible realm outshines ordinary eyesight in the visible
realm.[23]

Inner vision is often associated with remembering;
blindness to present demands frees the eyes of memory to
see metaphorically into the past. Hortensia claims that her
"dry eyes sometimes flower again . . . and the city comes
back to me" (280). Recall how Robles's eyes turn to ancient and valuable turquoise as he begins to look on his
past. Just before that passage, the pouches under his eyes
"glinted opaquely," indicating perhaps that his eyes, like
Hortensia's, are about to be used not as an instrument
through which to survey the outer world, but as an aid to
interior scrutiny. In this reverse poetics of sight, the frequent squinting of Ixca and others might represent an
effort to mesh interior and exterior vision. As he talks with
Rodrigo, Ixca "narrow[s] his eyes, concentrating the light
of his powerful body in the slits of his eyelids," suggesting
that his sight is accompanied by insight (205).

NARRATIVE AND SOCIAL STRUCTURE: THE COMMUNAL
IMPERATIVE

The bond between Federico Robles and Hortensia Chacón, visible in their marriage and their son, affirms their

common racial heritage. The emergence of that bond finds a parallel in the structure of the novel as the plot progressively reveals other hidden relationships. This expanding network symbolizes the ties that exist between all the inhabitants of the city "where the air is [no longer] clear." Some of the connections seem contrived, dependent on chance: Little Jorge Morales is dying exactly when Norma's house is burning, so that when his mother Rosa sends Teódula to make excuses for Rosa's not coming to clean that day, Teódula arrives just in time to witness what she is then able to interpret as a sacrificial pyre. And Ixca, Norma's former lover, ends up living with Norma's former servant.

The most amazing bond of all is that Manuel Zamacona is Robles's son, though neither knows it. As if to emphasize this connection, at one point Ixca taunts Robles about having no children, and Robles says that his child is the Revolution. On the one hand, there is simply a mistake; Robles does have a real child, though he is unaware of it. On the other hand, Robles is symbolically correct, for Zamacona represents the new generation of intellectuals who are products of the Revolution. That Robles and his son Manuel should meet to discuss the character of Mexico underscores the idea that all people in the city are related, yet often are ignorant of that relationship. This is the affirmative sense of Ixca's words at the end of the novel: "Here we bide. What are we going to do about it. Where the air is clear" (376). Individualistic philosophies, which help men like Robles ascend to solitary power, will not lessen urban alienation, just as capitalism will not solve the economic problems of the city's poor. Some kind of communal social system is needed. When Federico falls on his knees in front of the migrant worker Gabriel's coffin, his

knees buried themselves in the earth: surface-dry earth of forever-hidden subterranean lagoon, lagoon at the ancient, damp,

froglike core, the place of meeting between men. . . . Those mute
lives whose names he could not remember multiplied in mortal
pantomime until they covered all Mexico with all failures and
downfalls and assassinations and battles. Then they came back
again and spoke to him, recognized him, their own body. (341)

The words recall Pablo Neruda's poem, "The Heights of
Macchu Picchu," where the narrator speaks for all the
nameless people who built the great monument. Fuentes
will echo Neruda's poem in a later story, "The Son of
Andrés Aparicio."[24]

The communal nature of *Where the Air is Clear* appears at the start of the novel in the way Fuentes weaves
together the social fabric of his text. From Gladys García,
who sees a group of people waiting for a taxi to Bobo's
party, we move on to that party. From there, several
stories of guests spiral outwards into a continually expanding network of relationships. The taxi-driver who
takes one couple there serves as a point of entry into yet
another group. The fragmentation of the text into separate
sections, often headed by a character's name, resembles
closely the structure of Dos Passos's USA trilogy, a work
whose influence Fuentes has acknowledged.[25] At the end
of the novel, our glance falls once more on Gladys, as we
hear the same words we heard at the start: "Here we bide.
And what are we going to do about it? Where the air is
clear" (5). The design of the text is circular. On the one
hand, as I've just suggested, the words affirm the communal nature of city life. Ixca's wish to reach out and touch
Gladys' hand as he speaks the last words represents his
sense of unity with a fellow city dweller. On the other
hand, repetition of the question, "What are we going to do
about it" projects a stoic kind of resignation, an acceptance that we are back where we started and *can't* do
much about it.

Both instances of the question follow several pages of
what we might call communal odes to the city. Those odes

suggest that one solution to living in the city is to write about the experience; a writer, at least, will listen to and record all its voices. Both times it is Ixca who speaks, but he speaks in his role as city spirit; his voice is a collective voice. The songs contrast with the essaylike portions of the book.

In the introductory ode, Ixca invokes "the spirit of Anáhuac, who does not crush grapes but hearts." This is the ancient spirit he himself incarnates in the novel, and it is a frightening presence, one which demands blood. This initial invocation reenacts the ancient tradition of the poet's call upon his muse. Ixca's meditation resembles a prose poem: a rush of images pictures Mexico from the inside and prefigures subsequent images in the novel by yoking ancient and modern forms: "Kneeling, crowned with a wreath of cactus, flagellated by your own—by our —hand, your dance adangle from a feather plume and a bus-fender. Dead in a flowery war, a bar scrap. . . . countenance of dry earth and gold blood, . . . the sweetness of another skeleton" (3). Ixca conflates his and the city spirit's voice into one communal narrative. The final series of images leads up to the emblematic "Incandescent prickly pear. Eagle without plumes." The surprising combinations of words suggest the difficulty of describing a world that itself incarnates a number of paradoxical dualities: "city of carnivorous walls, . . . city of immense brevities, city of fixed sun, . . . city of merry lethargy, . . . city rigid between air and worms, . . . city new upon sculptured dust" (4). In their mixture of contrasting elements, these strange, even magical, images may represent the legacy of surrealism in Fuentes's work. Fuentes combines surrealism's techniques of the uncanny juxtaposition of images with an appreciation of native Mexican realities.

The final prose poem of the novel—subtitled "Where the Air is Clear"—includes a catalogue of heroes and a dreamlike recapitulation of Mexico's history. As he did in the prologue, Ixca shifts the mode of his speech to create

a communal voice in response to the challenge of urban
life. The narrative voice scrambles pronouns to destroy the
sense of an individual persona; the one dissolving into the
many. Joseph Sommers argues that "since narrative subject and object are both unclear, the effect achieved approaches that of the collective unconscious of Mexico
City."[26] The piece is the linguistic equivalent of a fiesta.[27]
During it, almost like a sacrificial victim, Ixca's voice dies
into the life of the community. The text symbolically accomplishes the ancient ritual the land demands: Fuentes
makes literary language assume the burden of rejuvenating the Mexican earth, a ritual largely abandoned since the
conquest. By the time the reader recognizes the historical
panorama, the individual narrator has disappeared and
history seems to speak itself. In a sense, Fuentes abolishes
the authority of the Spanish language. Latin American
events narrate themselves freely, no longer subservient to
the grammar of the conquest.

At one point in the epilogue, images from the prologue are humanized by association with characters in the
novel. It is as if in the course of the narration the images
have grown flesh: "Gladys García of carnivorous walls
. . . Librado Ibarra's immense brevity, Teódula Moctezuma of the fixed sun and the slow fire, Tuno of merry
lethargy . . . Gervasio Pola, rigid between air and worms"
(373). They are followed by snatches of dialogue taken at
random from the preceding pages so that the multivocal
impulse of the novel is compressed and intensified in the
epilogue. Numerous techniques and images illustrate its
strength throughout. We have seen Ixca and Robles both
speak—in their different ways—in the name of collective
humanity. Near the end, just before the overt scrambling
of grammatical voices in the epilogue, Ixca "became
. . . the city itself . . . the names and smells and all bodies
sprinkled the buried length of the great heavy unbalanced
valley, all tombstones, and above all, all voices, voices"
(362). These voices include newspaper headlines and

popular songs as well as spoken words or thoughts, even French and English expressions—the voices of other cultures.[28] The "tube-squeezed light of neon advertisements" may come closest to constituting a prophetic analogue for an urban language—frighteningly brash, perhaps, but excitingly modern, symbolically anonymous and multiple.

In recording the many voices of the city, *Where the Air is Clear* responds to the need for a collective language, to the image of a people waiting to be heard. The image appears with special clarity one day at the Robles mansion when "a dozen brown faces . . . squeezed together" at the end of Norma's garden come to receive her charity: "Manuel . . . thought of them as identical in all epochs, all ages. Like a subterranean river, indifferent and dark, flowing far below idea or change. . . . Hands touched *rebozos,* as if to cover up more and become still more anonymous" (215). Fuentes attempts to create a communal language and narrative structure, to do more than hand out old clothes to the waiting citizens, to give a renewed voice to the "subterranean river" that includes not just the poor, but all the inhabitants of the region where the air used to be clear.

Tradition, Repression, and Independence:
The Good Conscience

After the large canvas of *Where the Air is Clear,* Fuentes narrows his focus to center on the struggles of one individual in *The Good Conscience.*[1] The novel was clearly inspired by the great European realists; Fuentes mentions Galdós in particular and goes on to say that the novel is a typical *bildungsroman*—his own "sentimental education."[2] Its hero, Jaime Ceballos, thus recalls the heroes of

Stendhal, Balzac, and Flaubert, all of whom Jaime reads during the course of the story. The plural Spanish title, *The Good Consciences,* makes its ironic impact clearer than the English one, for it stresses the sheeplike natures of men who can rest easily even though they may be far from good. Early on, the narrator informs us that "the citizen of Guanajuato is . . . a practiced, talented, certified hypocrite."[3] The story concerns young Jaime Ceballos's attempt to resist this way of life, typical of a small provincial town.

The narrative begins by following the Ceballos family through Mexican history. Like Artemio Cruz, its members ally themselves with governors and ministers, consolidating their financial empire. During the French invasion of Mexico, one of three Ceballos brothers does not serve the emperor, but marches with the liberal armies and is captured and executed. In not following the common family pattern, he prefigures Jaime's adolescent rebellion. Just after Jaime's birth, his father, Rodolfo, urged on by his sister Asunción, turns against his lower-class wife, Adelina, allowing her to return home, but keeping Jaime. Asunción takes over Jaime as her child, since her own husband, Jorge Balcárcel, is unable to father a child. Uncle Jorge, the director of a bank, is a creature of habit and cliché, demanding his egg "boiled for exactly one hundred and eighty seconds," spouting conventional mercenary and sanctimonious sayings like, "Decidedly, private property is a postulate of Divine Reason," or, "A man's treasures are his family and his faith" (23). Furthermore, "The first rule in this family was that life's real and important dramas should be concealed. Asunción had secretly plotted to gain a child, Rodolfo had secretly felt guilt for abandoning Adelina, but everything was hidden" (26).

Jaime is the key to this hypocritical structure: "Asunción's substitute son, the pretext for Balcárcel's authority, Rodolfo's link with the past" (26). Predictably, no one wants him to grow up and destroy the pattern. Uncle Jorge reflects that "the son who because he is not really theirs must be watched over and chained to them more forcefully than if he had sprung from Asunción's barren womb" (76). But things cannot stay this way forever, as the curtains, moved perhaps by the winds of change and passion, suggest:

All these cloth arms lift and wave, topple over small tables, brush away bric-a-brac. It is as if heavy wings are trying to carry the house in flight. Then the wind ceases, the curtains are still, and the slow dust sifts again. (29)

Similarly, as Jaime sits in the sun on Easter Sunday, the sights and sounds of the town—vendors of all sorts, horsemen, beggars, cats—are interspersed with images that suggest his own awakening sexuality: one horse tries to mount another, and "long candles hang their reposing virility beneath the tarp of the vendor" (46).

Fuentes links this sensual growth to the awakening of a social conscience in Jaime, both urges repressed by provincial family life. That same Easter Sunday, Jaime gives food and shelter to a mine labor organizer who is hiding from vindictive bosses. He is distraught when his uncle discovers the man and turns him in. Just after he has felt great sympathy for this one authentic voice, now stifled, Jaime must listen to "the tongues of a hundred gratuitous preceptors, . . . all friends in the immediate world of his aunt and uncle"—the commercial, religious, government, and ranching interests, all competing for Jaime's attention (59). As he progresses through adolescence, the narrowness of life in Guanajuato, its stifling atmosphere, its hypocrisy, become increasingly intolerable for Jaime. He begs his father to explain his mother's situation to him, for example, asking to see her; but Rodolfo literally runs away. At this point, Jaime typifies the sensitive young man, isolated from his schoolmates, alienated from his

family and his society, immersed in books his elders consider inappropriate, dreaming of a glorious future.

During this period, he associates the intense religious
feeling when he contemplates Christ on the cross with his
intense sympathy for Ezequiel—the labor organizer—and
his suffering. It is as if Ezequiel represented Christ on
earth for Jaime and also something private, an alternative
to his family's mode, just at the moment when he has
discovered his own sexual force: "He saw Christ very
close, hanging upon nails. Ezequiel Zuno still closer, and
not mute like the crucified figure. . . . the body he had
discovered today . . . joined them all, Christ, Ezequiel, and
the candle" (55). And like Jesus, Ezequiel is led away to
his death by rough soldiers, while Jaime cries out in guilt,
almost as if Ezequiel were dying for Jaime's sins. In a sense
that is true, for Ezequiel dies for the sins of Jaime's class,
which oppresses workers to assure their own comfortable
lives. Jaime's real mother becomes another kind of Christ
figure for him:[4] "No, the words of the Bible did not explain faith, but those two names, those two living people
who had suffered hurt at the hands of . . . his family
. . . Ezequiel, and Adelina" (97). To align himself with
these figures, and to atone for his sins, Jaime enacts a kind
of penance in the desert, melodramatically lashing himself
with a thorny whip of braided cactus spines.

As the novel proceeds, it becomes more and more
evident that the way his elders treat Jaime stems primarily
from their own fears and inadequacies. The morning after
Uncle Jorge has had feelings of sexual guilt at not satisfying his wife and "a series of indecent visions which he
wishes and does not wish to disrupt," he speaks to Jaime
about his conduct, with particular emphasis on sexual
matters (76).

In attempting to weed out Jaime's deviations from
their own social pattern, Jaime's aunt and uncle try to
separate him from his one friend, a pure-blooded Indian
boy, who is socially unacceptable to the family. This Juan

Manuel represents the native strength from which the superficially respectable Ceballos family has become alienated—a fresh, clean force, the indigenous life idealized after the Revolution:

His Spanish possessed a certain cautious quality: It was a learned language. . . . He evoked a sense of strangeness. . . . Those dark eyes, wide open to the world and illuminated by an inner happiness, were lights in a face full of energy and strength of will. His simple gestures possessed a real elegance. (84)

Again here, as in *Where the Air is Clear* and *The Death of Artemio Cruz,* a man's strength and power are concentrated in his eyes. If, as Octavio Paz has suggested, Mexicans habitually wear masks, it is by their eyes that we must know them. Furthermore, Juan Manuel, like Fuentes himself, is already considering the force of language in Mexican society—pondering the stylistic differences between the passionate tumult of the philosopher José Vasconcelos and the "serene clarity" of the novelist José Luis Guzmán as opposed to the speeches of union leaders and politicians —"the other Mexican language: a language of lackeys" (91).

Throughout most of the novel, Jaime has taken religion seriously, wanting to imitate Christ's passion and suffering and love for others, while he sees those around him going to church as an empty social gesture, not a personal commitment. He succeeds momentarily in the context of the church, when the priest he talks with—the only adult who shows him some measure of understanding —falls on his knees and begs Jaime to pray for him after seeing Jaime's back covered with blood (as a result of his penitential flogging). The next time the priest sees Jaime, however, when Jaime says he had wanted to suffer to wipe away his mother's pain, the priest tells him that it was foolish to expect men to change because of his wounds and that henceforth he must simply love everyone, not judge them.

After this, a change comes over Jaime, his "eyes
. . . lose their ability to be astonished," and he thinks, "on
the one hand the complex theorems of love and sin, man's
fall and salvation; on the other life's vulgar plain reality:
to fornicate, to conform to class and breeding, to die"
(142). It is as if he has passed through a maturing kind of
fire, which has separated the real from the ideal in him,
making him a socially acceptable man rather than a saint
or a revolutionary. Unlike his liberal ancestor, who in a
sense symbolizes the part of Jaime that dies, he becomes
a man with a "good conscience." For a while, he feels
uneasy, remembering his earlier passion and rage at injustice, but he finally assumes the genteel role his family has
planned for him. As he says to Juan Manuel, "I'm going
to do everything exactly opposite to what I wanted. I'm
going to conform" (146–47). And as the novel ends, "the
great green portal of the Ceballos mansion opened, and
Jaime entered, to belong to their domain."

The potential for communal life that Fuentes implies
with the narrative techniques in *Where the Air is Clear* is
missing from *The Good Conscience*, where he portrays a
provincial society that suffocates generous impulses.[5]
Though life in the Mexico City of *Where the Air is Clear*
is hardly ideal, community there is not synonymous with
conformity as it is in *The Good Conscience*. Even so, the
individual "conscience" of Jaime provides a particle of
hope. Like Rodrigo Pola, he passes from idealism to conformity, but his own sadness at the process, as well as his
bonds with Ezequiel and Juan Manuel, partially redeem
him in the eyes of the reader and foreshadow the growth
of a not entirely provincial soul.

Fragmenting Forces in the Revolution and the Self:

The Death of Artemio Cruz

The Death of Artemio Cruz (1962) is Fuentes's best-known novel, an acknowledged masterpiece in the boom of recent Latin American fiction. The book focuses on the experiences of one man, but through them it portrays the dynamics of the Mexican Revolution of 1910–1920 and of Mexican society in succeeding years. The memories of Artemio Cruz on his deathbed form a meditation on his past life and his accomplishments. In parallel fashion, the novel as a whole reflects back on the Revolution and its aftermath. Cruz uses his memory to fight against death; the book might be said to fight for memory of the original ideals of the Mexican Revolution, forgotten and betrayed in later years. The novel is a successful portrait of both the man and Mexican society because it reveals the progressive fragmentation of both.[1] Artemio Cruz has become splintered; he is now several different selves. He speaks in multiple voices which appear on the pages as separate sections of text. These voices correspond, on the personal level, to the conflicting factions in the Revolution and in contemporary Mexico.

The book reveals a continual interplay of historical and individual forces. The brutality of the Revolution mirrors Cruz's brutality in business and personal affairs. Sometimes it seems as if the cruelty Cruz experienced as a boy and during the fighting in the Revolution explains his later ruthless behavior. At other times we wonder whether the Revolution might have achieved more lasting success if it had brought to power better men than Artemio Cruz. In short, is Cruz brutalized by society and the Revolution, or does he corrupt them?[2] Contemplating

Cruz, the reader remains suspended between sympathy and condemnation.

The Death of Artemio Cruz, published four years after *Where the Air is Clear,* condenses and intensifies the panorama of Mexican society in the earlier novel. The past pervades both texts. Progressive discovery of Artemio Cruz's personal past structures his story, and the Revolution provides the dominant historical presence in the novel. Memories of the Revolution are thus joined to the ancient—the "prehistorical"—Aztec traditions that show through the portrait of modern Mexico City in *Where the Air is Clear.* The three voices within Artemio Cruz correspond structurally to the many separate voices of the city in *Where the Air is Clear.* Whereas in the earlier novel, Fuentes weaves elaborate and often surprising connections between inhabitants of Mexico City, in *The Death of Artemio Cruz* and in *The Good Conscience* he stresses the divisions within one character. *Where the Air is Clear* constitutes a more polemical and explicit investigation of the Mexican national character than does *The Death of Artemio Cruz,* which represents a stocktaking, a confirmation of existing traits. Many of the central figures in *Where the Air is Clear* are quite young; we see them in the process of becoming. Artemio Cruz, on the other hand, approaches the end of his life, and we see what he has become.

CENTRAL EVENTS AND IMAGES

Just before the novel opens, Artemio Cruz has made a trip to keep intact a vast chain of graft. On his return to Mexico City, he collapses. From the beginning of the novel, he languishes in bed, surrounded by his family, thinking and remembering. In occasional counterpoint to Cruz's thoughts, a tape recorder plays back conversations with officials of American firms for which Cruz has served as a Mexican "front man." We hear of bribes, the suppression of riots, intimidation of the press, plans for American intervention in Mexico's commercial and political affairs. This background suggests what Cruz's life has become by 1959. Memories of his earlier life unfold against this setting in twelve sections. Cruz narrates these twelve sections in the third person, referring to himself as Artemio Cruz. Each of these sections is accompanied by a monologue in the first person and another monologue in the second person. The sections range backward and forward in time; if we straighten out the chronology, Cruz's story unfolds in the following manner.

Artemio Cruz is the illegitimate son of a plantation owner and a mulatto servant. He grows up in the country and joins the Mexican Revolution on the side of the rebels. In 1913, Federal troops kill all the Indians in one village, including Regina, Artemio's first love. One day in 1915, he is captured by a revolutionary force opposed to his own. That day he witnesses the execution of a fellow prisoner, Gonzalo Bernal. Sometime before Bernal is shot, Cruz left their common cell to bargain for his own safety. It is unclear whether or not he could have helped Bernal by remaining with him. Perhaps he would only have died as well. But Cruz will later feel guilty about having abandoned Bernal.

Cruz escapes, and in 1919, when the fighting is over, he gains entrance into the Bernal household by claiming that he was at Gonzalo's side when he died and that Gonzalo asked him to go see his family. His plan is to woo Bernal's sister Catalina, ingratiate himself with their father, and take over the hacienda. Old Bernal, deeply in debt, can no longer run the hacienda and tells Catalina she should marry Cruz so that he will save them from ruin. Catalina resists at first. She loves someone else, she resents Artemio's opportunism, and she does not believe his story about her brother. But she succumbs in the end to her father's wishes and to her own sensual attraction to Cruz, an attraction she herself does not fully understand.

Cruz steadily gains control of more and more land and wealth. Elected a federal deputy, he consolidates his financial empire through corrupt deals with American businesses. Catalina Cruz bears two children, Lorenzo and Teresa, and the family moves to Mexico City. Catalina's father dies. In 1939, Lorenzo is killed fighting with the international brigades for the Republican side in the Spanish Civil War. All this time, Catalina continues to resent Artemio and he turns to a series of mistresses.

This sequence of events is punctuated by a complementary structure of images that accents central moments and ideas. Mirrors, for example, appear throughout Cruz's story. He looks in one as he enters his office building, as he shaves in a hotel room in Acapulco, as he comes downstairs in his house. This succession of mirrors provides an emblem for the narrative that contains them. Cruz is doubled in mirrors as he is multiplied by the various voices of memory which record his past.[3] Mirrors also provide moments of reflection in a life of action. Generally, Cruz dislikes seeing his reflection, but is drawn to study it just the same. We sense a simultaneous desire and reluctance to know himself. Or perhaps Cruz dislikes the mirror's reflection of a single, aged, physical self—not the numerous possible selves of the imagination. This defeat of the imagination characterizes Cruz's memory of the moment before he lapses into his mortal illness. He sees himself reflected in the glass top of his desk, and he thinks: The "twin in the glass will join the other, who is yourself, join the seventy-one-year-old old man."[4] Mirrors stifle him and remind him of his age: "I am not old although once in a mirror I was old" (136). He is attracted to his image when he can concentrate on the "green eyes and energetic mouth"—both youthful and strong. But he is repelled by the sight of his own false teeth and turns away from the mirror to insert them (142).

His green eyes are another recurring image. They recall Artemio's Spanish heritage, suggesting aristocratic pride, power, dominance over others. They also reveal inherent force, liveliness, charisma, and sensuality. Catalina gasps when she first sees him: "Dear God, how can I help but respond to such strength, to the force in those green eyes?" (96). Moreover, Artemio's father had green eyes, as did his son Lorenzo. They suggest, then, the importance of personal heritage, just as Artemio's long meditation on Mexico will stress the significance of a national heritage.

THE REVOLUTION—AND AFTER: HISTORY AND THE LAND

From the novel's central focus on the conflicts within Cruz, the reader moves outward to the conflicts that divide Mexican society as a whole, and particularly to the problems posed by the Mexican Revolution. Fuentes has compressed about one hundred fifty years of Mexican history into the novel. As in Cruz's personal story, so in this historical panorama of Mexico the narrative digs back and back in search of origins. Throughout the book, the presentation of historical events follows two principles: the repetition of important moments of conflict and the revelation of persistent social patterns, though the people who embody those patterns may change. What's more, Cruz's individual life fits into an ancient mythic pattern as well as into these historical events, for he gives a New Year's party, symbolically closing his life, 52 years after he sets out on his own from Cocuya. (Aztec time was divided into cycles of 52 years each.) Here, as in the rest of Fuentes's work, mythic structures persist, but their contents are significantly modified by history.

Through the figure of Artemio Cruz's paternal grandmother, old Ludivinia Menchaca, the historical narrative may be said to begin in 1810, for she was "born in the year of the first Revolution, brought into the world behind doors battered by terror" (264). The first Revolution, the war of independence from Spain, begins a process that will lead to the next one, a hundred years after. Ludivinia Menchaca represents the old order, the landed aristocracy, which resisted reform movements even back in the middle of the nineteenth century. Artemio Cruz is born on her family's land, but denied its heritage. He goes off to fight in the Revolution against the order upheld by families like the Menchacas and finally ends up in virtually the same position as his grandmother, denying a voice to later revolutionaries.[5]

The figure of Miss Rosa in Faulkner's *Absalom, Absalom!*, who walls herself up in her house after the destruction of the Civil War, would seem to be a precursor of Ludivinia Menchaca, who does just the same after the mid-nineteenth-century struggles in Mexico. Ludivinia's room "was hot and musty and smelled of the tropics," a "nest of closed-in smells" (281); Miss Rosa's room was "a dim hot airless room all closed and fastened for forty-three summers." The two women even speak in much the same way: a sharp "yes" or "no" at the start of a paragraph, a list of rhetorical questions, a repetitive style.

Ludivinia's vision of "the green-eyed child," Artemio Cruz, outside her window, forms the link between the tumultuous period she lived through and the later Revolution. In between came the years of the dictator Porfirio Díaz. Díaz originally rose to power when he opposed the reelection of the former president, Benito Juárez, in 1870. In order to strengthen Mexico financially, the Díaz regime allowed many foreign concessions to enter Mexico, gave away huge properties made up of land taken from the Indians, denied freedom to the press.

The second Revolution began in 1910 when Francisco Madero opposed the reelection of Díaz. His sympathy for land reform gained him the support of the *campesinos* and their leaders, Pancho Villa and Emiliano Zapata. Madero became president in 1911, but his government was weakened by continued fighting and agitation for land reforms it failed to carry out. As a result of the general confusion, Victoriano Huerta took over in 1913 and Madero was killed by Huerta's forces. These acts provoked Venustiano Carranza and Alvaro Obregón to rise against Huerta and to uphold the original constitution against Huerta's politics of personal power. Carranza and Obregón were supported intermittently by the forces under Villa and Zapata.

In 1913, when we first see Artemio Cruz in the Revolution, he is fighting with the forces of Carranza against Huerta. By the day in 1915 when Gonzalo Bernal is shot, Villa and Carranza have quarreled, Villa has been defeated by Carranza's ally Obregón, and Villa's forces are in retreat. These Villistas capture Bernal and Cruz just before Carranza's forces catch up with them. When they are still in their cell, Bernal says that "as soon as Zapata and Villa are eliminated, only two caudillos [chiefs] will remain, your present leaders" (Carranza and Obregón). He asks Cruz, "Which one will you follow?" Cruz replies that "my leader is General Obregón" (188). This is the first of Cruz's fortunate alliances, for in 1920 Obregón overthrows Carranza, who is killed, and becomes president.

Fuentes suggests that early in the Revolution, leaders concentrated too much on ideas and ignored practical concerns: "the general found the best policy was to take immediately what money there was from the wealthy . . . and to leave to the final triumph of the Revolution the details of the land and workaday reforms. Now they had to get to Mexico City and chase the drunkard Huerta, the murderer of Don Panchito Madero, out of the presidency" (65). But as the story of the Bernal hacienda will reveal, these "details of the land and workaday reforms" are essential to the common people. Later on in the Revolution, the power struggle between different leaders and their factions diffused the earlier strength of revolutionary

reform. In the beginning, the Revolution passed through
the pueblos cancelling the peasants' debts and releasing
political prisoners. But "the purpose today is to glorify
leaders" now that "the men who believed the Revolution's
purpose was to liberate the people have been eliminated"
(186).

In addition to a survey of Mexican history, Fuentes
provides vignettes which evoke the natural scenery and
the artistic traditions of Mexico. Though Cruz is confined
to his room in Mexico City, his mind covers the country
in reverie. One section of narration constitutes a kind of
hymn to Mexico, the land and its traditions. This is the
really valuable inheritance Artemio Cruz's family will receive, not the money they are so eagerly waiting for. It is
also Cruz's own heritage:

Remember this country? You remember it. It is not one; there
are a thousand countries, with a single name. You know that.
You will carry with you the red deserts, the hills of prickly pear
and maguey, the world of dry cactus, the lava belt of frozen
craters, the walls of golden domes and rock thrones, the lime-
stone and sandstone cities, the texontle-stone cities, the adobe
pueblos . . . the Veracruz combs, the Mixtec braids, Tzotil belts
. . . you will inherit the land. . . . (266–68)

But Artemio Cruz knows that he has not added to this
heritage. He curses himself: "You will bequeath the futile
dead names . . . men despoiled of their names that you
might possess yours. . . ." (269). In an attempt to create
a personal setting appropriate for this national heritage, a
kind of return to the cultural past, Cruz has decorated his
mansion with Mexican antiques. He clings to the memory
of these possessions as he lies dying. The novel's description of the mansion (pp. 242–43, 249) forms an ironic
parallel to the earlier description of an elaborate church
from the colonial period (p. 31). That church represents
the real artistic heritage of Mexico. It endures in spite of
men like Artemio Cruz and their pseudo-antique houses.

SOCIAL CRITICISM

The betrayal of the Revolution by Artemio Cruz calls forth Fuentes's own revolutionary perspective. Four specific failings of postrevolutionary Mexican society recur throughout *The Death of Artemio Cruz:* class domination, Americanization, financial corruption, and the failure of land reform.[6]

A cluster of details at the start of the novel sets the critical tone. Here Cruz rides to his office in his limousine as his wife and daughter enter a shop:

The chauffeur was sweating in the heat of the sun and could not turn on the radio. He [Cruz], in back, reflected that he had not done badly in associating himself with the Colombian coffee-growers when the war in Africa began, and the two women entered the shop and the shop-girl asked them please to be seated while she advised the proprietress (for she knew who they were, this mother and daughter, and her instructions were to inform the proprietress the moment they entered). (13–14)

As in *Where the Air is Clear,* here the comfort of the rich who work in skyscrapers and ride in cars contrasts with the discomfort of the poor who either drive them or walk. Furthermore, there are parallels between this scene and the next one. As we switch scenes, we do not hear about Cruz's feelings for his wife or daughter or any conversation between the two women, but instead the detail about the proprietress hurrying to greet them. As Catalina and Teresa enter the shop, Teresa registers a feeling of despair as she is indoctrinated into this hierarchy of dominance by her mother, who motions to her not to make room on the sofa for the saleswoman to sit down with them.

A little farther on, another transition between Artemio Cruz's activities and those of his wife and daughter again provides a socially critical detail (and another mirror image):

Cruz moved toward the revolving door . . . he saw a man identi-

cal to himself, wearing the same double-breasted suit, but color-
less, . . . a man surrounded by beggars, who let his hand drop
at the same instant he in the vestibule did.

. . .

Again the outstretched hands of beggars disheartened her,
and she squeezed her daughter's shoulder to hurry her into
the artificial coolness and the scent of soaps and cosmetics
. . . she asked for a jar of "theatrical" cold cream and two lip-
sticks. . . . (17)

The beggars are noticed in passing—a flash in a revolving
door, a glimpse of hands outside a drugstore/restaurant.
The images form only small intrusions in the story. That
is part of the problem: the rich and powerful Cruz family,
and even we readers who follow their thoughts and actions, pass by people suffering social oppression—chauf-
feurs, saleswomen, beggars. We are all on the way to
something more "important." For Cruz, it is a meeting
with American geologists and financiers; for the women it
is the buying of cosmetics and the eating of nut waffles and
orange juice.

The counterpoint of these two scenes also underlines
the second point of social criticism in the novel. This is the
domination of Mexican finances and natural resources by
North American business, and the concomitant aping of
American culture in Mexico.[7] As Catalina and Teresa eat
their North American raisin bread and waffles with syrup,
they carry on a long dispute about how to pronounce the
last name of Joan Crawford. They get it wrong of course,
and to pile irony on irony, their food is served during the
discussion by a waitress in a Mexican folkloric costume.
This costume is designed to appeal primarily to the
American tourists who eat at the exclusive Sanborn's and
to Mexicans who imitate them. For Fuentes, "The great
cultural farce has consisted in disguising the past and
presenting it clad in the bright colors of folklore."[8] Mean-

while, back at his office, Cruz is extracting a two-million-peso bribe from the Americans so that he will be their "figurehead" for the exploitation of Mexican sulphur domes. Waffles served by a waitress in a Mexican costume parallel American interests filtered through a Mexican front man. Neither activity represents a true appreciation of Mexican culture or economics. Artemio Cruz is actually a denial of the popular idea that the Revolution has made Mexicans proud to be Mexican. After remembering the scene where he obtained a larger bribe than the Americans would like to have given him, he reflects that he is particularly satisfied to have imposed his will on them because he regrets "the geographical error that has prevented [him] from being one of them." Cruz admires the efficiency and comfort of the United States and finds "intolerable the incompetence, misery, dirt, the weakness and nakedness of this impoverished country that has nothing" (28).

The third point of criticism, financial corruption, is well illustrated by the example of Cruz receiving his bribe. That is only one of many such frauds. The fourth problem, the lack of meaningful land reform, appears as Artemio Cruz takes over the hacienda of his father-in-law, old Gamaliel Bernal. He does not give the peasants land, as they had been promised. Instead, Cruz drives off the smaller landowners, consolidating the surrounding land into an even larger unit than before. He then sells it off to farmers in exchange for urban lots he knows will increase in value. The farmers will not operate large enough haciendas to support the peasants in the area, who will then be forced to leave the land, since they own none themselves. Ironically, after all of this, Artemio Cruz is nominated for Federal Deputy in recognition of his efforts on behalf of agrarian reform.

PRIVATE POWER

We shall soon see how Fuentes represents memory as power, how Cruz's memory triumphs (temporarily at least) over his surroundings. The text that he narrates is perhaps his final attempt to dominate before he is definitively conquered by death. But besides this, struggles for power pervade the individual and social relations within the novel.[9] To move beyond Cruz himself is to notice that the hunger for power everywhere disrupts both public and private domains, both society and marriage. The original impetus of the Revolution was fragmented, its spirit weakened by the power struggles of its generals. In the political life that has followed the Revolution, this disruptive desire for power persists.

Private power struggles, fragmenting and disintegrating intimate relationships, are most fully developed in the "war between the sexes" that rages between Artemio and Catalina Cruz. Here again, Cruz's origins are significant. Ludivinia recalls that the boy's mother had been chased away by his natural father, Atanasio (296). Cruz continues this pattern of dominance in his own marriage. When he first meets Catalina, he wonders, "Did she feel the assertion of possession that he scarcely disguised?" (36–37). Catalina herself is divided between nights of passion and days of hatred. She, too, sees the relationship as strife: "At night you conquer me, but I defeat you during the day" (97). And she reflects that they have both lost "the dream, the innocence" of their lives (107). But Catalina says this to herself, not to Artemio. Her understanding of the situation remains inside her; it does not begin to bridge the gap between them. Similarly, Artemio does not dare to say the words that he believes might enable them "to forget and begin anew": "Don't hate me. Have compassion for me, beloved Catalina. For I love you. Weigh my guilt against my love and you will see that my love is the greater" (107). If this appeal were to fail—as well it might, given Catalina's attitude—he would have shown weakness, lost ground in the power struggle.

This tension between Artemio and Catalina is only one manifestation of the continual play of opposite forces in the novel. Like Artemio Cruz, who is divided between past and present, body and mind, lover and dominator, husband and father, brutality and tenderness, Mexico is divided between "sons of bitches and poor bastards," rich and poor, Spanish and Indian heritages, modern buildings and ancient rituals, women and men, revolutionary ideals and everyday problems. Compressed into the mind of one man, as he lies dying, these divisions take on urgency and universal significance.

THE SELF: "MEMORY IS DESIRE SATISFIED."

The situation which the reader confronts on the first page of the novel, when he learns that Artemio Cruz is on his deathbed, shapes the story that follows. The title is also a directive: before we open the book, we know that Cruz will die. From this the events draw psychological urgency, since we sense that the narrator does not have "all the time in the world." Much of what we hear is a kind of "return of the repressed" before it is too late. Though Cruz is not a practicing Catholic, he has grown up in a country where final confessions are traditional. We might regard this book, then, as a final confession in a nontraditional mode, where the reader, not the priest, will condemn or absolve Cruz.

This certain approach of death at the end of the novel permits memory freedom of action within a closed form. Emotional recollection, not logical chronology, orders the events. We go back and forth in time, searching with Cruz for some kind of truth about him.[10] This process is highlighted by the fact that we see his origins, his birth, only near the end of the book.[11] The element of suspense is projected toward the past, rather than toward the future. The consequent closeness of birth and death warns us about the shortness of all human life and the necessity of choosing our actions well.

The very fact that he can recall the events of his past is a satisfaction to Artemio Cruz. For Cruz has divided himself in order to survive; he has cut out of his everyday existence most of his emotion for Catalina, his despair at Regina's and Lorenzo's deaths, his disappointment at losing Laura—a woman with whom he had a serious love affair, perhaps even his own fear of death. But, as he says, keeping up a proud exterior forever is killing: "Pride. Pride saves us. Pride kills us" (195). So that, now, he is glad that memory can revive these emotional experiences. They help him "survive" spiritually his own coldness and postpone the literal coldness of death. This is the sense in which "memory is desire satisfied: / and with memory you will survive, before it becomes too late / before chaos prevents memory" (58). Duplicating the self in memory's narrative thus conquers, for a time, the reflections of the body in mirrors. But the triumph of memory is not eternal; the chaos that threatens it is death.

NARRATIVE TECHNIQUE

This confrontation between memory and death continues throughout the novel. It motivates the most striking aspect of *The Death of Artemio Cruz*—the division of the text into three different modes of narration, and three different verb tenses. The interest of the novel depends to a large extent on the carefully orchestrated interplay between the different voices of Cruz. Fuentes's formal innovation succeeds particularly well here because narrative strategies correspond to psychological configurations.

Except for occasional intrusions from Catalina's thoughts, and a chapter recounting Lorenzo's experiences in Spain, Artemio Cruz narrates the entire book. His sickness and imminent death are recounted in the first person and the present tense, his meditations and desires in the second person and the future tense, and the events of his past life in the third person and the past tense. While the persons and tenses of the voices are clear, the perspectives of the voices elude exact description, for they share many images and ideas. They are often categorized as three distinct parts of the mind: consciousness, the subconscious, and memory.[12] Fuentes has explained that in addition to Cruz's first and third person voices,

there is a third element, the subconscious, a kind of Virgil that guides [Cruz] through the twelve circles of his hell, and that is the other face of his mirror, the other face of Artemio Cruz: the You that speaks in the future tense. It is the subconscious that clings to a future that the I—the dying old man—will never know. The old I is the present while the He digs up the past of Artemio Cruz. It's a question of a dialogue of mirrors between the three people, the three times that constitute the life of this hard and alienated character. In his agony, Artemio tries to regain through memory his twelve definitive days, days which are really twelve options.[13]

The use of these three different voices permits the juxtaposition of different scenes, figures, and images. They demonstrate the coexistence of Cruz's separate selves—immediately, from the inside. For instance, in a first person sequence—in Cruz's room—Cruz sees Catalina and Teresa rummage first through his suits, and then through his shoes, in search of his will. Cruz greatly enjoys their ridiculous physical—and moral—position. "To see those two women on all fours among the scattered suits, their wide buttocks elevated, their cheeks fluttering with an obscene panting, fumbling through my shoes. Bitter sweetness closes my eyes. I raise my hand to my heart and close my eyes. 'Regina . . .' " (157). The contrast between Regina's disinterested love, narrated earlier in the past tense and evoked later in the future tense and the present greed of Cruz's wife and daughter is clear and forceful.

The first voice the reader meets is the *I* of Artemio Cruz dying; it concentrates on the unpleasant physical sensations he experiences: "My stomach . . . ah! . . . and my chest continues sleeping with the same dull tick-tick-tick that taps in my wrists . . . I—am—body, I" (5). These unpleasant sensations provide the impetus to escape the physical present and take flight through his other voices. Memory is power for him now. The motivation is made explicit early on. At one point, for example, Cruz's eyes feel like lead, and after "another injection," he asks himself, "But why?" and continues, "No, no, let me think of something else, quick, something else, for that hurts, it hurts, it" (end of section). After this painful present, Cruz switches to another self—in the future: "You will close your eyes and you will see again, but you will see only what your brain wants you to see: more than the world, yet less. . . . Desire will send you back into memory and you will remember" (55–58). The episode in the past tense that directly follows this meditation contains the love scenes with Regina during the Revolution. Just before the injection that provokes the reverie, he has said, "I have forgotten your face, who loved. Oh, God, I have forgotten that face. No, I don't have to forget it. Where is it? . . . how can I summon you up to be with me here?" (55). The memory that follows accomplishes that desire.

In these first person sections, particularly near the end, the reader participates in a moving battle. Cruz's voice fights for the right to define him against other voices which threaten to take over the description of him—Catalina, Teresa, the priest, the doctor. His secretary Padilla is his ally in this battle, for Padilla manages the tape recorder that plays Cruz's voice when it was stronger than it is now—better able to drown out the others. The use of interior monologue here, as in *Ulysses,* besides presenting a character's inner depths, is also a sign of his solitude.

The second voice the reader hears is the second person, the *you*—"*tu*" in Spanish. This "*tu*" is the second person familiar, the form of intimate address. In addition to presenting a private side of Artemio Cruz, direct address draws Artemio Cruz and the reader together, and strengthens the idea that Cruz represents all Mexicans, perhaps even all men. Even after the reader has learned that Cruz is speaking to himself and not to the reader, the sensation of being implicated in the story persists.

In the first transition from an *I* section to a *you* section, Cruz reveals the reason why the *you* is addressed in the future tense: he adopts the future because it denies the presence of death. He wants to look ahead and to see something besides his presently arriving death; but the only things he has to distract him from the present pain of the dying process are memories. He therefore puts them in the future tense, the tense of hopes and plans, the only action he can manage now: "In your half-darkness your eyes would prefer to look ahead, not behind, and they do not know how to forsee the past. Yes: yesterday you will fly home from Hermosillo" (8). The "Yes" that separates the past tense from the future means yes, Cruz has found a way to satisfy his desire to believe in a future for himself.

The second person sections contain the fullest memories of Cruz's son Lorenzo, including lyrical descriptions of their ride together on the coast at Veracruz before Lorenzo leaves for Spain. This is Cruz's most persistent happy memory. In one of these memories of Lorenzo, Cruz modulates between past and future tenses. It is as if he wants to shape his hope in the future rather than accepting its end in the past: "you rode your horses; he asked you if you would ride together as far as the sea: he will ask you where you are going to eat and he said—he will say—papá, he will smile lifting his arm" (159). Once again he succeeds; the passage continues in the future. This voice of the future that speaks of the past represents a triumph over time: "You will invent a time that does not exist, and measure it . . . and you will end by thinking that there is no other reality than that created by your mind" (198).[14]

The futurity of these sections represents, as I have noted above, a potential Artemio Cruz, who is possible only in thought and who is soon to be extinguished by death. Such passages constitute Artemio's attempt to pardon himself by holding out the idea of the better person he might have been.[15] Cruz includes in them an alternate set of events—what this secret self wishes he had done:

> you will choose to leave him [Lorenzo] in Catalina's hands, . . . you won't push him to . . . that fatal destiny which could have been yours . . .
>
> you will tell Laura: yes
>
> you will tell the fat man in the blue room: no
>
> you will elect to stay in the cell with Bernal and Tobias, to share their fate . . .
>
> you will be a peon
>
> you will be a blacksmith . . .
>
> you will not be Artemio Cruz, you will not be seventy-one. . . . (237–38)

But it is clear that Cruz's effort to revise the past cannot succeed; he has done what he has done, and he knows it. His failure to redeem himself in his own eyes makes the story of his death all the more moving. Cruz's judgment of himself is ultimately more important—and more condemning—than our external judgment of his business deals, his cowardice, his coldness, his infidelity.[16]

The third voice we encounter, the *he,* constitutes another example of memory as escape from death. These memories present the finished past and lack the sense of potential change included in the *you* sections. But they still provide Artemio Cruz with an alternate—and an extended—time frame. As I've mentioned earlier, these twelve sections are dated, and they recount Cruz's story through the events of twelve key days that span his life. The hard facts they contain lead us to judge him more harshly than the events he longs for and imagines or the emotional needs he reveals.

So far I have emphasized the *different* functions of these three voices. But at the end, as Artemio Cruz dies, they are necessarily compressed into one: "Artemio Cruz . . . Name . . . heart massage . . . hopeless . . . I carry you inside and with you I die. The three, we . . . will die. You . . . die, have died . . . I will die" (306). The future tense is the last one to go—always the greenest, the most hopeful. But its last expression is joined to the *I* of the present, to inescapable death. The technique of alternating the three voices in small sections rather than presenting three long narratives foreshadows this final compression. It heightens the tension the reader experiences between sympathy for Artemio Cruz and judgment of him, between allowing him to live as he wishes in the past of his potential goodness or to die as he must in the present of his accomplished harm. As Fuentes has said of Artemio Cruz, "Good or bad, the reader must choose."[17] The shifting perspectives make the choice engaging, but difficult.

STYLE AND LANGUAGE

The different voices that represent Artemio Cruz speak in a variety of styles. Although the entire novel theoretically takes place in Cruz's mind, only the first and second person sections are rendered in a stream-of-consciousness form of narration, where the reader follows directly the pattern of Cruz's thought. The third person sections do contain thoughts, but these thoughts are filtered through a voice that also narrates exterior events. These events, in contrast to Cruz's more lyrical reveries in the second person sections, are recounted in spare prose. This is the language of the practical Artemio Cruz, the language of action: "He stood and lightly touched his wounded forehead. He ought to go back to the wooded thicket, there he would be safe. He staggered" (71).

Even the description of Artemio's farewell to his first love, Regina, though it contains a foreboding contrast between a violently killed coyote and beautiful flowers, reveals the same simple sentence structure: "It was early. They went out on the street, she in her starched skirt, he in his felt sombrero and white tunic. They lived near the barranca: bell flowers hung over its void, and a rabbit killed by the fangs of a coyote was rotting in the foliage. . . . Their hands joined" (65). Compare this style with the baroque images and sentences in Cruz's reveries about the cathedral (p. 31) or the rich produce of Cocuya (p. 136).

In the second person sections, Cruz's thoughts often resemble incantations, ritual songs of praise or lament, to Mexico (pp. 266–67; see above, 54), to Cruz's former self (in the "you will choose" section, 237–38; see above, 64), to the body (when he remembers how all his organs used to function properly, pp. 83–84). The words of such sections may even be arranged as in a poem. One such "minipoem" plays on a slang obscenity that has particular significance in Mexican culture. The section begins:

You will say it, it is your word and your word is my word:
. . . imprecation, snapping greeting, life word, brother word,
memory . . . resumé of our history, . . .
    Fuck your mother
    Fuckin' bastard
    We fuck 'em all
    Quit fucking around (137)

There are twenty more lines in the same vein. The thematic importance of this chant merits a small digression here. First, the obscenity is an affront, a challenge to the polite reader, a gauntlet of language thrown down. It also constitutes a poetic recognition of a brutal aspect of Mexico's heritage. And beyond this, it is a recognizable act of homage to Octavio Paz.

The Spanish word here translated as "fuck" is the verb "chingar." In *The Labyrinth of Solitude,* Octavio Paz explains that: "in Mexico the word has innumerable meanings. . . . But . . . the ultimate meaning always contains the idea of aggression . . . an emergence from oneself to penetrate another by force. . . . The person who suffers this action is passive, inert and open, in contrast to the active and aggressive and closed person who inflicts it. The *chingón* is the *macho,* the male; he rips open the *chingada,* the female."[18] However schematic this formulation, Paz uses these terms to suggest that in a metaphorical sense, all Mexicans are *"hijos de la chingada"*—sons of a violated mother. This is because the Spanish conquistadores violated the native women, just as Spain invaded the new world, and from that violation came the mestizo race, the dominant population of Mexico.

The relevance of the expression to Artemio Cruz should be immediately clear. He is literally an *"hijo de la chingada"*—born from the violation of a native servant by the descendant of a Spaniard—and he returns to the expression throughout his story. For him, "You are what you are because you knew how to fuck 'em without letting them fuck you" (138). Mexico's history begins with the violation of her "mother" earth by foreigners, and the pattern of violence continues in men like Cruz, who have absorbed the word *"chingar"* and made it their plan of action. Dominate or be dominated. The philosophy extends to the idea of "one life for another." This is why Artemio Cruz feels pain when he repeats the words "I survived." Cruz doesn't merely survive; he survives by climbing somehow on the deaths of others—of Regina, or Gonzalo, or Lorenzo.[19]

A related habit of speech is Cruz's repetition of words, a sort of mental stutter, particularly in the *I* sections. The very first of these sections provides a good example: "Iron hammers in my ears and something, some-thing, something . . . I am this, this am I . . . I am this eye, this eye I am . . . and I am these cheeks, cheeks, cheek-bones where the white whiskers are born. Are born. Face. Face. Face, grimace . . ." (4). This repetitive style projects a sense of desperation, an effort to grasp even the physical realities of life, which are quickly slipping away.

Through these stylistic variations Fuentes integrates some of the rhythmic and sensual power of poetry into his prose. This lyricism augments the novel's emotional force. At the same time, the classical elegance of the rigorous *tripartite* narrative voice holds in place the often baroque richness of the text.

2

Short Fiction and Theater: Magical Realism, Symbolic Action

Fuentes has always been fascinated by what he calls "the world of the second reality": "I have always attempted to perceive behind the spectral appearance of things a more tangible, more solid reality than the obvious everyday reality." He claims that this continuing interest stems from his childhood taste for authors like Robert Louis Stevenson and Edgar Allan Poe.[1] For him, "reality is reality plus its mirrors. . . . All reality duplicates and prolongs itself magically."[2] In this kind of "magical realism," supernatural events appear to grow out of the environment rather than descending upon it from beyond. This sense that reality is opening out into a fantastical domain is particularly strong in the novella *Aura*, where Fuentes expands an apparently ordinary newspaper advertisement in a magical way.[3]

Fuentes uses magical realism in two distinct but related capacities: to underline extreme psychological power and to suggest the presence of ancient cosmic forces. The rooms in *Holy Place* and the house in *Birthday* (another novella), for example, are invested primarily with emotional energy rather than with supernatural presence. The final metamorphoses in these works thus represent personal psychological force rather than divine power. The same is true for the terminal magic in *Aura:* it is primarily human enchantment. In *A Change of Skin* on the other hand, the scene in the pyramid, like the scene in *Where the Air is Clear* where Norma Robles is destroyed by fire, suggests the existence of more impersonal powers. In *Terra Nostra* and *Distant Relations* the sources of magic are less easily identified; miracles happen and people react. Events seem emblematic rather than motivational.

In discussing Aztec civilization, Fuentes contrasts the Mexican gods who are not like men with the classical deities who are. The Mexican gods are "the other; a separate reality." This separation provokes a "paradoxical encounter between what can't be touched or affected by men (the sacred) and the human, physical, and imaginative construction of those sacred spaces and times."[4] Fuentes's distinction between the world of men and the world of gods, then, roughly corresponds to the psychological and the cosmic kinds of magic in his fiction.

Alejo Carpentier has argued in his well-known discussion of *"lo real maravilloso"* ("the marvelous real") that indigenous American culture and nature provide its writers with a wealth of surprising images. They constitute a spontaneous, homegrown kind of surrealism that contrasts with the artificial variety practiced by European surrealists.[5] Instead of deliberately juxtaposing a sewing machine and an umbrella on a dissecting table, for example, or covering a spoon with fur, the American artist may simply describe what his environment contains, a colonial baroque church facade where an angel plays the maracas or a local legend in which a condemned popular leader transforms himself into a bird and takes flight as he is executed.

As we have seen, Fuentes draws much of his magic from Mexican mythology. Our surprise at the juxtaposition of seemingly incompatible images in his fiction often results from the proximity of two different cultures, from the intrusion of ancient beliefs or figures into modern scenes. It is almost as if the ancestral presences that lurked behind the scenes in *Where the Air is Clear* come out into the open in "Chac Mool," *Aura,* and *All Cats are Gray;* and Fuentes's description of his fantastic stories as recounting "the reappearance of extinct forms, hidden underground," recalls Teódula's ancestors hidden under the floor in *Where the Air is Clear.*[6] This exposure to other worlds or second realities of myth and magic occasionally lends Fuentes's work a dreamlike quality in which unreal events take place without rational explanations. When he says that a novel by the Czech writer Milan Kundera will only exist fully if the reader "knows how to open the windows of dream it contains," Fuentes suggests the kind of participation many of his own texts require.[7] He has set the windows of dream in his house of fiction.

According to Tzvetan Todorov, texts in the fantastic mode must inhabit that region of uncertainty between the uncanny, which seems strange yet can be explained by the laws of the universe as we know it, and the marvelous, which violates those laws.[8] It thus operates on the frontier of two genres. The fantastic only lasts during the reading process, Todorov argues, because a reader opts for either the uncanny or the marvelous after finishing the text. Fuentes's works range from the uncanny to the marvelous, and often play between the two. Many of them, like *A Change of Skin, Holy Place,* and *Birthday,* are difficult to classify since marvelous events may be interpreted as dreams or hallucinations. With regard to Fuentes's shorter fiction, the earliest stories establish themselves as marvelous with clearly impossible events. *Aura,* on the other hand, fits well into Todorov's category of the fantastic. Indeed, as we shall see, much of *Aura*'s effect depends on its atmosphere of incipient magic and on the reader's consequent suspension between the uncanny and the marvelous.

The Witches of Desire:
Aura

Fuentes's fondness for "the world of the second reality" attracts him to witchlike figures, for they seem able to communicate with that world.[1] *Aura* might be called Fuentes's "portrait of the artist as an old witch" or enchantress, a subject he will pursue at greater length in *Holy Place* and which he prefigured in *Where the Air is Clear* with Teódula Moctezuma. I say "portrait of the artist" because Consuelo's creative power, like that of an artist's, is enchanting and frightening. She pursues a "second reality," "the infinite of desire and the imagination," as does Fuentes himself.[2]

Aura, like the future-tense sections of *The Death of Artemio Cruz,* begins by appearing to address the reader directly: "You're reading the advertisement: an offer like this isn't made every day."[3] Fuentes underscores the initial impact of the second person narration by starting with the very words that implicate readers explicitly, "You're reading," as indeed we *are*.[4] As in *The Death of Artemio Cruz,* though we realize soon enough that the narrator is "really" talking to himself, the direct address challenges us and draws us quickly into his story. We identify with the "you" and experience the increasingly bizarre events of the story through his eyes.

The narrator, a young historian named Felipe Montero, answers an advertisement that seems tailor-made for him. An old woman, Consuelo, wishes him to edit her dead husband's papers in return for room and board and an attractive salary.[5] As Felipe reads the papers, which contain love letters from General Llorente to his young fiancé, Consuelo, he becomes increasingly enamored of Consuelo's elusive niece Aura, who lives with her aunt. At the end of the novel, as Felipe clasps Aura in his arms, she has become the old aunt, and he himself the long dead husband.[6] *Aura* is thus the portrait of a need—Consuelo's need to feel young and loved again, like that of Artemio Cruz, a need to deny time's annihilating force. The magical transformation underlines the urgency of her desire.

The story builds masterfully toward its final conflation by means of an increasing number of connections between Aura and Consuelo, together with hints that Aura is aging. This progression, combined with a haunting atmosphere and delicately bizarre images, make *Aura* one of Fuentes's most successful works. In the love letters he reads, Felipe learns that Consuelo is fifteen, Aura's age, when she first meets General Llorente; the general speaks of her green eyes and green dress—like Aura's, the color of youthful passion. Just after this, Felipe says: "Now you know why Aura is living in this house: to perpetuate the illusion of youth and beauty in that poor, crazed old lady. Aura, kept here like a mirror" (89), a mirror Consuelo creates, not one that creates *her*. Then Felipe puts the manuscript aside and goes down to find Aura. Shortly thereafter, he has a dream where Aura "turns toward you and laughs silently, with the old lady's teeth superimposed on her own" (95–97). Felipe's dream, in addition to signaling his growing awareness of the convergence of the two women, might also suggest his participation in the process.

As the story progresses, the identification of the two women becomes more intense. Aura asks with a "warm voice" in Felipe's ear whether he will swear to love her forever, "even though I grow old? Even though I lose my beauty? Even though my hair turns white?" (109–11). After Felipe swears that he will, he reaches out to touch Aura, but she has gone to sit at the feet of Consuelo, who has apparently been watching their lovemaking and "moves her head in rhythm with the old lady's: they both smile at you, thanking you," before leaving together (113). Near the end of the novella, when Felipe finishes the

memoirs of General Llorente and looks at the photographs that follow them, he sees Aura in the pictures of
the young Consuelo. In the second photograph, she appears with the general:

Aura doesn't look as young as she did in the other picture, but
it's she, it's he, it's . . . it's you. You cover General Llorente's
beard with your finger, and imagine him with black hair, and you
only discover yourself: blurred, lost forgotten, but you, you, you.
(137)

Felipe's discovery of himself in General Llorente prefigures the final scene where he again swears to love the
woman he holds in his arms forever. He has become the
General, saying to himself, "You love her, you too have
come back" in a triumph of love over time, "when the
memory of youth, of youth re-embodied, rules the darkness" (145).

From the beginning of the tale, haunting details suggest that mysterious forces may be at work. Felipe feels as
if the advertisement is intended especially for him—and
no one except him answers it, even though the salary is
attractive. The front door of the old house has a knocker
with a dog's head that seems as if it were grinning at him.
It "opens at the first light push of your fingers." As he
enters the house and smells a "thick drowsy aroma," he
feels as if he were entering some uncanny domain, leaving
the real world of the street behind, and tries "to retain
some single image of that indifferent outside world" (11).
Hints of black magic appear with the presence of killed—
sacrificed?—animals and fetishlike objects. One night
Felipe hears "the painful yowling of a number of cats"
(37); the next morning he gets a brief glimpse of a group
of cats, "all twined together, all writhing in flames and
giving off a dense smoke that reeks of burnt fur" (59).
Later on, Felipe comes on Aura beheading a goat while
Consuelo performs some kind of ritual. Another night, he
finds a strange naked doll "filled with a powder that trick-

les from its badly sewn shoulder" beside his plate. He suspects it of containing "a secret illness, a contagion"—a love potion? we wonder (99). One early incident seems particularly significant in this context. When Felipe first meets Consuelo and she is explaining the editing project to him, she has a rabbit beside her. It goes away, and when Consuelo calls it, " 'Saga, Saga, where are you?' " Felipe asks, " 'Who?' " Consuelo then replies, " 'My companion.' " " 'The rabbit?' " asks Felipe. " 'Yes,' " says Consuelo, " 'She'll come back.' " Just after this, when Felipe hesitates at Consuelo's stipulation that he must live in her house to do the editing, Consuelo summons Aura, who appears instantly "without the slightest sound." Consuelo then says, " 'I told you she'd come back.' " When Felipe, confused, asks again, " 'Who?' " Consuelo replies " 'Aura. My companion. My niece' " (25). She seems to have changed rabbit into niece in her moment of need. Consuelo, then, is a witch, who possesses or creates Aura to seduce Felipe for her. And as Felipe is drawn into her magic circle, so too the reader is drawn deeper and deeper into the increasingly magical story.

That Felipe follows at all, and ultimately succumbs to Consuelo's desire, suggests not only the power of her magic, but also the universal nature of such desire itself. Felipe's sense that he is destined for this job indicates perhaps his natural attraction to the house on "Donceles" —"Maidens"—Street. When he looks for the first time into Aura's green eyes, he thinks:

They surge, break to foam, grow calm again, then surge like a wave. You look into them and tell yourself it isn't true, because they're beautiful green eyes just like all the beautiful green eyes you've ever known. But you can't deceive yourself: those eyes do surge, do change, as if offering you a landscape that only you can see and desire. (27)

In Aura's green eyes, Felipe recognizes a landscape of rejuvenation. Finally, of course, Consuelo's desire for youth and love must also be Felipe's and Aura's—and everyone's: to be loved even when we are old. In the closed realm of desire that is Consuelo's house, time seems to bite its tail, to approach a circular pattern where events repeat themselves. At the end of the novella, Consuelo promises Felipe that together they'll bring Aura back; and near the beginning Consuelo's face looks "so old it's almost child-like" (17). The time of aging is not strictly one directional here.

In addition to the universal archetype of the witch or enchantress (and the strangely wonderful powers of desire she commands), *Aura* also reflects a particular aspect of Mexico's history. A historically oriented interpretation of the novel might emphasize not the triumph of love, but the tyranny of the past. In her musty old house, Consuelo's power over Aura and Felipe can be seen to represent colonial elements in Mexican society that have survived beyond their natural term.[7] Like the ancient Aztec presences in *Where the Air is Clear,* this survival—the marvelous power of the past—is both terrifying and admirable. Rodríguez Monegal suggests that Consuelo "symbolizes the reconstruction of old Mexico on top of the insolent and modern structure of present-day Mexico. . . . The memory of a dead time is embodied and lives, even though it be a monstrous life."[8]

The isolation of the house and its special atmosphere removes *Aura* from the contemporary scene that pervades much of Fuentes's work. Manuel Durán points out that in *Aura,* allusions to the commercial world serve principally to establish a contrast between the outside city streets and the interior of the house. The novella thus remains "at the edge of the almost irresistible contamination" by pop art in Fuentes's texts. According to Durán, Fuentes seems to be saying that there is a limit to this contamination and that limit is the sacred. Its magic fires do not admit neon rivals.[9] What "contamination" there is comes from other earlier—Fuentes might say eternal—sources.

Aura is frequently compared to *The Aspern Papers* by Henry James. There, a young man in search of a valuable set of papers goes to live in a mysterious old house with an old woman and her niece. When the old woman, who has an uncanny hold on her niece, dies, the niece offers herself in marriage as a condition of the young man's access to the papers he covets. But the young man refuses, and, in contrast to what happens in *Aura,* past remains past and desire unsatisfied.[10] There are also a number of striking parallels between *Aura* and "Rappacini's Daughter" by Hawthorne: they share the old house, the mysterious garden, the mortally seductive charms of a feminine inhabitant for the young male guest.[11] (In the case of "Rappacini's Daughter," it is the young woman's father rather than her "aunt," who "creates" her, perverting nature with his science.) It would seem that for James, and even more for Hawthorne, the powers represented by the witchy women are demonic or destructive and therefore to be avoided, whereas for Fuentes, they are fascinating, even attractive, because they open onto the "world of the second reality," which provides an alternative to our own.[12]

As I have suggested earlier, *Aura* seems to be a classic example of magical realism, where the magical grows out of the real. Here the psychological reality of the desire for eternal youth and love motivates a magical event. As General Llorente wrote prophetically to Consuelo in a letter, *"Que ne ferais-tu pas pour rester toujours jeune?"* (what wouldn't you do to remain forever young?, 84). In its progression through increasing strangeness toward a final fantastical transformation, the very texture of *Aura* illustrates the genre.

"Many Returns of the Day":
Birthday

Fuentes's novella *Cumpleaños (Birthday)* shares *Aura*'s magical atmosphere but does not build toward a climax in the same way. The text is more fragmented and continues the experimental mode of *A Change of Skin*, published several years earlier. A birthday marks the passage of time: the stark one-word title here accentuates the work's abstract focus on time without a softening social context. The conspicuous absence of the "happy" most frequently modifying "birthday" suggests the inexorable rather than the joyful nature of birthdays and reflects the longing for eternal life that appears in the novel. *Birthday* is a total fiction that abandons rational chronological or causal progression in favor of a dreamlike multiplication and conflation of times, places, and figures. Contradictions and paradoxes are often recounted with the dreamer's mixture of acceptance and puzzlement: "I didn't know if I was dressed or nude. It didn't matter," says the narrator; obstacles are "at the same time infinitely slim and absolutely thick"; "I've lost the way. Nevertheless, the noises are now the ones I dreamed. But the shapes are deceptive."[1]

The novella opens as a husband and wife, George and Emily, wake up and creep into their son Georgie's room to sing "Happy Birthday." The scene changes after the song, and until the very end of the book, we follow a confusing series of scenes that concern an old man, a boy—who seems to grow into a young man—and a woman in an old house.[2] At the end we are back with George, who feels "that a wound is developing a scar on his forearm" (113). The mark and the name George link him with the old man in the preceding text, which might then be interpreted as George's dream, though Fuentes does not suggest this directly.[3]

In a repeat of the doubling suggested by the names of Georgie and George, the two men in the house often seem to merge, to exchange places, or to be inhabited by a transparent narrative voice—memory itself, perhaps. At one point, this voice says that "the memory of the old man was all that the boy and the man had reminded me of, it's true; what's more, it was all that I'd forgotten. But to remember all of it is to forget it all again" (89). The fluid narrative voice that snakes in and out of characters who in turn are also fluid, like that in *A Change of Skin* and *Terra Nostra,* illustrates Fuentes' theory of "de–I–ification"—the disappearance of a defined narrator—which I will investigate in more detail later on.

A narrator who seems to be "everyone and no-one" can serve to introduce an important presence behind *Birthday.* In one sense, the novel does constitute a birthday celebration, for it is Fuentes's tribute to Borges on his seventieth birthday. Borges is half English, and his family calls him Georgie, so that the "Happy Birthday dear Georgie" at the start of the book is directed to him.[4] But not only to him. In the course of the text, Fuentes does to Borges what Borges—in many of his stories—has done to himself. He disrupts traditional notions of time and makes Borges/George into a man of all ages, merging him with a boy, an old man, and the thirteenth-century theologian, Siger de Brabante.[5] Like many of Borges's stories, but conceptually somewhat less lucid, *Birthday* is an abstract meditation on time, and particularly on the idea of reincarnation. The figure of Siger, who is evoked at the end, "awaiting his new incarnation," seems to represent time itself, which in the words of the epigraph, "hungers for incarnation." Besides being incarnated in the figures of Siger and of George, time at one point flowers in a series of images that puts welcome flesh on abstract meditation:

The sum of natural time, I had already said, is atemporality: the brevity of a hare is compensated for by the permanence of a mountain, the time of the sea is limited by that of a shrimp and expanded by that of the skies that it reflects. Eternity is an illusion of compensated times, a continuum in which beings with short lives are added onto those with long lives and the latter in turn re-engender the former. If I had been a butterfly—I said to myself—I'd already be dead; if I were a river, I wouldn't be born yet. (101)

The house which the three figures in the novella inhabit is repeatedly called a labyrinth—Borges's most characteristic image. This dwelling at times appears to be old, at other times, under construction. Perhaps it represents a new "house of fiction," one that builds on previous structures.[6] Wanderers in Borges's stories—like all explorers of all labyrinths—feel confused though they sense the existence of a design in the paths they traverse. So here, as the narrator continually explores confusing corridors, the boy laughingly tells him that "this place will end up having a shape, but you won't know it" (108). At this point, the narrator, who merges into the dreamer George, recognizes the streets of London. Like Borges's labyrinths, this one reaches out to encompass the world. And *Birthday* ends—like many of Borges's stories—with a historical postscript that sheds doubt on its own veracity: "Siger de Brabante . . . fled to Italy and sequestered himself in a house on the outskirts of Trani. . . . There, he was assassinated by a mad servant in 1281. Some chroniclers dispute the accuracy of this date" (115). The truth, like the narrator who is everyone and no one, is everywhere and nowhere.

Finally, in Siger, Fuentes has chosen rather a Borgesian figure, as if to confirm Borges's own idea that writers create their own precursors.[7] Like Borges—and Fuentes—Siger made several disturbing speculations regarding time and eternity. Indeed, the heretical notions of Siger occupy a central place in *Birthday*. Near the end, the narrator speaks in what we assume to be Siger's voice and embroiders on his "three theses that scandalized the world": 1) "if the world is eternal, there can have been no creation"; 2) "if truth is double, it can be infinite"; and 3) "if the human race has common intelligence, the individual soul is not immortal, but mankind is" (93–94). All of these ideas point toward a denial of an omnipotent supreme being, toward a displacement of origins and individuals by continuities and communities.

Siger's three theses develop the subject of reincarnation, the secret of which is that "the world is eternal because it dies renewing itself; the soul is mortal because it lives on its intransferable uniqueness" (101). By the end of the novel, it begins to dawn on us that the shifts of identity, where the two Georges seem to change places as dreamer and dreamed, correspond to different reincarnations of Siger, a man who wants to achieve immortality. He achieves his aim by projecting himself into other lives. At the end of the novella, Siger explains to "George" that he'll pass on his breath to another body and already speaks in the plural: "Now we have what we've wanted most. It's my turn to be reborn, thanks to you" (106). Now we get the answer to a riddle that reverberates through the latter part of the story: when does a door cease to be a door? When it is a horizontal door—a tomb. But in a sense even a tomb can be a door, to another incarnation. In this context of reincarnations, as William Siemens has pointed out, when the woman who has accompanied Siger in the old house appears to George in the park, she can be seen as a kind of messenger transmitting Siger's soul to George.[8] The idea of reincarnation suggests an additional resonance for the title of the novella. Just as birthdays mark specific moments in the life of a person, so individual people mark particular instances in the life of a soul that journeys through different bodies.[9] Siger, after remembering and anticipating all the things he has been or will be, "each time with a different body but a single mind," an-

swers the narrator's question of "Who are you now?" with
"Now I'm you"—the narrator of this story (104).

This last thesis, especially, provides one theoretical
basis for the notion of a continually changing communal
narrative voice that we find here and in much of Fuentes's
other work. Fuentes might say, with Siger, that "I plotted
all the impossibilities: I thought about reversible times and
the simultaneity of space, I came to believe that what took
place had never taken place and what never happened was
already recorded by history" (99). Within the narration,
which seems to have no clear beginning or end, times are
reversed: George the dreamer/narrator sees himself as an
old man—and perhaps also as a boy. The labyrinthine
house is simultaneously itself, the city of London, and the
(now) proverbial house of fiction. The whole narration,
dreamlike as it is, finds itself confirmed, "recorded by
history," in the mind of Siger. In *Birthday* Fuentes has
constructed narrative analogues for Siger's theses, and like
those theses, whose notions of multiple times and souls
were heretical, Fuentes's text with its plurality of times
and voices constitutes a kind of narrative heresy.[10]

The Bedroom and the Public Square: *The One-Eyed Man is King* and *All Cats are Gray*

Both of Fuentes's plays, *El tuerto es rey (The One-Eyed
Man is King)* and *Todos los gatos son pardos (All Cats are
Gray)*, are highly stylized, symbolically charged dramas,
yet they represent two different modes. The first play is
relatively spare in allusions, concentrated in time and
space, and has a cast of two. The second concerns mythical and historical figures, ranges over centuries, and im-

plies, if it doesn't actually employ, a "cast of thousands." Thus, they illustrate the range of private and public concerns Paz attributes to Fuentes in his 1972 statement at Fuentes's inauguration into the Colegio Nacional. In addition to portraying the dynamics of power and passion, both dramas investigate the nature and function of language and literature in human affairs.[1]

In *The One-Eyed Man is King,* Donata waits with her servant Duque for her husband's return from a trip to the casino at Deauville. Donata and Duque argue, cajole, fight —in short, play innumerable verbal games. The final game is Duque's apparent impersonation of the returning master and his subsequent death at the hands of a guerilla band because he cannot prove that the house belongs to him—as indeed the "real" owner might not have been able to do because of his debts. The play takes place in an old mansion, where, as in *Aura* and *Birthday,* desire and frustration intensify in a confined space. But unlike Consuelo, neither Duque nor Donata command sufficient magic to fulfill their desires. The play's confinement and harassment, with the implied—yet not implemented—alternative of personal commitment, recalls Sartre's play *No Exit,* where "hell is other people."

Duque's name—"Duke"—suggests at the outset that there is no appreciable difference between servant and mistress; they share the need for communication, emotional fulfillment, and domination. And indeed, at the end, when Duque impersonates the returning husband, he refers to himself and Donata, whom he calls María, as brother and sister, his servants, his children. Is this wishful thinking on his part? Or a final "truth" that is stranger than the preceding fictions?

The play itself dramatizes the absence of a central figure of authority and the fictions people create to fill the vacuum. Fuentes suggests in his introduction that *The One-Eyed Man is King* explores the relationship between God and man: "Who is this lord who sees and knows everything, this great absent one who fixes the rules for behavior in his house so severely and then abandons those who live there to all the temptations of freedom? . . . The worst sin of the lord is in his lack of solidarity with his creatures."[2] In contrast to this seigneurial abandonment is Duque's suggestion to Donata about total commitment: "If everyone were to choose one person and take complete, true responsibility for that person, that would be healthy" (90). At one point, Duque seems to impersonate a Lord who attempts solidarity, claiming that he "drinks, fornicates, robs, assassinates, and humiliates" himself "in order to abolish the difference" (99). We might note that this drama of absence leads up to *Terra Nostra*, which is also built around a missing father figure, for there Fuentes has skipped a generation in the ruling dynasty, making Philip II's grandparents Philip the Fair and Joanna the Mad his parents.

The title of the play recalls that of Fuentes's volume of short stories, *Songs of the Blind*, with its portrait of man's imperfections and troubles, and its implied wish for a comprehending vision. Fuentes's occasional references to Aztec brutality and to the persistence of blood sacrifice in Mexico suggest that he is not really lamenting the loss of an original paradise but rather Mexico's failure to "envision" and enact a way of life commensurate with the promise of the land. A meditation on sight and blindness at the center of the play recalls the dynamics of the seen and unseen in *Where the Air is Clear*. Duque says that "it's dangerous to see, Madame, it's very dangerous; nothing is seen with impunity; nothing lets itself be seen without stealing part of our look. And thus from look to look, our eyes burn up and one day we wake up blind. We've seen nothing. We've seen it all" (64). Blindness here, like Hortensia Chacón's, represents a certain amount of experience, but not her kind of invaluable insight. This account suggests that living itself leaves us blind and confers no "second sight." The title, "the one-eyed man is king," completes a proverb which appears in *Where the Air is Clear*. One snob asks another what they are doing in Mexico City if they could live at the center of the world in New York or Paris. Her friend answers, "Masochism, my dear . . . and the pleasant axiom that in the land of the blind—" (*Where the Air is Clear*, 128). The saying comments on the nature of power and vision, suggesting that —as we shall see in *All Cats are Gray*—the strength and insight of he who wields the power may be less important than the weakness and stupidity of those who submit to it.

All Cats are Gray dramatizes the Spanish conquest in Mexico. It builds toward the time when Cortés, aided by his native lover/interpreter Marina, enters Mexico City; after Moctezuma is killed, Cortés is then himself divested of his power by the Spanish crown.[3] Here, as in *Terra Nostra*, Fuentes attempts to adjust the imbalances of history which have made the indigenous inhabitants of Mexico the objects of "culturicide," their conquerors objects of "personalicide."[4] In fact, he restores psychological interest not only to the Spaniards but to the Aztecs as well. In modern Mexico, Moctezuma is generally—following Bernal Díaz's early account—imagined as the archetypal Mexican hero, gloriously defeated by circumstances, and Marina as the traitor who brought about the defeat; she is *La Chingada*, the woman violated by the conqueror, who then betrays her own people and is seen by Octavio Paz and others as symbolic of Mexico itself. Fuentes in a sense "unmasks" this traditional legend to reveal new forces at work; they are possibilities, not certainties, perhaps even alternate masks of his own devising. Fuentes wishes to shake up the Mexico that habitually sees itself as the heroic Moctezuma to provide us all with the disquieting recognition of the opposite in the self.

The concept of masking and unmasking is central to the production.[5] At the start of the play, Moctezuma is surrounded by cloaked "augurs"—or prophets—who

briefly remove their body masks—or cloaks—to represent
Aztec gods. Near the end of the play, these same augurs
remove their cloaks to appear nearly naked, as men, not
gods. They resemble Federico Robles in *Where the Air is
Clear,* who finally prefers the naturally fragrant Hortensia
to the artificially perfumed Norma, and suggest that what-
ever divinity may exist resides in man. The naked augurs
rejoice in a nationalistic spirit of affirmation: "We've
learned to fight, this time, and again, and again and again,
though each time we are beaten. . . . We will fight
. . . For a face . . . For a name . . . For land" (165–66).
They are on the right track, but they may be a bit too
zealous. They stone Moctezuma, killing him and thus
making way for Spanish rule to mistreat the people. The
final scene of the play lays yet another mask on the eternal
skeleton of Mexican history: ancient gods and men are all
dressed as modern figures—Cortés as a U.S. army general,
Marina as a call girl, and Moctezuma as the president of
Mexico. Earlier in the play when the augur who stands for
the ancient god Quetzalcóatl takes off his cape, we see that
"a white featureless mask covers his face" (27). On the one
hand, that mask suggests "a communal face" representing
the Mexican people who will overthrow all the Moc-
tezumas and Cortéses imposed on them; it also suggests a
benevolent ruler like Quetzalcóatl, who will be selfless.[6]
On the other hand, it suggests that the true face of Quetzalcóatl has yet to be revealed—or, perhaps, that it must
not be revealed to a passive audience but created by an
active people. It is a blank page to be written on by Mexico's future historical events.

In *All Cats are Gray,* Moctezuma is a tormented soul,
continually vacillating, and terrified of accepting responsibility for the defense of his own people. As Lanin Gyurko
has pointed out, Moctezuma is a plurality of conflicting
selves; the battle cannot be fought against Cortés because
the emperor is consumed in continual war against himself.[7] Thus, he wishes to see Cortés as a god—the long-

awaited Quetzalcóatl—and therefore to attribute his own defeat at the hands of the Spaniards to fate. In this sense, Quetzalcóatl resembles the absent master in *The One-Eyed Man is King* and El Señor's missing father in *Terra Nostra;* the worlds of these works become godless, fatherless voids to be filled by the chances of man and history, which in the Hispanic world, according to Fuentes, have still engendered paternalistic despotism. From the very beginning of the play, Moctezuma sweeps feebly with a broom, attempting halfheartedly to "put his house in order." We might consider that with this portrait of the weak and indecisive Moctezuma, Fuentes situates the tragedy of the conquest within the Mexican character. In paving Cortés's way, Moctezuma resembles the "front man" Artemio Cruz who facilitates the North American economic conquest of Mexico. It might be argued that Moctezuma speeds up the process of integrating Spanish and Indian systems of belief by associating Cortés with Quetzalcóatl; he is a kind of translator—a male Malinche. But as we have seen, Moctezuma is a translator because he is afraid to speak for himself. He says: "This captain [Cortés] is Quetzalcóatl; he must be. Otherwise, you would destroy the magic reason of our religion . . . and condemn me to madness" (94). In fact, he slows down the process of true integration by allowing the Spaniards to dominate his kingdom.

Just as he reduces the traditional image of Moctezuma, Fuentes resurrects and elevates the long-maligned Malinche.[8] In her efforts to make Cortés see the value of her culture and people, to help him establish a multicultural society, she represents the positive side of the art of translation. She begins the play with a long monologue that draws her history out of her three names: Her parents called her Malintzín—"witch, goddess of bad luck"; Cortés called her Marina, for the ocean over which he had sailed; and her people called her "Malinche: traitor, the white man's tongue and guide" (13). Later on she explains

to an incredulous Cortés that Moctezuma considers him
a god and tries to persuade him that she can rule Mexico
benevolently with him: "Don't destroy this land, don't
violate it" (100). But Cortés thinks these ideas a sacrilege
and refuses the role of benevolent divine ruler in favor of
violent human conqueror. Marina receives only insults for
her efforts, the augurs cursing her in the perverted form
of a "Hail, Mary" "full of rancor, the devil be with you,
cursed are you among all women" (175).

Marina's power is the power of language: "Power and
the word. Moctezuma or the power of fatality; Cortés or
the power of the will. Between the two banks of power, a
bridge: language, Marina, who with words converts the
history of both powers into destiny" with the same linguistic skill she unraveled her own history from her names.[9]
When Marina tells Cortés that "only what is named exists," she pleads for him to use the power of words to
merge the two cultures of Mexico and Spain. But Cortés
repeats her very words, and from them rises in a crescendo
of domination: "You say that only the named exists. Listen to the words with which I create the world: . . . faith,
honor, courage, cunning, violence" (157). They are the
code of medieval Spain, and he tells her they mean nothing
apart from his individual passion. This selfish linguistic
action is what Fuentes, like Marina, fights against in his
own works to establish a new language freed from the
codes of conquest, one that includes many voices.

Destructive political powers win here, not the constructive power of the word. Both Cortés and Moctezuma
are defeated by their own personalities and by the power
that Cortés covets and Moctezuma rejects. Moctezuma
wails near the end of the play, "Well, what have we done,
the two of us, except to touch the same sphere of power;
I, to give it up; Cortés, to take it? Moctezuma conquered,
Cortés victorious; both, slaves to the power that we pre-
tend to dominate" (168). Prophetic words, for Cortés himself is soon divested of his power by agents of the king.

Cortés and Moctezuma share a constricted sense of time. Like Ixca Cienfuegos in *Where the Air is Clear,* Moctezuma looks to the myths of the past for guidance and does not adapt to present necessities. Cortés looks toward what he hopes will be a rich future for his heirs, much as the unreformed Federico Robles envisions the bright future of postrevolutionary business, ignoring ancient Mexican traditions. As we shall see in his essays, Fuentes believes that Mexico must move toward the future with an awareness of the past in order to construct a satisfactory present. In their narrow visions, their inabilities to achieve a temporal and a cultural synthesis, Cortés and Moctezuma are both gray cats in the night of the conquest, no matter what masks they may wear.[10]

Like *The Death of Artemio Cruz, All Cats are Gray* speculates on the relative strengths of individual will and historical circumstance, and as in many of Fuentes's works, the balance rests somewhere in between the two. In the weak, indecisive Moctezuma and the shortsighted Cortés, Fuentes seems to suggest that while one man—or two—cannot change the course of history, he can certainly stem the tide or swell it. Individual integrity is not swallowed up by the current of history, but rather contributes to its flow.

With the final scene of *All Cats are Gray,* Fuentes illustrates clearly his sense that ancient patterns still prevail. The play ends when a youth whom we see sacrificed as Cortés arrives in the Aztec capital returns as a student shot by contemporary soldiers (in a symbolic reenactment of the Tlatelolco massacre in 1968). Again, as in *Where the Air is Clear* and *A Change of Skin,* Mexico has exacted a sacrificial victim. No one speaks in this scene; perhaps the absence of words indicates that Mexico has not yet found a voice to call a halt to the violence. Again, a dark view of the nation. If we look for a glimmer of optimism in the play, perhaps the primary source must come from its impact on its audience, some of whom may be moved to try and break the vicious cycles of recurring sacrifice. We also have the momentary hope for the people's persistence expressed in the unmasking of the augurs. When asked about his similarly negative portrait of Mexico in 1999 in *Terra Nostra,* Fuentes responded, "Well, I think that one can be excessively pessimistic in a novel [or a play, presumably] in order to shake up certain consciences."[11] And once shaken, these consciences may eventually act.

Scenes from the City:
Short Stories

The stories in *Burnt Water*—the first collection by Fuentes in English—illustrate Fuentes's characteristic concern with public and private realms; but here, confrontations in private apartments or rooms prevail over visions of streets, markets, churches, plazas, or parks.[1]

The title *Burnt Water,* as Fuentes explains in his introductory note, is the translation of an Aztec expression describing the volcano-ringed lake surrounding the ancient city of Tenochtitlán, the predecessor of modern Mexico City.[2] This striking image continues Fuentes's penchant for the paradoxical fusion of contraries, his fondness for luminosity and for the persistence of ancient traditions in contemporary Mexico. It recalls that similarly evocative image in *Where the Air is Clear,* when Federico Robles's eyes are "fugitive with light, trembling, like turquoise wings aflame in darkness" (*Where the Air is Clear,* 81).

Taken all together, these stories resemble a fresco of life in Mexico City, but a fresco whose separate scenes fit into niches like those in Orozco's decoration of the city's National Preparatory School. Moreover, Fuentes's vision often penetrates the surface of this cityscape to reveal different cultural layers so that we can imagine this text, like the larger mural of *Where the Air is Clear,* as a palimpsest. The principal superimposed inscriptions come from Aztec times, from the Colonial period, from the pre-Revolutionary era of Porfirio Díaz, and, of course, from recent years. This layering makes the passage of time visible in space and reveals Fuentes's historical consciousness, his desire to bring the past forward to the present. Once again, two influential precursors are Faulkner and Octavio Paz. Fuentes has said that "in Faulkner everything is in the chronic present. Even the remotest past is present."[3] For Paz, "past epochs never vanish completely. . . . Sometimes the most remote or hostile beliefs and feelings are found together in one city or one soul, or are superimposed like those pre-Cortesian pyramids that almost always conceal others."[4]

The notion of layers recurs throughout Fuentes's stories; these layers may implicate times, places, or people. In "Mother's Day," when General Vergara and his grandson are raising hell in a bar, they are also reliving the General's war experiences: "Yaqui Indians faithful to Obregón had hidden in those holes, be careful, don't spill that cold brew, and everyone was staring at us as if we were crazy, a loudmouthed old man and a kid in his pajamas, what's with them? there they were, ramming their bayonets into the bellies of our horses . . ." (44). The entire story of "The Doll Queen" concerns the narrator's troubled imposition of past memories on present realities. He is clearly "in search of lost time," and even looks for it, as Proust's Marcel does, in parks. "In a Flemish Garden" inserts a Belgian garden, even Belgian weather, into Mexican soil and atmosphere: "The very rain stirs colorings in the grass I want to identify with other cities, other windows" (18). After this vision, the narrator rushes to the opposite side of the house and looks out the street-side window to see "a blast of jukeboxes, streetcars, and sun, the monotonous sun. A Sun God without shading of effigies in its rays, a stationary Sun Stone" (18). But when he returns again to the garden, the rain is still falling. Different ages in the city's life are consistently juxtaposed through descriptions of buildings or memories. The characters in "Mother's Day," "The Two Elenas," and "These Were Palaces" all live in old buildings that have been altered in some way through time. In "Palaces,"

it was little Luisito who did the talking, it was he who imagined the city as it had been in colonial times, it was he who told the old woman how the Spanish city had been constructed, laid out like a chessboard above the ruins of the Aztec capital. (94)

"The Mandarin" thinks to himself that "only those who can perceive the nocturnal scent of the lost lake really know this city" (153). A few pages later, he feels ashamed "that a country of churches and pyramids built for eternity should end up contenting itself with a city of shanties, shoddiness, and shit" (155). This character's face, like the city he inhabits, is layered as well:

His features were so markedly Oriental that they obscured the Indian mask underlying them. It happens with a lot of Mexican faces. The stigmas and accidents of known history recede to reveal the primal face, the face that goes back to Mongolian tundra and mountains. In this way Federico Silva was like the lost perfume of the ancient lake of Mexico: a sensitive memory, practically a ghost. (156)

Another kind of "layering" is the doubling, the confusion of identities, that occurs in "A Pure Soul." There Juan Luis superimposes his sister Claudia onto his lover Claire so that he can possess the forbidden Claudia in the flesh of the accessible Claire. Here as in many of his works, Fuentes creates a modern version of the myth of Quetzalcóatl, who fled Mexico after being tricked into incest with his sister. (Juan Luis lives in Switzerland.)

The first story in *Burnt Water*, "Chac Mool," records the "takeover" of one Filiberto by a statue of the ancient

rain god—the Chac Mool—he had bought at the flea mar-
ket. The Chac Mool has emerged into the twentieth century, come alive, so to speak. But with this life comes old
age—and presumably death.[5] "In a Flemish Garden"
similarly describes the occupation of an old mansion's
garden by the ghost of Charlotte, the wife of King Max-
imilian (who after the French invasion occupied the Mexican throne from 1864–1867, before being executed by
Juárez). Here this ageless "witch" achieves virtually the
same thing that Consuelo does in *Aura*—the revival of her
husband through a young man.

These first two stories are fantastical, even allegorical. They come from Fuentes's early collection, *Los días
enmascarados (The Masked Days,* 1954).[6] Because, like
Aura, they contain eruptions of the fantastic into everyday
life, these early stories can be included in the general
category of magical realism. With its resemblance to parable, its metamorphosis, and its intrusion of an ancient
deity into the modern world, "Chac Mool" bears a striking resemblance to two stories by Julio Cortázar, "Ax-
olotl" and "The Idol of the Cyclades."[7] The tales warn
modern children not to play with sacred ancient fire for
it may still be smoldering and ready to ignite. These stories, together with novels like *Where the Air is Clear* and
Carpentier's *The Kingdom of this World,* seem to constitute a kind of subcategory of magical realism that asserts
the continuing power of ancient beliefs and their attendant
rituals.

The rest of the stories in *Burnt Water* portray various
psychological or social deviations; they are not magical,
but often very strange. "The Two Elenas," "A Pure Soul,"
"The Doll Queen," "The Old Morality," and "The Cost
of Living" originally appeared in the collection *Cantar de
ciegos (Songs of the Blind,* 1964).[8] The title and the epigraph for *Songs of the Blind* come from a blindman's
begging song that ends the fourteenth century *Libro de
buen amor (The Book of Good Love)* by the Archipreste

de Hita: "We cannot earn it/ With these leprous, blind,/
Poor, and crippled bodies." (What the blindmen cannot
earn is a bit of breakfast.) The lines suggest, in addition
to the two physically deformed characters in the book, a
controlling image of emotional deformity.[9] Many characters are misfits; others simply do not tolerate ways of life
that differ from their own. Their "blindness" and isolation
contrast implicitly with the vision that sees them all.[10]

In "Mother's Day," a young man admires the vitality
of his grandfather, who fought alongside a number of
revolutionary leaders, changing his loyalties—like Artemio Cruz—as the leaders rose and fell. In this story we
sense the frustration of postrevolutionary generations who
feel they've missed the only real "boat" in modern Mexican history. They have been born too late and have to take
the leavings of the Revolution—memories of the fight or
wealth made in its aftermath. In "The Two Elenas," a
man lives with his wife, who toys with the intriguing idea
of a *ménage à trois,* while—unbeknownst to her—he
sleeps with his mother-in-law. "A Pure Soul" concerns
another triangle, this time involving the tortured though
not overtly incestuous love of a sister, a brother, and his
fiancé. "These Were Palaces" describes life in the run-
down apartments that now occupy what was an ornate
palace. It concentrates particularly on the emotional affi-
nity between a little boy in a wheelchair and a crazy old
woman who looks after stray dogs. In contrast to the
people who live in this ruin, "The Mandarin" keeps up his
splendidly outmoded residence—even though it is flanked
on both sides by skyscrapers—until he is finally robbed
and murdered. A similar brutality ends "The Cost of Living," when a teacher is knifed to death for attempting to
distribute leaflets calling for a strike. In "The Doll Queen"
a young man seeks out a former childhood playmate, only
to discover that her parents have buried her alive so to
speak in their apartment because she is now a cripple.
Since Amilamia's parents now think of her as dead, they

worship her as she used to be in the form of a doll en-
shrined on a baroquely decorated altar—a grotesque per-
version of the Mexican Day of the Dead festivities when
families construct elaborate altars to honor recently
deceased relatives.

Except for "Chac Mool," "The Old Morality" is perhaps the most schematic story in the collection. It recounts the disruption of an eccentric but happy household
by traditionally moral but inwardly corrupt meddlers. As
Manuel Durán has pointed out, the provincial atmosphere, with its moral and sexual hypocrisy, links it with
The Good Conscience.[11] The young Alberto lives contentedly with his grandfather Agustín and Agustín's scandal-
ously young lover on their ranch until his dead mother's
three sisters get the juvenile judge to declare the place an
"atmosphere of shameless immorality." He then goes to
live with his unmarried aunt, who seduces him. This he
half enjoys, claiming that the severe spinster has softened
through sensual affection. Thus, although he thinks that
on the whole he prefers life back at the ranch, he can't
quite decide to send his grandfather a letter saying, "Come
get me please. It seems to me there's a lot more morality
at the ranch" (152).

In addition to professing a worn-out moral code, the
aunts, called Milagros (Miracles), Angustias (Anguish),
and Benedicta (Blessed), talk like old morality plays. They
are introduced like stock characters and act accordingly,
calling Grandfather Agustín "blasphemer," "heretic,"
"whoremonger" (141). The same is true for Agustín,
Micaela (Agustín's mistress), and an attendant group of
priests; everyone repeats the same routines and rather
enjoys them. Agustín shouts daily insults at the priests;
they leer at Micaela and run away when Agustín lifts
Micaela's skirts, and the narrator observes how "about the
same things happen" each day "and we're all very happy"
(139). This is true comedy in the sense that an ebullient
round of life goes on; but it has a message, too: "immorali-

ty"—which may in the end be regenerative—is dressed up as "morality." The story recalls *Huckleberry Finn* in its contrast of the natural and spontaneous life with the cleaned and pressed (and repressed) "moral" life. And there's even an aunt to do the "sivilizing."

Fuentes occasionally creates a specific connection among the layers of his verbal city. A voice that records a collective memory, speaking for someone more than its owner, appears in several stories. In "The Doll Queen," for example, Amilamia's parents beg the narrator to recall her for them. In "These Were Palaces," Luisito seems to possess a kind of collective memory and imagination. He remembers his own past in a big house his family once owned before they moved to Mexico City. But he also "remembers"—imaginatively—the crumbling palace they now inhabit as it once existed: Old Manuelita

made a great effort to remember everything the boy told her and then imagine, as he did and when he did, a majestic palace: the entryway before there was a lottery stand, the carved marble façade stripped of cheap clothing stores, . . . free of the advertisements that disfigured the ancient nobility of the building. (98)

And later on, when she is alone in her room, Manuelita "rereads" these texts: "This is the way she communicated with him, by remembering the things he remembered and forgetting about her own past" (98). Luisito and Manuelita share a hidden communal memory that comforts them because it allows them to escape from their drab lives.

This memory is similar to the memory they imagine their stray dogs might possess, both of them "carnal" and "incandescent," though in different keys. After Luisito watches some boys cut off one dog's tail, he looks at the other stray dogs and says to his little sister that "the dogs of the sun" are "telling each other something, . . . these dogs are going to remember the pain of one of their own pack, . . . but Rosa María's shoe-button eyes were like stone, without memory" (101). Luisito's sister clearly lacks his sense of communal memory. The expression "dogs of the sun" implies that their communicative force survives from Aztec times. The dogs will add the recent cruelty of these teen-agers to all their past sufferings.

Later on in the story, Luisito wants to keep his mother from gossiping about the fracas Manuelita caused by bringing her stray dogs into the church for comfort. He does this by threatening to reveal some old letters his mother wrote—but did not send—in which she painted a falsely rosy picture of her life to an old flame. These letters, like his and Manuelita's stories, are really imaginary narratives that grow out of memory and desire. He joins his mother to Manuelita by telling her that everyone needs such imaginary worlds to survive the one they inhabit. The imaginative narratives of Luisito and Manuelita—and the hypothetical memory of their dogs—can be seen as a paradigm for Fuentes's conception of narration itself which, as we shall see again in "The Son of Andrés Aparicio," thrives on collective memory. Fuentes implies that this kind of memory is particularly strong in Mexico City: "In a place that had been a palace centuries ago little Luis found it easier to imagine things, and remember" (97).

It seems appropriate, then, that this volume which records the collective voice of Mexico City should end with a story that pays homage to Pablo Neruda and specifically to Neruda's poem, *The Heights of Macchu Picchu,* for that poem proclaims its intention to speak for the voiceless multitudes who built the ancient fortified city of the Incas. "The Son of Andrés Aparicio" follows Bernabé Aparicio from outings with friends in his poor barrio through a love affair which even he perceives as rather dreary to his association with the "Chief" of an underworld organization that lives off crime and terror. Words from *The Heights of Macchu Picchu* appear (unidentified) at two crucial points in the text. Several significant details draw the two works even closer together: Macchu Picchu is an ancient citadel built of stone on stone; the Chief's house—located in the section of Mexico City called Pedregal after the stone on which it is built—resembles a modern fortress, in monumental style, with cement ramps and a sunken pool; it, like Macchu Picchu, was built for the rich by the poor. Pedregal is in one sense then a lost city, not as Macchu Picchu was before its discovery, but before the journey of the poet to recover its massed voices. But the primary lost city here is the barrio where Bernabé grew up: "It had no name and so it didn't exist as a place" (188). It corresponds to the modern urban wasteland Neruda's climber leaves behind in his ascent toward the heights.

Let us return to the actual quotations from Neruda. When the Chief commands a token theorist in his band to read aloud "any book at all, the one he liked most," the theorist then reads "in a trembling voice" three sets of lines from Neruda's poem. The last ones, "Stone within stone, and man, where was he? / Air within air, and man, where was he? / Time within time . . ." signal the awakening of a social conscience in Neruda's poet/climber/quester when he contemplates Macchu Picchu as he begins to assume his role of literary spokesman for the nameless masses. The lines herald the end of the poem where, "I come to speak for your dead mouths," where he invites these mouths to "speak through my speech, and through my blood." But Bernabé is not ready yet; when the Chief asks him, "Did you understand anything, boy? Bernabé shook his head" (217). The Chief burns the book, but that cannot erase the language of conscience. For like the proverbial mole of the revolution, it resurfaces. After Bernabé learns about the Chief's past harassment of his father, "he dreamed, unable to separate his dream from a vague but driving desire that everything that exists be for all the earth, for everyone, water, air, gardens, stone, time," and wakes up with Neruda's phrase, "And man, where was he?" in his mind (228). The dream is a dream of solidarity.

It, like Neruda's words, and the stray dogs in "These Were Palaces," signals a connection with past injustice.

Once again, narrative depends on personal memory. At the beginning of the story, Bernabé has not been able to put his thoughts into words because, above all, "he couldn't remember his father's voice" (190). In a pep talk to his terrorist Hawk Brigade, designed to whet its appetite for student blood, the Chief subverts Neruda's constructive sense of solidarity. He appeals to the street boys' resentment against the rich, encouraging them to "get your revenge for . . . the abuse you've taken all your miserable lives" (224). He invokes memory of past injustice to divide and destroy, not to unite and reform. From the Chief and his second, both, we hear the philosophy of the "fat man" in *The Death of Artemio Cruz:* dominate or be dominated. The journey of the poet in *The Heights of Macchu Picchu* culminates in his assumption of speech for the dispossessed. Bernabé's journey ends less decisively. In order to survive and not revolt, he must suppress and forget. In this atmosphere, even his mother's words "meant the opposite of what they said" (231). Nevertheless, he is grateful that his mother gives him "his father's most handsome suspenders, the red ones with the gilded clasps that had been the pride of Andrés Aparicio" (231). They are presumably a sign that he may eventually inherit his father's passion for reform along with his red suspenders. And so he ends up poised between his own desire for comfort and the memory of the injustice his father fought, between his mother's meaningless words and his father's red suspenders.

In echoing Neruda, in "rewriting" *The Heights of Macchu Picchu* in prose so to speak, even including a fragment—a stone—from the earlier structure, Fuentes achieves in his text a literary equivalent of the architectural layers in the Mexico City of the stories, with its palaces turned apartment houses, its lake covered by asphalt. The record of historical time informs the arrangement of literary space, for the writer's page, like the Mexican soil, is a palimpsest, covered with successive cultural texts. And the recognition of past inscriptions enlivens recent creations.

3

Poetics and Politics: The Essays

The traditional cross-fertilization of fiction and essay in Latin American letters operates with particular force in Fuentes's work.[1] In addition to incorporating intellectual history into his fiction, Fuentes often continues his narrative treatments of given subjects in his essays. Key words, images, and ideas move from one to the other. The essay "X-Ray of a Decade: 1953–1963,"[2] for example, surveys many of the social problems that underlie *Where the Air is Clear,* while discussions in that novel tend toward the form of essays. And two of Fuentes's most successful political essays—"The Death of Rubén Jaramillo" and "Lázaro Cárdenas"—include extensive fictional recreations of scenes. For the sake of convenience, I have followed Fuentes's own division of his essays into two groups. *Tiempo mexicano (Mexican Time,* 1971) contains articles on political, social, and economic events; *Casa con dos puertas (The House with Two Doors,* 1970) essays on art and literature.[3]

The essays in *Mexican Time* view Mexican society from a broad historical perspective. They combine critical analysis with suggestions for reform and occasional homage to a significant leader. Fuentes writes consistently from the left but also critizes Mexican leftists for being too doctrinaire. He appears more utopian in his political essays than in his novels or his literary criticism. The essays are often intended as calls to action, while the novels represent testimonials, confirmations of an unsatisfactory state of affairs. In one case, optimism can be useful; in the other it is simply self-deceptive. Fuentes also frequently adopts an oratorical, journalistic style in his political pieces—lists of complaints or objectives, series of rhetorical questions, repetitions of key words for emphasis, inflammatory language, and resounding denunciations. As he points out in the introduction, this is avowedly partisan writing. The essays, particularly when they propose specific reforms or bear witness to injustices, illustrate Fuentes's idea that because channels of public communication in Latin America are not well developed, intellectuals must speak out.

TIME AND HISTORY

The first essay in *Mexican Time* begins by defining "Mexican time." As we have seen in *Where the Air is Clear,* for Fuentes "there is not just one time [in Mexico]: all times are alive, all pasts are present" (9). This presence of the past represents an unconscious wish of the land and the people. Furthermore, previous times must be kept alive because "no Mexican time has been fulfilled yet. Because Mexico's history is a series of 'subverted Edens,' . . . which we wish at once to revisit and to forget" (9–10). Fuentes's political essays—and his fiction in a different domain— attempt to fulfill the potential of Mexican time. Fuentes encapsulates his sense of the coexistence of different kinds of time by turning a visual image into a catchy phrase:

The crumbling adobe walls of huts in the Mexican fields display advertisements for Pepsi-Cola with surprising regularity. From Quetzalcóatl to Pepsicóatl: onto indigenous mythic time is superimposed western calendar time, the time of progress, linear time. (26)

When he takes a more linear view, Fuentes discerns four traditions within Mexican history: indigenous mythic views of the cosmos; Spain's notion of coterminal power and divinity (which developed from the Roman tradition of legitimate succession); stoic individualism that buys serenity and personal satisfaction with loneliness; and western European positivism that identifies bourgeois interests with those of the state. A fifth, and as we shall see, a saving force in Latin America, according to Fuentes, is the utopian tradition. It puts community values above the interests of power (39). This tradition has not prevailed so far; instead, Mexico has combined "paternalism, [the] perpetual hope for protection," with "personalism, [the] eschatology of the individual savior." These vertical power structures have perpetuated centralized authority in Mexico: "Aztec Emperor: Spanish Viceroy: Señor Presidente" (129).

To begin his historical panorama, Fuentes tells the story of the benevolent feathered serpent god Quetzalcóatl, who fled the land after being tricked into incest with his sister, promising to return and bring prosperity. Thus, "the history of indigenous Mexico is the history of absence and waiting. . . . Hernán Cortés, by disembarking in Mexico on the day foretold for the return of Quetzalcóatl, fulfilled the promise by destroying it" (22). The colonial culture that resulted from this conquest was hybrid. Still, the colonial period as a whole was an anachronism; it "prolonged the organic order of the middle ages," denying both indigenous antiquity and European modernity—rationalism, individualism, mercantilism (28).

These latter forces took over with a vengeance in the twentieth century. Even the Revolution could not stop them. Fuentes's description of them implies his criticism of contemporary society and his suggestions for its reform:

The Mexican revolution broke the medieval Spanish heritage that still chains the majority of Latin American countries. And it adopted, in the end, a politics of capitalist accumulation and rapid industrialization by means of heavy foreign borrowing and postponement of the demands of the campesinos who had been the soldiers of the Revolution and of the workers who provided a cheap labor force. (143)

Even so, Fuentes celebrates the Revolution itself—though a bit reluctantly, since he often criticizes the revolutionary rhetoric that has accompanied the reactionary policies of one government after another: "Only the Revolution—and for that reason, in spite of everything, it deserves a capital R—made present all Mexico's pasts. It did this *instantaneously,* as if it knew that time was short for this fiesta of incarnations" (11).

Fuentes argues that throughout its history, Mexico has always been masked—"in its very origins by a skin of rock, mosaic, and gold," which preceded the "icy and baroque viceregency," which was followed by "the formal dream of liberalism, by the deceptive peace and progress of the Porfirian period." Mexico has only broken through its masks with the Revolution when it discovered itself.[4] There "acts coincide with words and appearances with real faces; the mask falls and all the colors, voices, and bodies of Mexico shine with their true being" (83). Fuentes recalls an image that symbolizes Mexico finally seeing its own face during the Revolution: Zapata's soldiers are surprised and delighted with their own reflections in the huge mirrors of the Porfirian aristocracy's mansions in Mexico City. Once again, Fuentes reluctantly acknowledges the significance of the Revolution: "Perhaps only for that the Revolution had been worth it: it had given them faces, identities. Look: it's me. Look at yourself: it's you. Look: it's us" (62). The negative side of this self-recognition, Fuentes explains, has been a heritage of chauvinistic isolationism (83).

In postrevolutionary times, Fuentes marks two particularly significant dates, the second really a consequence of the first. In 1940, with the end of President Cárdenas's term, the period of revolutionary reforms was over. Up until then, these changes had benefited the bourgeoisie: agrarian reform meant better methods, increased production, more men in the factories, less in the fields; Cárdenas's nationalization of oil resources meant cheaper fuel for industrialization. But after 1940, Fuentes maintains, the bourgeoisie has been complacent, satisfied with its accumulated wealth and power.[5] In 1968, the government opened fire on a student demonstration and killed large numbers of people. Fuentes thinks that social pressure had built up to a point where either repression or social reform was needed. The country had been—and still is—divided in two: "The urban industrial world exploits the indigenous campesino world via many forms of internal colonialism." In addition, young people born after 1940 are disillusioned and impatient because they have never seen the positive action of revolutionary reform, but only "quantitative development without real political or social progress" (147–48).

CRITICISM AND REFORM

Fuentes's criticism of Mexico focuses consistently on several issues. Many of them stem from his dislike of a monolithic power structure that prevents different voices from being heard. Such a structure betrays the Revolution by imposing uniformity on diversity. International corporations, the president, the government bureaucracy, union leaders, all represent the interests of the upper middle classes. Fuentes welcomes dissent from this bloc in the form of student demonstrations or labor strikes; they are a sign of life. A central problem, according to Fuentes, is the one party system in Mexico. The Partido Revolucionario Instutional (Institutional Revolutionary Party) was

originally designed to unite the country after the divisive
Revolution. But now the myth of " 'national unity'
around the powers of the Institutional Revolution" serves
to smooth over what might prove to be useful distinctions
among classes or factions, and particularly between left
and right (147). Without this myth, open controversies
might lead to some social change. The Revolution has
become—via the PRI—"an Institution that renders homage to the indigenous and revolutionary past with words
and to the 'progressive' and bourgeois present with acts"
(11).[6] Fuentes detests this double-speak whereby "freedom is political monopoly by the PRI, abundance is misery, revolution is counterrevolution" (75). Contrary to his
ideal, the press is characterized "above all [by the] absence
of problems." The same is true for labor: "the union leader
is, by definition, a man who doesn't create problems. But
he is also something worse: the man who prevents problems from being created" (73). Fuentes cites figures to
show that almost all of Mexico's resources are privately
controlled. This means that the state can dispense few
social services to the poor. In addition, much of the country's wealth flows out to the international corporations
with which the private sector is linked.

All of this is why Fuentes sees Mexico as having
"arrived at urban industrial society only to ask ourselves
if the effort was worth it." Mexico's arrival at industrialization coincides with revolts from inside industrialized
nations against their technocracy, pollution, and urban
ghettos (33). According to Fuentes, when Mexico's
dreams are fulfilled, they are subverted: the long-awaited
return of Quetzalcóatl turns into the conquest and the
consequent death of indigenous culture; and "the dream
of Benito Juárez leads directly to the nightmare of Porfirio
Díaz" (11). The notion of the subverted dream recurs
frequently in Fuentes's essays; it's one of the nasty tricks
time plays on us. In his discussion of the Czechoslovakian
writer Milan Kundera, Fuentes maintains that "the illu-

sion of the future has been the idyll of modern history. Kundera dares to say that the future *already took place,* under our noses, and it smells bad."[7]

What to do? Since Fuentes criticizes the Mexican government for its monolithic, univocal nature, many of his suggested reforms aim to take account of the plurality of Mexican society. Fuentes's principal objective is to create a strong, independent governmental structure that combines a widely based democracy with long-term social planning. This would represent the fulfillment of the old utopian tradition denied so far by paternalistic power structures in Mexico: it would constitute "the human plan" of "personal freedom plus communal ties" (137).[8]

Since return to the benevolent reign of Quetzalcóatl is impossible, and submission to the commercial regime of Pepsicóatl is undesirable, Mexico must work out a new program that will allow her to develop and at the same time not eradicate her diverse cultural heritage. According to Fuentes, this will require "a political reform of great decentralization" (38). Fuentes has mentioned that in an effort to strengthen the "popular community tradition" ("always beleaguered" by the other tradition of centralized, paternalistic power, but "surprisingly resistant"[9]), he and Octavio Paz among others helped to start a kind of grass-roots labor organization to voice workers' complaints. Fuentes stresses, however, that such an organization must be led by laborers, not intellectuals, or it will not succeed. He has also suggested that the PRI divide up into two parties.[10] That way the left would have a distinct voice. Together with the decentralization of power would go the decentralization of population in the cities. This would alleviate the decline of the countryside. Similarly, Fuentes believes that the correct evolution of Marxian socialism is toward the increasing autonomy of different sectors of society.

But Fuentes does not wish to see the state disappear. On the contrary, it is the only entity strong enough to

defend the economically oppressed sectors of the population against private wealth and international corporations.[11] Fuentes believes that the left must propose modest
yet concrete objectives; to achieve them it must unite
urban groups with democratic ideals—students, teachers,
intellectuals, professional people—and exploited workers
and *campesinos* (158). "The PRI is powerful because the
left is divided. . . . They [leftists] want utopia tomorrow,
but nothing will happen until they are willing to work bit
by bit."[12]

Two presidents have moved in this direction, according to Fuentes: President Cárdenas in the late thirties, and
President Echeverría in the early seventies. Fuentes includes a tribute to Cárdenas in *Mexican Time*.[13] He accompanies the former president on a trip to the
countryside, where Cárdenas encourages the people to
keep on working for agrarian reform, democratic unions
and local government, good state schools. Fuentes recreates moving scenes where *campesinos* swarm around Cárdenas, asking questions, bringing up problems, or
sometimes simply giving him "the biggest ovation I ever
heard." Fuentes begins by evoking a traditional prome-
nade in Guanajuato at dusk. We hear several voices prais-
ing Cárdenas's democratic spirit and then asking him
questions. Finally, Cárdenas himself speaks, but only in
response to these questions from the people, not in domination from above. This form of dialogue illustrates the
political structure Fuentes advocates.

Throughout the piece, Cárdenas questions the right
of a person or a group to speak: where does the Mexican
press that has betrayed the Mexican Revolution get the
right to speak against the Cuban Revolution? Fuentes
suggests that the right to speak derives from moral
thought and action. The power of language demands responsibility; it sounds a hopeful note throughout the essays. On this same trip, Fuentes visits an old Zapatista
who tenaciously guards yellowed titles to communal lands

as a defense against their unjust seizure: "They don't have
these papers. We do. These papers prove our right to exist.
They are in my custody, and I will never lose them, even
though it cost me my life." Fuentes imagines the man "as
a wandering guardian of the seals, humble, hidden, anonymous, but sure of his true power and of his final victory,
because he held in his hands the final proof of legitimacy:
the written word" (124).

Another essay in *Mexican Time*, "The Death of
Rubén Jaramillo," pays homage to Rubén Jaramillo,
spokesman for the *campesinos* in the state of Morelos.
Here Fuentes alternates between recreation of the brutal
murders of Jaramillo, his pregnant wife, and three sons,
and testimonies to his almost saintly life as an agrarian
reformer. The technique causes the reader's rage at the
injustice of the murders to grow slowly and steadily, nour-
ished by the *campesinos*' own emotions. Near the end,
Fuentes characteristically links this present violence to the
past. Following the savage killings of Jaramillo and his
family, Fuentes evokes the nearby ruin of "Xochicalco,
the altar of death." He imagines the sculpture of Quetzalcóatl killing all it touches on the frieze that surrounds the
ancient temple. Once again, Mexico has demanded a sacrifice. "Different judges, officials, priests; the same Mexican barbarity, the same Mexican terror by night and in the
sun. Sitting in the golden chair, the new powers . . . preside
over the old blood ritual" (120). But the governor, general,
landowner, businessman demand blood not to pacify the
gods, but to increase their own wealth and perpetuate the
misery of the *campesinos* who provide it.

Fuentes catches himself at the end of this vision
though, which might well belong to *Where the Air is Clear,
A Change of Skin,* or *Terra Nostra.* He says no to the
fatalism he has just pictured—"deconstructs" his own
text. For this is an essay not a novel, and to be effective
it must at least suggest the possibility of reform: "No, it's
not the fatal barbarity of the gods; it's the combatable

injustice of man that assassinated Rubén Jaramillo and his family" (120). This is perhaps Fuentes's most moving essay; it is extremely effective as fiction, but it is also inspiring and serves as an implicit call to action.

As in the case of Cárdenas, Fuentes suggests that the highest compliment he can pay Jaramillo is to transmit his people's genuine love for him in their own words. Thus, he uses simple language with carefully chosen repetitions and short sentences. This language reproduces the dignity of the *campesinos* that speak to him, most of them talking like the first one, "sitting in the shade of his miserable porch at the back of a miserable one-room shack used for everything: cooking, eating, sleeping" (112). After each story he says, "That's what . . . told us." The words "the chief is dead. Now we are all Jaramillo" reappear throughout. They too are an implicit call to action. By killing Jaramillo, the forces of oppression have split him into many: these are the voices Fuentes records; in recording them, he multiplies them in the minds of his readers, who will wish to carry on the fight.

POLITICAL RHETORIC

Throughout these essays, Fuentes's mode of thought and his style are relentlessly dialectical. In their very essence then, they combat the monolithic and authoritarian political system he laments. Like the revolutionary rhetoric he describes, but in a different way, Fuentes's own writing might be termed "double-edged." Such a style suits Mexican history well, for according to Fuentes, that history has been a series of dreams simultaneously accomplished and betrayed. A similar reversal describes "the supreme paradox of the Spanish colonization": Mexico "was colonized by a country that soon became a colony of Northern European mercantile powers" (30). Latin America itself has paradoxically chosen the ideology of its exploiters—

anti-utopian, liberal positivism (31). Fuentes characterizes
the very idea of utopia as "there is no such place and there
is such a place: that's the most profound and secret root
of Hispanic American culture" (29).

As it reveals dualities in Mexican society, Fuentes's
prose incarnates the dialectical mode of thought on a
linguistic level. Examples are numerous, occasionally
amusing, and often catchy. They constitute a highly epi-
grammatic style, full of quotable phrases. Too full, one
might say, except that clever slogans contribute to an
effective political style.

Here, as elsewhere in his writing, Fuentes emphasizes
a point with an ABBA structure of chiasmus. Young people disillusioned with society, for example, "see what they
don't want; want what they don't see" (149). (A = see;
B = want; B = want; A = see). Earlier on, Fuentes declares
that "we can't return to Quetzalcóatl; Quetzalcóatl won't
return to us either. Like Godot, Quetzalcóatl went away
forever and only came back disguised as a Spanish con-
quistador or an Austrian prince" (33). And again, with
regard to his own texts: "*Cruz* is a story about the death
of life. *Aura* is a story about the life of death."[14]

Such conceptual reversals tend to make Fuentes's
expository prose opaque; they disrupt the linear arguments that generally characterize political writing. This
chiastic design of the text forces us to double back on what
we've read and consider alternatives. The process suggests
a discourse that takes more than one line of thought into
account, one that plays with words. This element of play-
fulness—perhaps even of self-parody—enlivens the critical mode. On the other hand, the symmetry of the design
gives a sense of inevitability to a pronouncement.

Fuentes himself has pointed out that the chiastic
structure resembles a mirror, a self-reflexive space.[15] A
mirror is often terrifying because it returns a character to
himself, to a presence that he may have wished to forget
or to go beyond. Furthermore, the chiastic reversals I

quoted above, describing the repeated patterns of conquest and sacrifice in Mexico, like the persistence of myth in Fuentes's work as a whole, reveal yet again his concern with a return of the past. They are one of the tricks of history: their sense of inevitable progression and return reminds you that what you thought you controlled controls you. The future turns out to duplicate the past. Thus Fuentes's chiastic designs are usually frightening, and suggest ominous returns of the past or of the self. But they can also hold out a promise of the return to a *better* past. In this sense chiasmus represents a "mythic" pattern in the most general way; it returns us momentarily to a kind of textual *illo tempore,* a primordial time, abolishing linear progression. This is the aspect of the design that structures *Aura.* Consuelo can be imagined as achieving her desired return to the past through a chiastic progression: Consuelo and the General as young lovers (A); Consuelo alone after the General's death (B); Consuelo alone, but having conjured Aura (B): and finally, Consuelo and Felipe as the General rejuvenated (A). In doubling back on itself to end where it began, chiasmus suggests a continuous series of cyclical transformations. This space that Fuentes cuts out of traditional linear prose works against the linear time of progress he claims has been superimposed on indigenous time in Mexico. It is a rhetorical structure that yearns for the cyclical time of myth to conquer the linear time of history. It corresponds to Fuentes's political desires for an eventual fulfillment of the utopian dreams of community with which the New World began.

Fuentes further disrupts the linear progression of sentences by expanding oppositions into lists. Again, examples abound, but one will have to do: the parable of Quetzalcóatl" illustrates the tension "between freedom and necessity, between consecration and profanation; between identity and anonymity, that hides in the ancient art of Mexico" (22). Reversals and lists of oppositions illustrate Fuentes's own use of the innovative language that he praises in other writers. But they occasionally create problems for readers and in this too they correspond to Fuentes's beliefs. Unlike the hated union leader who "prevents problems from being created," Fuentes uses language in just the opposite way.

Individual images themselves often play ingeniously on ancient Mexican symbols, plumed serpents and masks appearing frequently:

Mexico imposed the mask of Quetzalcóatl on Cortés. Cortés rejected it and imposed the mask of Christ on Mexico. Ever since, it has been impossible to know who is worshipped at the baroque altars in Puebla, Tlaxcala, and Oaxaca. But the confusion has been overcome by blood: the indians, accustomed to men dying in honor of gods, felt amazed and defeated by a god that had died in honor of men. Christ or Quetzalcóatl, the Galilean crowned with thorns or the serpent crowned with feathers? (22–23)

Note the two intertwined chiastic designs here (Mexico-Cortés-Cortés-Mexico; men-gods-gods-men). In another essay, Fuentes stresses a point by stripping away Quetzalcóatl's feathers: Mexico must either widen what are now too narrow tunnels leading toward integral economic development and authentic social justice, "or we'll be strangled, like the figure of Laocöon, in a hermetic, dark circle with no exit, devoured by serpents with no plumage."[16]

A style that plays as it argues, in addition to coining quotable phrases and disrupting linear thought patterns, provides comic relief from relentlessly critical argument. Here Fuentes takes over a foreign advertising jingle to play on an earlier invasion: "There's a Malinche in your future; put a Cortés in your tank" (15). Furthermore, in contrast to the long homages he pays to Cárdenas and Jaramillo, Fuentes punctuates his political arguments with quick satirical portraits. As often in *Where the Air is Clear,* devastating details characterize the social position and attitudes of a particular type. During the regimes of presidents Ruiz Cortines and López Mateos, the government "raises the temple of national unity, a church that passes hosts out to some, tacos to the majority, the same sermons to all, excommunications to malcontents, absolutions to penitents, preserves the paradise of the wealthy, and promises it to the poor" (67). Even more biting is the glimpse of President Diaz Ordaz retiring to the presidential palace after the killings in 1968: "Tecatecuhtli [the Aztec word for a dignitary] retired to a mansion that cost the country more than forty million pesos, with machines to filter the smog (. . . and what about the smoke of the shots, and the mist of tear gas?), with a private movie theatre, and flawless marble walls, like mirrors. To admire himself all the better. 'With peace, everything is possible.' 'One single road: Mexico and the Mexican Revolution' " (154).

A RADICAL POETICS

In his best-known literary essay, *La nueva novela hispanoamericana* (*The New Hispanic American Novel*, 1969), Fuentes surveys "el boom," the recent explosion of Latin American fiction to which he belongs. He argues throughout that contemporary Latin American novelists invent a new language and that this effort represents a form of decolonization, a healthy profanation of sacred Spanish traditions.[17] He begins by discussing general concerns and then analyzes the works of five contemporary novelists. The final chapter argues that innovative language is often a socially disruptive force, "an enemy word."[18] It suggests alternatives to the status quo.

Fuentes writes with a constant awareness of the Latin American novel's problematic history: its virtual nonexistence in the colonial period, its continual dependence on the European novel. One traditional problem is that nature, which often helped European writers discover themselves, particularly in the Romantic period, frequently took the role of protagonist in Latin American novels. This resulted in part from the influence of European naturalism; but Fuentes stresses the overwhelming impact of the new world environment itself. Like the characters who disappear at the end of José Eustacio Rivera's *The Vortex* (1924), the novels themselves were swallowed by the jungle, mine, or river.[19]

For Fuentes, the Mexican revolution, and the novels it engendered—Mariano Azuela's *The Underdogs* (1916), Martín Luis Guzmán's *The Eagle and the Serpent* (1928), and later Agustín Yáñez's *The Edge of the Storm* (1947), and even Juan Rulfo's *Pedro Páramo* (1955)—have been essential in the formation of a lively tradition because they introduce ambiguities into Latin American fiction. Those novels begin to break down the former stereotypes of the barbarous jungle and the barbarous dictator against the noble savage or the enlightened reformer. In these novels of the Revolution, villains and heroes often change roles; "heroic certitude becomes critical ambiguity, natural fatalism contradictory action, romantic idealism ironic dialectic" (*The New Hispanic American Novel,* 15). Fuentes believes that what he calls bourgeois realism—a psychological and descriptive way of observing social and personal relations—has run its course. For him, the future lies with writers who create a "second" or "parallel reality" through myths that return for their expression to "the poetic roots of literature" (19).

To move toward this future through the creation of a new language is to say what history has kept quiet, to profane and contaminate the sacred rhetoric—of church or academy. Humor is an essential part of this linguistic renovation. In the humorous wordplay and slang of novels like Julio Cortázar's *Hopscotch* or Guillermo Cabrera Infante's *Three Trapped Tigers,* "for the first time, our books

know how to laugh" (30). Laughter, like love, is revolutionary because it disregards rules:

Our literature is truly revolutionary insofar as it denies the established order the words would like, and opposes to it the language
of alarm, renewal, disorder, and humor. The language, basically,
of ambiguity: of the plurality of meanings . . . of openness. (31)

The openness is really triple: the Spanish language opens
itself to deformative enrichment from local expressions;
Latin American literature and world literature both open
themselves to mutual interchange.

Much of Fuentes's analysis of Latin American literature illustrates the theories of French critic Paul Ricoeur;
Fuentes cites his description of the word, or the literary
text, as a mediating force between synchronic structure
and diachronic event in language—between language as it
has always been used and the ways in which a particular
era or author transforms it, between general rules and
individual works.[20] Such a duality naturally attracts
Fuentes, and he characteristically expands it into a series
of oppositions, or "universal antinomies" of language: the
systematic versus the historic, anonymous versus individual speech, institution versus innovation, obligation
versus selection, and so on. The scheme suits Fuentes's
study of the growth of Latin American literature particularly well, for it allows for oscillation between Spanish
institutions and Latin American innovations.

KINDRED SPIRITS

Fuentes's notion of a "second reality" that criticizes as it
recreates this world attracts him to several fellow artists.
The names of William Faulkner, Luis Buñuel, and José
Luis Cuevas[21] appear frequently throughout Fuentes's
critical writings. He has included an essay on each of them
in *Casa con dos puertas (House with Two Doors,* 1970).

(The title comes from Fuentes's evocation of Balzac's "house with two doors," where the past enters and the future exits. I imagine the two doors representing Fuentes's own dual heritage of native Mexican and European literary traditions, as well as his dialectical mode of thought.) As always, we catch glimpses of Fuentes's own fiction through his descriptions of other works.

The second reality Faulkner creates—his Yoknapatawpha County—is of course more traditionally realistic than the worlds of Buñuel and Cuevas; his "real greatness" according to Fuentes is that "his characters are he, you, and I." Even so, Faulkner's "poetic radicalism" reveals "our *other* identity, the one we scrupulously hide" (70). The characters in Buñuel's movies, like Séverine in *Belle de Jour,* who is constantly looking toward the outside of the screen, "perceive a world beyond their own skins." They are moved to act in order to transform this perception in accordance with "their incandescent desires" (198). The work of Cuevas reveals similar "characteristics of transfiguration." It suggests "another person, another shore, another land . . . that tension between my appearance and the suspicion that there is another appearance which denies me and yet complements me."[22]

Intimations of other worlds reflect Fuentes's sympathy with surrealism, and his preference for disturbing rather than serene art and literature, for texts that are not comforting or traditionally beautiful: "It is only after a radical rejection of the worn out notions of beauty, harmony, and variety, that Cuevas goes out in search of identities for men who have become relativistic, humiliated, obsessive, out of place, and eccentric" (29). Buñuel's eroticism is of a disturbing variety, not "copulation," but "illumination, temptations, and secret restlessness" (202). Throughout his discussion of Buñuel, Fuentes stresses his surrealistic uniting of oppositions: "the unsatisfied, condemned, dangerous, secret look, against the comfortable, conformist, consecrated one; the eyes of the total world,

contaminated, longing, revolutionary, against the blindness of the established order" (198).

This dialectical vision also characterizes Fuentes's
own thought and style here, as it did in the political essays.
Lists of oppositions and chiastic reversals proliferate to
support a dialectical mode of thought, intentionally provoking and disquieting. And Fuentes often expands oppositions into progressions or transformations through time.
In the essay on Cuevas, for example, he elaborates on
Octavio Paz's idea that each stage in Mexican history
tries—and fails—to deny the preceding one: the conquest
tried to deny the indigenous world, the Revolution nine-
teenth-century positivism. The development of the novel
from Balzac through Proust to Faulkner forms another
variety of progression: "Balzac's man without a past, all
future, has made way for Proust's man who is pure past;
and he has led to Faulkner's man who is past only in the
present and for that reason, once again impending future"
(68).

Characteristically, Fuentes matches man's transformations through time by creating structurally similar series of changing images. He describes one of Cuevas's
precursors as abolishing

in a supernatural leap . . . the distance between what is and what
appears to be, between what one suffers and what one desires. A
fusion of opposites separated by literal positivism; death is a
fiesta, a fiesta is an impossible luxury, luxury is a deadly attrition,
an excess, a revel without daybreaks, a long night of smiling
skulls who ride bicycles.[23]

The images generate one another to create an interlocking
chain of verbal fireworks that celebrate the supernatural
leap toward another world. Furthermore, in this particular case, the technique suits the subject of the essay, for
Fuentes later maintains that Cuevas himself "serializes his
images so that the spectator will be forced to help the
painter in searching for a multiple identity."[24] We shall

see that the multiplication of figures in *A Change of Skin* and *Terra Nostra* urges the reader of Fuentes's texts toward a similar complicity.

Open-ended structures that allow readers or viewers different interpretations are one of many forms of artistic freedom that Fuentes consistently praises. Others include the novel's exploration of linguistic resources—wordplay, poetic diction, slang, regionalisms; violently surprising images that destroy traditional thought patterns; the dialectical fusion of opposites formerly "separated by liberal positivism." This last point is one example of Fuentes's persistent desire to reconcile social revolution and individual freedom. And also to conflate artistic and social renovation, to believe that "the authentic avant garde is always revolutionary" (204). Fuentes, like Buñuel, wishes to go beyond formal considerations to the social implications of art. Thus he points out that Buñuel's perception of objects is "a critique of property"; his "anarchic comedy parodies and exposes the meaning of the capitalist economy: the object of objects is not service but frantic self-consumption" (204–205).[25]

Finally, Fuentes creates striking and even poetic generalizations that, while they are often puzzling, perhaps even annoying, are also thought provoking. This example comes from his short tribute to Octavio Paz. It celebrates poetry as collective speech, a source of hope in an era of dictators and technocrats: "At bottom it's a question of knowing if we will say (like poetry) you are myself [*"mi yo eres tú"*]; or (like power), I am you [*"yo soy tú"*]" (155).

In addition to these general insights, Fuentes can capture the sense of an individual artist's work in a few words. Thus the figures Cuevas paints are "simultaneously heavy and airy . . . heavy as though they wanted to stay *until* they are identified, airy as if they wished to fly *in order to* be transformed."[26] Fuentes ends his essay on Buñuel, perhaps his most inspired critical piece, with a well-chosen and moving quotation from Buñuel himself:

"The final meaning of my films is this: to say again and again, in case anyone forgets it or thinks otherwise, that we don't live in the best of all possible worlds. I don't know if I can do more than that" (215).

DE-I-IFICATION

In his recent critical work, Fuentes uses a comparative perspective to open up a theoretical space for himself, a space not limited by (though free to intersect with) national geography. In *Cervantes or the Critique of Reading* Fuentes proposes a theory of "multivocal" reading and writing in the works of Cervantes and of Joyce. Fuentes says several times early on that Cervantes presents a "critique of narrative creation contained within the work itself: a critique of creation within creation."[27] Later on, he explains that in *Don Quixote,* this "critique of creation is a critique of reading," and "in *Ulysses* and *Finnegans Wake* it is a critique of writing" (97).

According to Fuentes, Don Quixote starts out attempting to transpose his notion of a unified chivalric code derived from "one way of reading" ("la lectura única") onto a multiple reality. He believes that there is no discrepancy between heroic deeds in books and in the world. Behind this belief lies his "univocal vision of a world structured by God" (75). But in the second part of the novel, Don Quixote finds out that someone has written of "things that happened to us alone"—i.e., things that only God could have seen. Because of Don Quixote's encounter with his apocryphal double, "the signs of the singular identity of Don Quixote are multiplied. . . . His integrity is destroyed by the readings he is submitted to" (76–77). He is thus the first modern hero—scrutinized from various points of view, read, and forced to read himself. Reading becomes multivocal in two ways here: within the fiction as Don Quixote sees himself multiplied, and without it as he is defined by the multiple intepretations of his readers.

The irony in this situation arises of course, as Fuentes points out, when now that Don Quixote is read, rather than imposing his reading of romances on reality, the world begins to imitate the world of his book. But in so doing, it only imitates itself and reveals its underlying injustice and cruelty. And for Don Quixote, when he finds equivalents—but deceptive equivalents—to his imaginary world in the real world, his illusion is destroyed. He then suffers "a nostalgia for realism"—realism in this case being the idea that in the world of "one *way* of reading" ("la lectura única"), or "legal reading," nothing comes between the word and the world, no apocryphal Quixotes trouble the imagined realities: "Before, everything that was said was true . . . even if it were fantasy" [*"todo lo dicho era cierto . . . aunque fuese fantasía"*] . . . what shatters this realism are plural readings, illicit readings" (80–81).

Don Quixote must finally define himself, then, not by the univocal kind of reading that "gave him life," but by "the multiple readings that took it away in longed-for reality but conferred it on him forever in the book and only in the book" (81). Fuentes has shifted the idea of multiple readings from inside the fiction to outside it, from characters in *Don Quixote*, including Quixote himself, to generations of readers who perform diverse interpretations on the novel he inhabits.[28] When Cervantes has Amadis of Gaul talk to Lazarillo de Tormes and Don Quixote read about himself, he has vanquished univocal reading forever (83). But even though he adopts this polyvalent "modern" outlook, Cervantes also affirms ancient moral notions of justice and love (93).

Fuentes parallels this plural kind of reading, which Cervantes establishes in the *Quixote*, with the idea of a similar plural kind of writing that Joyce develops in *Ulysses* and *Finnegans Wake:*

Joyce's critique of writing is a critique of individual writing, of the writing of the I, or unique writing, as Cervantes' critique of reading broke up unique and hierarchical reading, epic reading. And the novelty of "Joyceización" (Joycification) is that it inscribes "desyoización" (de-I-ification) in the total process of the economy of language. (108)

Fuentes again carries this de-I-ification out of the text, for he says that the last question posed by Cervantes is "who writes books and who reads them?" The story of someone who claims Cervantes and Shakespeare were "really" the same person serves Fuentes as a metaphor for the multiple authorship of all texts:

But I *am* convinced that it's the same author, the same writer of all books, a wandering and multilingual poligrapher, called according to the fancies of time Homer, Vergil, Dante, Cervantes, Cide Hamete Benengeli, Shakespeare, . . . Kafka, Borges, Pierre Menard, Joyce. . . . It's the author of the same open book that . . . is still unfinished . . . el libro de todos, de tutti, de alles, de tout-le-monde, of everybody. (96)

For some of his formulations regarding this new kind of writing, Fuentes takes off from the French critic Hélène Cixous, who maintains that Joyce's work is always "an odyssey, whose hero is many heroes."[29] According to Fuentes, Cixous explains how in Joyce's writing, "The subject wants to be an author, an ego; [but] Joyce annuls it with a radical critique of writing that converts novels into books written by one/plural, by everyone and by Joyce, by Joyce who is everyone and by everyone who is Joyce, Everyman" (107). Finally, again following Cixous, Fuentes characteristically joins linguistic to economic theories. The luxury of words, unlike the luxury of things, Fuentes notes at the end of his essay, belongs to all: "Words are the first and natural instance of communal property. Therefore, Miguel de Cervantes or James Joyce can only be owners of words to the extent that they are

not Cervantes and Joyce, but everyone: they are the poet"
(110).

This last notion of the poet as everyone reminds us
of Borges's place in all this. Fuentes's verbal play with the
idea of "one/plural" suggests that he is practicing a
Borgesian reading of Joyce through Cixous. Borges is an
early exponent of "de-I-ification," as Fuentes himself
recognizes: "Cervantes, author of Borges; Borges, author
of Pierre Menard; Pierre Menard, author of the Quixote"
(95). Borges writes many parables of authors who seem to
possess multiple identities and who thus transcend nation-
ality. The narrator of "The Immortal" ends his story by
saying, "Shortly, I shall be No One, like Ulysses; shortly,
I shall be all men; I shall be dead." Tired of the debate
about "Argentine" versus "universal" literature, Borges
cites Gibbon's marvelous example of "the Arabian book
par excellence," the Koran, which contains not a single
camel.[30] Fuentes's essays represent a similar phenomenon
in the realm of critical discourse. Fuentes himself has
noted in the introduction that the collection is devoted to
reencountering the Spanish literary heritage that Mexico
renounced while it searched for its own independence and
identity. (Fuentes celebrated that independence in *The
New Hispanic American Novel.)* Though he does not discuss Latin American literature explicitly in *Cervantes or
the Critique of Reading,* we recognize Fuentes's Latin
American voice in his analyses of European texts, in his
investigations of his own literary origins.

4

Later Novels: Psychology, Pop, and the Past

It is difficult to divide Fuentes's works into clear stages, for characteristic themes, symbols, and techniques persist throughout. In Fuentes's later novels, illicit desire continues to disrupt social convention in the face of psychological and social repression; the war of the sexes goes on; the rich exploit the poor; foreign interests exploit Mexico; violence seethes or explodes, claiming sacrifical victims; and the popular language of movies, advertisements, hit songs invades the literary text. If there is a distinction to be made within this last group of novels, it would be between the greater attention to individual psychology in *Holy Place,* which places it nearer *The Death of Artemio Cruz* and *The Good Conscience,* and the concentration on large historical concerns in *Terra Nostra,* aligning *it* with *Where the Air is Clear. A Change of Skin,* published in the same year as *Holy Place,* mediates between the two domains.

Ancestral presences still continue to haunt Fuentes's modern cities and towns though in his most recent work they may emerge increasingly from the European rather than the Aztec past.[1] Together with ghostly figures, they contribute to an atmosphere of mystery, either sacred or profane. Nonrational modes of perception and communication—myths, rituals, strange coincidences, dreams, obsessions, fantasies—now often structure the narrative. They cause ever greater disruption of traditional linear progression, and consequently require increased reader participation in the construction of the story.[2] This disruption reaches a peak with *A Change of Skin* and *Terra Nostra;* it decreases subsequently in the more traditional mode of *The Hydra Head,* picking up again in Fuentes's most recent novel, *Distant Relations.* Like *The Death of Artemio Cruz,* Fuentes's later works tend to radiate out to different times and places from an evocative anchor space that sets the pervasive tone: Claudia's house in *Holy Place,* the town of Cholula in *A Change of Skin,* the Escorial in *Terra Nostra,* Mexico City in *The Hydra Head,* and Branly's club in *Distant Relations.*

The continuing disruption of linear chronology in these later novels accompanies an increasing disintegration of individual identity. Two sources of inspiration seem important here. Manuel Durán writes that Fuentes's later works propose "oriental" or "primitive" ideas concerning "the transmigration of souls, doubles, and the recurrence of types, faces, attitudes." In this they go beyond individual experience.[3] Fuentes also reads recent French critical theory, which frequently questions the traditional autonomy of the individual author or text, as I have already suggested in my discussion of *Cervantes or the Critique of Reading.* Rather than a particular individual's search for a specific identity, Fuentes often conflates and/or multiplies identities in his portrayal of larger historical questions. Similarly, intertextual references to earlier works of art or literature suggest that as Paul Valéry said, "the lion is made of assimilated sheep," that books are made out of other books.[4]

A Modern Idol:
Holy Place

Holy Place is an intensely focused work. It belongs to the tradition of short psychological novels that includes Gide's *The Immoralist,* Mann's *Death in Venice,* and Ernesto Sábato's *The Tunnel,* which Fuentes has called the best psychological novel in Latin America.[1] In *Holy Place,* Fuentes concentrates primarily on a single relationship— between the movie actress Claudia Nervo and her son Guillermo. In its close attention to the development of individual problems, *Holy Place* resembles a case study; a young man has fixed his sexual desire on the figure of his mother and as a result he seems unable to love another woman.[2] As often in a case study, the complications of this relationship are fascinating to unravel. The entire novel is in one sense Guillermo's monologue directed toward his mother though she is not always there.[3] Guillermo presents a number of scenes in their lives, always speaking in the present and including long stretches of dialogue. In his alternating obtuseness and perspicacity, Guillermo fulfills the conditions for an ideal first-person narrator set down by Henry James: intelligent enough to refract experience in a complex and interesting way, but also more confused than the reader regarding his own situation. The reader thus experiences a sense of discovery concerning the narrator's behavior.

Claudia and Guillermo live in Mexico City, she in a large mansion, he in a luxurious apartment paid for by her. In flashbacks we learn that Guillermo's father lives in Guadalajara with his own mother, and that Guillermo had lived there too until Claudia kidnapped him and eventually won custody. Guillermo attended the best schools in Switzerland, where he met Giancarlo D'Aquila, whom he admires and who tries to seduce him in his ancestral palace one Christmas. Now Guillermo is back in Mexico and seems to do nothing except long to see Claudia, who is too busy to pay him much attention. Near the end of the novel, Claudia goes to Italy to shoot a film, and sometime thereafter Guillermo follows her there.

After this Guillermo's mental pictures are even less clear than before, some of them possible scenarios, others of them presumably closer to "fact." He mentions entering a sanitorium in Rome, and then leaving it for Mexico. One assumes Guillermo has gone crazy after his arrival in Rome, perhaps on learning that Giancarlo is now Claudia's lover. Guillermo imagines various solutions to his situation in the form of dreamlike scenes: the three of them live a tense yet ecstatic life together; Claudia abandons everyone but him; he becomes a cannibal and devours Claudia. But none of them works out; they represent desires and fantasies, not reasonable alternatives. The novel ends with a strange twist. Guillermo, now back in his old apartment in Mexico City, appears to have been changed into a dog. He waits around to be fed by his old pair of servants who now abuse him with kicks and cuffs, and imagines that one day he might tear Claudia and Giancarlo to bits.

The scenes we see throughout the novel are chosen by Guillermo, and his choices are motivated alternately by honesty and wish fulfillment. As often in confessional novels, Guillermo both covers up and exposes his neuroses. The last view of Claudia as she steps onto her plane for Italy allows Guillermo to keep on fantasizing about her feelings for him. Her next to final words to him are: "I love you but I don't need you." When Guillermo, crushed by this one-liner, rushes after her, she adds, "Don't believe everything I tell you. It's only my legend," and tells him goodbye.[4] Just after her departure, he returns home and projects Claudia's old films, saying to himself:

Terrible and beautiful and faraway, the dissolves I ordered follow. Claudia, you are the general's mistress . . . and you are, in my editing, the cabaret singer in a false and smoking Macao, . . . the Mayan princess . . . and your faces follow one after the other on my screen and there I have you forever. . . . The camera didn't rob you of your face: it preserved it for me, your son, the starnapper. (121–22)

He kidnaps her on film as she had earlier kidnapped him for life. Guillermo is chained to his pain, and keeps returning for more. Through his attachment to his mother, he has constructed a system for the continued frustration—and therefore the perpetuation—of his own desire.

Just as Claudia is fixed on film, so Guillermo is fixated on her. Guillermo's arrested development is dramatized by his fondness for a scene in one of Claudia's movies: a small child runs into her arms, and she "protects him forever" (121). The only girl we see him with is one of his mother's group of followers—Bela—a copy of Claudia in a smaller size, and consequently less satisfying. Even Giancarlo, with his daring and brash manner, his carelessly elegant clothes is (as Guillermo revealingly admits), "yes, a kind of masculine counterpart of my mother" (62).

Guillermo's difficulties are compounded because his financial dependence on Claudia reinforces his emotional attachment to her. His adoption of her style leads him to want expensive clothes and dogs, a fancy sports car, a glamorous apartment. When we first see Guillermo, he steps out of a Lancia ("which she gave me") wearing a Gucci blazer and slacks ("which she bought me"), and pulls a Pall Mall out of his pocket. Fuentes takes a stab here at upper-class Mexican taste, dependent on foreign merchandise. Claudia's house, "like all Mexican houses," is protected by "a wall topped with broken glass." But ironically, that seems to be about its only Mexican characteristic. The typically Mexican glass defends typically foreign luxuries—"an English lawn," trimmed hedges, "clean Scandinavian furniture."

Even more important than Guillermo's financial attachment to Claudia is his tendency to erase his own self-image with hers. Several times Guillermo is physically eclipsed by Claudia. At a party, she and her leading man both stand, "arm in arm, in front of me, hiding me, and I move to one side" (18). Again, Guillermo remembers that when Claudia kidnapped him, "she pressed me against her and said that she was my mother and I raised my eyes and found, . . . my own child's face turned into something else, into lips that kissed me and then separated from me" (19). The image brilliantly foretells his future in compressed form. It suggests the painful dynamics of identification, of love and separation, of attraction and subsequent rejection.

Finally, in the scene just before Guillermo is transformed into a dog, he "voluptuously" sinks into the clothes in Claudia's cupboard, "which still hold her perfume, the same as my kidnapping, the same as my childhood . . . my mouth is satin, jewelry, and vinyl, my tongue, calfskin and crocodile, my palate, glacé silk . . . she lets me see myself as her" (140). He puts on her lace panties, which he deforms, and stumbles in her high-heeled shoes, clawing the mirrors in his fall, as if to protest against his captivity in her image. This extreme dependency clashes with the natural maturing process and causes hostility. Not surprisingly, then, this scene, which begins in adulation, contains the opposite. There are references to witch hunts, and Guillermo imagines himself informing on his mother. He wonders if, at her trial, "to show myself like this, show that I am her, that she usurps my identity, that she has turned me into . . . this ravenous dog who can no longer hold himself up on these high, gigantic heels" will be enough to condemn her. Again in this scene, as in *Aura,* a character's metamorphoses trace a chiastic progression, in this case a return to the self: Guillermo (A) dresses in Claudia's (B) clothes, sees his reflection as Claudia (B) in her mirror, but then finally stumbles, rediscovering himself (A).

Though he is certainly not content, Guillermo nonetheless manages to tolerate this love/hate relationship, to exist in this state of war between two sides. It is the addition of a third that pushes him around the bend. The erotic triangle formed by himself, Claudia, and Giancarlo disrupts both Guillermo's illicit desires and the defenses he has constructed to control them. On the one hand, Giancarlo has simply usurped the place Guillermo dreams of occupying in Claudia's life. On the other hand, Claudia has taken over Guillermo's one friend, his alternate object of desire—perhaps even his attempt to create a sensual life for himself apart from Claudia. In yet another sense, Guillermo possesses Claudia symbolically through Giancarlo, who refers to Guillermo as "brother." This destroys Guillermo's carefully orchestrated worship of the Goddess Claudia—his protection against his own sexual frustration. The continuously postponed desire he lived on has been partially destroyed, but only vicariously; he has not experienced the release of tension that normally accompanies the satisfaction of desire. Guillermo is left with nothing, and collapses.

MYTHOLOGIES REVISITED

Following in the tradition of Freud, Fuentes describes these psychological conflicts in mythological terms. He continues his interest in ancient Aztec gods and goddesses, but in the story of Claudia and Guillermo, he combines them with classical figures. *Holy Place* takes as its mythical context a different version of the Ulysses story from the one Homer used.[5] This is the variant recounted by Apollodorus where Ulysses's son by the witchlike Circe returns to Ithaca, kills his father, and occupies Penelope's bed, while Telemachus remains with Circe.[6]

The novel opens as Guillermo and Giancarlo are discussing the prudent Ulysses who stopped his men's ears and had himself lashed to the mast so they would not be drawn in by the sirens. The ending of the myth—"the classic male, the faithful wife, the prodigal son. And they lived happily ever after"—seems to bore the young men; their desire for Claudia makes them wish to disrupt the harmonious family group—already partially broken down by Claudia's leaving Guillermo's father. And Giancarlo suggests moving beyond traditional forms of behavior—"to listen to the song of those who wish to break the natural order, which is also the resolvable, predictable order of the myth. Turned into a ritual" (12).

Both Guillermo and his friend are heading toward encounters with an experienced siren, and unlike Ulysses, do not seem to value either prudence or natural order. They prefer the kind of emotional adventure that disrupts order. The young men seem unaware that as they avoid the myth of Ulysses, Guillermo, especially, draws near the myth of Oedipus. Here, as elsewhere, Fuentes suggests that desire freed from repression often disturbs established patterns—like "a song which . . . is . . . the hidden, forbidden part [of nature], absent from the accepted inventory of things" (13). Giancarlo's invitation to listen to forbidden songs suggests the homosexual love he will later propose to Guillermo. This kind of desire, like Guillermo's passion for his mother, has traditionally been "absent from the accepted inventory of things," excluded from the family house, which, like the Ceballos mansion in *The Good Conscience,* remains "a final receptacle of subdued desires" (20).

Guillermo thinks that "if Ulysses had yielded to the song, he wouldn't have been prudent; there wouldn't be a story; there would be another story" (13). *Holy Place* is this other story—the alternate version of the myth. It will not be classical in tone. But it will include other myths and rituals, both ancient and modern. It has a twentieth-cen-

tury siren, and even an enchanted grotto—Guillermo's
room, where he returns, "like the Incas, to renew [his]
energy" (29).

Just after this first scene, which introduces the subject
of myth, Claudia herself appears as a modern goddess.[7]
We first see her "sitting on a black leather stool"—a
modified throne. She wears black lounging pajamas "with
wide sleeves embroidered in gold with Tarot figures"—the
richly casual and yet symbolically significant dress of her
own sanctuary. Even Claudia's complexion suggests the
figure of a much-worshipped idol: "a blend of old ivory
and newborn light"—ironic echoes of Buddha and Christ?
Claudia seems harsher than Teódula Moctezuma in
Where the Air is Clear for some reason; perhaps because
she has no Ixca to sacrifice for her. She must obtain her
own victims. Unlike Teódula, who represents the hidden
force of the demanding goddess and who therefore lives
alone, her ancestors under her floor, Claudia is surrounded by a crowd of worshippers, a degraded public version
of the ancient tradition.

Like an ancient god or goddess, Claudia seems to
change her form at will: "She hugs herself and she's a dark
panther"; "she places her arms akimbo and, standing,
crosses one knee over the other; she's a heron" (16–17).[8]
And this goddess in her sanctuary is preceded by her
images—her portraits suitably "framed in burnished gold
and patinaed silver," like ancient icons.[9] Claudia is a well-
established twentieth-century cult, with its attendant ritual: a film star surrounded by her satellites.

Claudia characterizes herself as a kind of national
idol, occupying the mythic space left vacant by the disappearance of traditional beliefs: "You know I bear the
weight of the nation's honor on my shoulders . . . I don't
have to tell you: before, Mexico was Pancho Villa, now it's
me" (31). Like Teódula Moctezuma, she most resembles
the powerful and dangerous figure of the principal Aztec
mother-goddess: "Tlazolzeótl was the native goddess of

death, fertility, and filth; her hands smeared with blood and excrement were also the hands . . . of purification" (40). She both gives and destroys life, as Claudia has given birth to Guillermo and then virtually destroyed him. Like Artemio Cruz, Claudia is a practiced dominator. At the beginning of this scene, Guillermo ponders the beliefs of certain tribes that a man is born of three different mothers, as he watches his mother in front of a three-way mirror. His words recall the three different figures the Aztecs had for Tlazolzeótl—Tonantzín (our mother), Coatlicue (skirt of snakes), and Cihuacóatl (snake woman).[10]

SACRED SPACES

The same introductory scene that prefigures Claudia as a mythic siren also suggests the nature of the "holy place" that Claudia and Guillermo inhabit. On the first page of the novel, boys at Positano have come "at dawn," and "planted the stakes in the sand to mark the playing field: the holy place," for their weekly "ritual" soccer game on the beach (11). Various "places" in the book are "holy" or sacred, in various ways, most of them ironic. The two most important are Claudia's house and Guillermo's apartment.[12]

Besides the physical sanctuaries in *Holy Place*, the title designates the existence—or at least Guillermo's desire for the existence—of a symbolic emotional enclosure. Such a space, protected from the conventions of society, would shelter Guillermo and Claudia alone, together. Guillermo sees this enchanted private domain disappear and dissolve into public territory as Claudia moves away from him at the airport. She "goes out into the sun, outside the enclosure, the space restricted to consecrate and protect us—temple, palace, apartment—out to the handkerchief-waving public" (118).

Claudia's house in Mexico is a temple dedicated to a

goddess, decorated with her images. The inner sanctuary
there contains her most important relics—her clothes,
which still retain the scent and the imprint of her body.[13]
The sanctuary is lined not with paintings, but with mirrors, for Claudia worships herself. But Claudia is also
revered in a subsidiary "holy place"—Guillermo's apartment. The description of this "enchanted grotto"—the
site of Guillermo's private cult—suggests first Guillermo's
worship of Claudia. But it also represents the state of
Guillermo's soul in terms of the aesthetics and philosophy
of late-nineteenth/early-twentieth-century decadence.

Guillermo has decorated his rooms like the apartment of the actress Sarah Bernhardt—an early twentieth-
century French analogue for Claudia. She was perhaps
most famous for her role in Oscar Wilde's *Salomé*.[14] Guillermo has an Aubrey Beardsley print that shows Salomé
about to kiss the lips of John the Baptist. This figure of the
passionate and deadly Salomé is Guillermo's private icon
of Claudia in his preferred style. Furthermore, the "serpents on all the scarlet silk walls" prefigure the dangerous
and passionate nature of their relationship. The designs of
"untied knots" and "knotted parallels" suggest its incestuous and endlessly complicated form. The Salomé is surrounded by other period pieces: "Tiffany lamps,"
"Guimard furniture," "Lalique plates," "a dropped ceil-
ing of carved boxwood" (29).

Guillermo's state of mind as well as his surroundings
duplicates the philosophy of decadence. Its exponents take
the emotional risks of listening to the sirens' song. Guillermo's posture of exhaustion ever desires yet more exhaustion through new and dangerous emotional experiences.
Though they may have escaped—as they seem to wish—
the happy ending of the Ulysses myth, Guillermo and
Giancarlo reenact this modern myth, which requires an
unhappy ending. Guillermo claims he returns to his grotto
to renew his energy. But really he renews the energy of his
neurosis, and his philosophy of decadence.[15] Many of the

epigraphs in *Holy Place* come from authors who wrote about passion in settings of extreme richness verging on decadence: Baudelaire (also unusually attached to his mother), Huysmans, Fitzgerald. Four are taken from *The Great Gatsby*. They imply a parallel between the wild extravagance and emotional bankruptcy of Fitzgerald's wealthy New Yorkers and the Mexicans in *Holy Place*. In addition, Gatsby's love for Daisy, while not incestuous, is fixed, like Guillermo's, on one unattainable object.

At the end of *Holy Place*, following Guillermo's metamorphosis into a dog, the two vulgar servants, Gudelia and her husband Jesus, destroy the elegant furnishings they cannot possibly appreciate. They slap each other, laugh, make love, eat tortillas and beans from paper plates, and generally enjoy themselves. They are lusty, healthy, "normal" people—everything Guillermo was not, reminding us of the proverbial statement made by the decadent poet, Villiers de l'Isle-Adam: "living? our servants will do that for us." This is just what happens here. Guillermo, literally refined out of existence, can only "sniff and whine and lower my head and hide in a corner, behind the stained curtains" (143). This "holy place" has been desecrated by Guillermo's neurosis as well as by Claudia's cruelty.

Guillermo's final transformation recalls Kafka's novella, *The Metamorphosis*, where Gregor Samsa wakes up one morning as a cockroach. (Fuentes lists Kafka first among the great pioneers of nonrealistic art he mentions in *The New Hispanic American Novel*.) Kafka and Fuentes both use a fantastical event to accent a psychological problem. And both transformations appear to dramatize a metaphor. In Gregor's case, he and his family seem to have been thinking of him as less than human, perhaps even as insignificant and unsatisfying as an insect, when presto he becomes a cockroach. Similarly, at one point Claudia says to Guillermo as he kneels at her feet, "Get up. You look like a lap dog" (42). And Guillermo certainly seems to be leading "a dog's life" by the time of *his* "metamorphosis." Tzvetan Todorov claims that this kind of transformation is an important component of the fantastic in literature. He describes it as the "collapse (which is also to say the illumination) of the limit between matter and mind."[16] Fuentes's selective use of fantasy in *Holy Place,* like Kafka's in *The Metamorphosis,* emphasizes the mind's power to distort events and situations as a result of intense suffering. The blurring of distinctions between matter and mind through fantasy constitutes a particularly effective ending for a novel that resembles a case history leading to a breakdown.

Breaking Mental Habits:
A Change of Skin

A Change of Skin, like *Birthday* and *Terra Nostra,* is a highly experimental novel. The title indicates the nature of the experiment, for the characters and the narrator are fluid; they continually "change skins," or switch roles. It is as if the metamorphosis in *Holy Place* were multiplied several times, and then dreamed over again. The temporal scheme of the novel resembles the organization of time in *The Death of Artemio Cruz;* from a situation in the present, the narrative makes excursions back into the past. But the time frames are less clear than in the earlier book. Descriptions, events, conversations—in the past or in the present—form a collage of juxtaposed fragments with few explicit connections between them.

In the present—or the foreground of the collage—Javier, and his wife Elizabeth, are driving from Mexico City to the beach at Veracruz with Franz and his young lover Isabel. Their car breaks down in the town of Cholula, and they are forced to spend the night in a small hotel.

During the night, the couples switch; Isabel sleeps with Javier and Elizabeth with Franz. But they return to their original rooms, and at midnight, Isabel leads them all to explore the ruins of the ancient Aztec pyramid in Cholula.

From this situation, the pasts of Javier and Elizabeth and Franz emerge. These characters, like Artemio Cruz, return to key periods and scenes in their lives in an attempt to understand how they have arrived at their present confusion and sadness. Isabel, a student, is too young to succumb to this weight of the past. As she says, "No waiting! If I want something, I take it, do it, or drop it."[1] Through thoughts, monologues, dialogues, conversations, dreams, we learn that Elizabeth and Javier met in New York while Javier was studying there on a scholarship from Mexico. They married, sailed for Europe, and spent an idyllic few months on a beach in Rhodes before returning first to Buenos Aires, and then to Mexico City where Javier now teaches literature at the university. Earlier, he had planned to write a novel, but has given it up.

The scenes from Franz's past center on his experiences as an architecture student in pre-World War II Czechoslovakia and his wartime activities as a Nazi architect. Just as the war was beginning, he had fallen in love with a Jewish girl named Hanna, who was taken away to a camp and never returned. Franz was tortured by guilt, but nevertheless helped to design the concentration camp of Terezin. When the war was over, he returned to Prague to search for Hanna, but could not even find her grave. In order to escape persecution for collaboration with the Nazis, he pretended he had died, changed his name, and emigrated to Mexico.

Even this summary is somewhat misleading, for Fuentes destroys traditional realistic events and characters. Events may be presented as possibilities; they can shift around, occasionally contradicting each other. At one point, Javier, Elizabeth, Franz, and Isabel are exploring the interior of the ancient pyramid, when an earthquake causes a rockslide. Elizabeth and Franz are "trapped on the other side, where there is no way out," while Javier and Isabel escape together. The latter pair return to the hotel, and Javier strangles Isabel with a shawl Elizabeth has given her earlier in the day. But in a scene that we assume follows this one, Isabel says that she has just seen Elizabeth and Javier talking together. Events like these are embedded in scenes that resemble dreams or hallucinations. These scenes dramatize the fears or desires of the characters. They present central themes, rather than contributing to the systematic development of a story. Here, even more than in Fuentes's earlier novels, rules of temporal logic do not apply.

PRESENT SELVES, ANCIENT PATTERNS

The preceding sequence of events, for example, might be seen as dramatizing several conflicting desires. Isabel projects her desire to have Javier to herself as Elizabeth's death in the pyramid. But perhaps Isabel herself is simply a projection of Elizabeth's desire to seem younger and more attractive to Javier. Javier, for his part, has quarreled with Elizabeth earlier that night, and projects *his* wish to escape her as her death. After the rockfall, when they hear the trapped Elizabeth and Franz screaming, Javier and Isabel embrace: " 'Now we will love each other,' he says. 'We'll have to love each other . . .' they go down the tunnel holding hands, see the exit shining in the distance like an incandescent point." But when Javier reaches that "incandescent point," things become more complicated: "Javier can read Isabel's mind . . . Yes, she is telling herself, I can be . . . his strength, . . . I will be able to hold off destiny, fate, circumstances, . . . until I offer them to him transformed by me, Isabel" (379). He realizes that this "new" life will not work. Isabel "doesn't understand that Ligeia [Elizabeth], his poison, his toxin, is also his life, his habit, . . . that he prefers Ligeia, with her barrenness and her routines, to someone else who would be equally barren and have worse routines" (380). He now wants Elizabeth back, and senses that Isabel can never replace her, though she may "give me Ligeia's hell again." And what's worse, by her insistent demands on his time, she will probably curb his freedom even more than Elizabeth did. He projects these thoughts as his strangling of Isabel.

Later on, Isabel's report of the conversation she overhears between Javier and Elizabeth represents another view of the marriage—perhaps Elizabeth's projection *through* Isabel of her desire to stay with Javier. According to Isabel here, Elizabeth and Javier "were just sitting there, holding hands . . . She was telling him that it didn't matter, that life had to go on" (457). In this version, they comfort each other during difficult moments. A sentence that comments on the rockfall sums up the way we might regard these events: "Someday it had to happen" (377). The events have a psychological force—they "had to happen." But they have no definite hour—"someday."

Javier's thoughts just before he strangles Isabel introduce the doubling of characters that accompanies this doubling of events: "Isabel, bring me an aspirin . . . now . . . Isabel who is Ligeia . . . she will be Ligeia . . . and she knows it" (381). Fuentes has said that the novel is full of doubles; the most important are the figures of Franz/ Javier and Elizabeth/Isabel:

In a sense, for the Narrator, I don't know if for anyone else, Elizabeth is what Isabel *can be* and what she must *not* be at the same time. Isabel is a repetition of Elizabeth in another time, another rhythm. And so you have the theme of the man who is always looking for *another* woman from his own only to find once again a reflection of that woman.[2]

The women switching lovers, rooms, and shawls suggests that one person undergoes several changes of skin because

the skin covers several distinct yet related personalities.[3]
As for the men, Franz and Javier meet at the center of the
pyramid just before the earthquake. They begin to wrestle,
but end up "joined at the belly and the thighs, still embracing each other without now admitting their true intention, a violent embrace of hatred transforming itself"
(377). This mysterious communion between two halves
of one personality seems to bring on the earthquake, as
if the confrontation were too painful or too difficult to
accomplish.[4]

The scene at the center of the pyramid recalls the
Aztec rituals celebrated there, and so the ancient notion
of sacrifice merges with the idea of a journey toward the
self. Mircea Eliade's description of a rite of passage suggests the persistent tradition to which the scene belongs:
"The center is then the sacred place par excellence.
. . . The road leading to the center, . . . toward the self,
. . . is arduous, sown with perils, because it is, in fact, a
rite of passage from the profane to the sacred; from the
ephemeral and the illusory to reality, and to eternity; from
death to life; from man to divinity."[5] But though the
explorers in *A Change of Skin* may sense the presence of
powerful telluric or divine forces and may indeed have
desired a rite of passage in the pyramid, as individuals they
remain in the profane realm. And Franz passes not from
death to life, but in the other direction.[6] Still, the ancient
echoes of cataclysm and rejuvenation are there; they suggest that these events follow an old pattern; for the narrator thinks about what he calls "The Great Cue" as he
approaches "The Great Pyramid of Cholula": "Every
cycle of fifty-two years a new pyramid was raised on the
base of the old one, for the end of a cycle required, as
homage to the arrival of the new, that the old should
disappear" (294). The text itself thus moves beyond the
limits of its individual characters, creating a kind of linguistic festival.[7]

Here, as in many of Fuentes's works, mythic time and

space underlie present events and places; figures and images reverberate toward the Aztec past. As if to suggest that the characters have participated in a modern version of an ancient ceremony of death and rebirth, closing one cycle and opening another, when Elizabeth and Javier put Franz's body in the trunk of their car, they find a baby underneath it. The baby, however, is devoured by a dog. This dog, and others that wander in both 16th and 20th century Cholula, recall the Aztec god Xolote, who descended to the underworld to make living men out of the bones of the dead. Furthermore, the entire novel transpires under the sign of the god Xipe Totec, worshipped as the god of spring and rain, originally flayed to benefit man. Both of these deities, then, are concerned with the process of death and rebirth, and Fuentes ceaselessly moves the reader between the two, never allowing one or the other to prevail. That the present action of the novel takes place on Palm Sunday adds a Christian layer of death and resurrection to the collage.

THE CHANGING OF SKINS

Two images near the beginning of the novel provide visual analogues for its conceptual shifting of identities. Elizabeth and her brother Jake are looking at old pictures of their father, and "could not believe that the man with sideburns and beard and the gabardine coat and the young man in a vest and derby with a pearl in his tie were the same person" (91). On the next page, in a different sequence, Franz remembers "façades that had been added as decorations to the still older medieval structures beneath. Smooth ancient stone, covered by yellow or rose plaster that today was falling off, allowing the original gray to be seen" (92). Faces and buildings change, and so, of course, do the people they cover. But more significantly, emotions change, and perhaps more than just their skins.

The idyllic love scenes between Javier and Elizabeth in their room by the sea in Greece contrast with their violent quarrels in the hotel room at Cholula. Elizabeth remembers waking one morning under Javier's loving gaze, after a passionate night: "You took me in your arms and lifted me as I opened my eyes. . . . and I was small and tender in your arms. On that one moment I have lived. Always hoping that someday it might come back. But not anymore" (339–40). On the other hand, during their argument in Cholula, when Javier tells Elizabeth to "stop yelling. They'll hear you all over the hotel"; she replies, "Let them hear! Let them hear how love can be lost and what kind of hatred comes to replace it!" (332). Much of Javier and Elizabeth's discord results from the fact that each often wishes to mark or change the other to fit his or her own images and desires. Javier wishes Elizabeth were younger, less demanding, not herself, but Woman. Elizabeth wishes Javier were more original, more successful, like some of the movie heroes she admires.

The narrator who presents these fluid figures and feelings changes his skin as often as they do. An omniscient voice recounts Franz's activities in Germany, and scenes from Javier's childhood in Mexico in the third person. What sounds like another voice refers to himself in the first person and appears in Cholula and in Mexico City. He addresses Elizabeth and Isabel in the second person; he calls the first Dragoness, the second Pussycat. This narrator filters much of the story through his conversations with Elizabeth where she recounts her memories. At other times, he appears to speak with the voice of Franz or of Javier. Although his voice may change, it is not asexual or androgynous; his nicknames for the women, plus his addressing them in the second person, establish a predominantly male narrative voice. Thus, as John Lipski has explained, the narrative voice is at the same time an omniscient entity and an externalized consciousness of the individual characters.[8]

At the start of the last chapter, just before he signs off, the narrator shifts our perspective for the last time by saying, "You told me all this that afternoon, Dragoness, when they let you visit me" (458). "They" are presumably the guardians in an insane asylum. The narrator claims that they would be surprised to hear that "the absolute silence of the first days is merely the announcement of a universe of sounds which at first are heard one by one, then fused into a pattern, an order." He says that "I play the mute idiot and keep all I hear to myself. All the voices that come through the stone. The panting of lovemaking, the shouts of a quarrel. The snapped commands, the fall of clods of earth" (459). So it's just possible that these sounds—"real" sounds, or hallucinations?—constitute the book we have been reading, this "universe of sounds."

A narrator like this, who hears sounds through walls, represents humanity at large. (Fuentes has said that "the Narrator could be everyone."9) His generalized voice delves into the collective past in order to explain the present. This composite narrative is confusing, for it includes many dreamlike sequences and nightmarish obsessions, which tend to float free at times, unattached to individual psyches.10 Fuentes has explained that this unanchored effect is intentional however:

All the traditional psychological elements are in the novel, but they are all there to be destroyed. . . . The novel turns against itself. It is finally tragically parodied by these young people who appear at the end, who restate, rewrite, relive, rethink, reimagine the novel *to destroy it.*11

At the end of the novel, the slippery figure of the narrator signs himself Freddy Lambert. Fuentes has noted that the name combines the first name of Friedrich Nietzsche and the last name of the hero in Balzac's *Louis Lambert.* This narrator's continually changing stance corresponds to Nietzsche's fondness for contradictions, to his adoption of different points of view. Freddy Lambert's identification with Franz and Javier resembles Balzac's portrayal of himself in *Louis Lambert*.[12] The literary nature of the composite name suggests that in addition to the voices of these particular characters, or of men and women in general, this voice includes the voices of other storytellers in other books.

Similarly, just as Isabel is a younger version of Elizabeth, so Elizabeth is a newer version of earlier literary figures: Javier calls her Ligeia, echoing Poe's story where a man's first wife comes from death to take over the body of his second. The allusion, added to her other nickname of Dragoness, suggests the proximity of love and death. Javier fears that this dangerous, devouring aspect of feminine charm has drawn him away from his writing.

The composite name of Freddy Lambert, combined with his continual shifts in perspective, annihilates the traditional notion that one narrator composes one story, and perhaps, by implication, that one author writes one novel. Fuentes presents the reader with several possible novels; which one he reads depends on his interpretations of the events.[13] According to Fuentes, he designed the book to be completed in this way by the reader:

In *Cambio de piel* the purpose of the narrator is to create two, three, four, five infinite instances of fiction, to establish that this is a novel, about a novel, about a novel, about a novel. . . . Cienfuegos . . . is asking the reader to read so as to be a witness; whereas in *Cambio de piel* the narrator is asking the reader to read so as to write the novel. . . . He [the reader] is a co-creator of the novel.[14]

In this context it is interesting to note that Fuentes has dedicated *A Change of Skin* to Julio Cortázar, whom he greatly admires. Cortázar is a pioneer of reader participation in Latin America. His novel *Hopscotch* (1963) forces the reader to collaborate in the composition of the text by including—or choosing to exclude—a series of "optional" chapters at the end of the book.

Besides references to novels and poems, *A Change of Skin* records the persistent, ubiquitous, and often strident voice of popular culture, particularly of films and songs.[15] This language represents Fuentes's desire to "legitimize all the vulgarity, the excess, and the impurity of our world, to rid them of the bad pejorative smell that allows our 'aristocracies' to stick their noses in the air." [16] His desire forms part of a trend in Latin America and the United States. Recent texts by Cabrera Infante, Cortázar, Vargas Llosa, Manuel Puig, Luis Rafael Sánchez, Donald Barthelme, Robert Coover, Thomas Pynchon, and Kurt Vonnegut, among others, incorporate strikingly "unliterary" forms of speech—the languages of film, journalism, sports, advertising, clichés, officialese, street talk —into their novels.

At one point, Fuentes suggests his own attempt to merge élite and popular forms in this text: Elizabeth looks at a drawing by José Luis Cuevas that resembles a "devil-clown, as though Chaplin and Mephistopheles had joined hands to create a new being, a saintly criminal, an erotic ascetic—an assassin who gives birth, a liberator who tyrannizes" (211). The mixture of classic and pop is the right medium to express Fuentes's persistent fusion of contraries in our world, his sense that criminals may be saintly, or devils clownlike—an "awareness that incompatibles no longer exist" (211).

As we have seen, Fuentes presents the reader of *A Change of Skin* with many questions: Are Franz and Elizabeth really trapped in the pyramid? Does Javier really strangle Isabel? Is a voice they hear in the pyramid really the narrator's? Are the two couples really one? Does all of this really exist only in Freddy Lambert's imagination? The answer, of course, is that there is no such thing as "really." These contradictions force the reader to accept the entirely fictional nature of the novel:

The only way to understand this novel is if you accept its absolute fictional nature. Absolute, right? It's a total fiction. It never aims at being a reflection of reality.[17]

As Julio Ortega points out, *A Change of Skin* constitutes the novel Javier might like to have written, one that shows what the world did not discover for itself. Out of Javier's desire for form as a replacement for reason in an irrational world, the novel orchestrates a form he could not as yet have envisioned, a form that points toward a "new space" of "invented reality."[18]

Like Fuentes's earlier intricate narrative designs in *The Death of Artemio Cruz,* this "total fiction" exists in a specific historical context. As we delve into the pasts of the characters, we touch on important historical moments. Here, as often in Fuentes's work, the connection between personal present and historical past is violence. The violent scenes of love and hate between Javier and Elizabeth parallel the violence done to human beings in the massacre of Aztecs by Spaniards during the conquest, which in turn parallels the extermination of Jews by Nazis during World War II.[19] "Who was Cuauhtémoc? Baldur von Schirach, brothers, leader of the Tenochtitlán Jugend" (431). There is, however, a great difference between the personal and the mass violence. Elizabeth and Javier *may* (though they usually do not) emerge from their violent scenes purged, even rejuvenated, ready to go on in new skins. The other violence is terminally destructive and leaves permanent incapacitating scars. In the first chapter of *A Change of Skin,* as the characters arrive in Cholula, the narrator evokes the day when the Spaniards opened fire on the population of Cholula, and destroyed most of the town. This scene of racial violence remains in the background while we witness scenes in concentration camps and examples of cruelty to Elizabeth's Jewish family in New York. Kids yell at her "Liz is a kike," and a group of hoodlums kills her paralyzed brother Jake by overturning his wheelchair, shouting "Kike Christ-killer" at him (281).

In addition to the sections of the novel that narrate Franz's wartime experiences in Eastern Europe, a whole series of scenes comments on the guilt of the Nazis. A rock band called the Monks appears from time to time throughout the book. For several long sections just before the end of the novel, the narrator drives around with these Monks, while they conduct a mock trial of Franz. One of them acts Franz, another Elizabeth, another the judge, and so on, in a kind of parodic mirror of the novel itself. More "changing of skins." Franz's accusor is called Jakob, "the son of Hanna Werner who died in a gas chamber at Auschwitz in October 1944" (443). (Recall that Franz and Hanna were lovers before the war.)

Jakob says sarcastically during this dreamlike "trial" that "to live in a cell built by Franz Jellinek was to be safer than on a Lufthansa flight." The figure of the accused (the Monk playing Franz) cries, " 'How can you know anything? You were a child, a baby. . . . That time was not your time. You can't know that time. It's forgotten, gone, lost forever.' " But Jakob jumps up and opens an old trunk, seizing fistfuls of papers: " 'It's all here, Franz. Nothing happened that was not carefully recorded. These papers remember. Here. And here. And here' " (446). The scene suggests an additional resonance for the title; Franz has changed his skin—his identity—in order to survive. He would like to forget the past, to absolve himself of responsibility for his actions, to believe that, as he has said earlier, "history never flowed through me. . . . I just happened to be around" (354). But Jakob has sought him out, and confronts him with his past. And, as in one of his essays, where an old man carefully guards the ancient titles to communal lands, Fuentes has words from the past preserve the hope of justice in the future.

The culmination of this "trial" suggests an alternate interpretation of the earthquake scene in the pyramid. Fuentes has said that the novel centers around a sacrifice in a pyramid. Presumably, Jakob has exacted his ven-

geance and killed Franz there. The figures of Javier and
Franz grappling and embracing represent the confrontation between the innocent present and the guilty past of
the accused. Jakob and the earthquake are complementary
signs of the universal judgment that condemns him to
death. Why has Fuentes chosen a young rock group
to condemn Franz? Perhaps to suggest that, contrary to
Franz's hopes, these young people are *not* too young to
remember his crimes because such atrocities leap across
time or because communal memory is stronger than individual recall. And that even such an apparently apoliti-
cal and amoral group as a rock band, aided by the written
word, responds to injustice and retains the right to judge
a criminal. For better or worse, the Monks may represent
the "arrival of the new," Franz the old that "should disappear" every fifty-two years (294). If one compares this
sacrifice with that of Norma in *Where the Air is Clear,*
individual guilt seems to play a greater role here; the
sacrifice achieves a kind of poetic justice that Norma's
death lacks.

In this novel, as in his other works, Fuentes includes
criticism of recent as well as past history. During his
"trial," some of the monks tell Franz, "Just head north to
Laredo and cross the border. That's where the busy factories are today. You can get yourself a job making napalm
or detergents that wipe away the color of the skin" (445).
Mexico does not escape, though; at one point Javier says
that "In Mexico everything is a ruin because everything
is promised and no promise is kept. In the United States
all promises have been kept. Yet it is a ruin just the same"
(81). For Javier, who sees his future lover Isabel turn into
his past lover Elizabeth, as Fuentes has said in his essays,
the future has arrived, and we do not like it.

A Change of Skin contains several snappy dialogues
like this one, which satirize modern Mexican society. Here
Elizabeth and Javier are arguing about the Mexican character. She says that " 'Death and fiesta, they are your two

poles, *caifán,* and everything in between is ceremonial rigidity.' " Javier replies that " 'If we're stiff, Elizabeth, it's because we're scared stiff. Mexico is a country with a tiger sleeping on its belly and we're all afraid that at any moment it may wake.' " " 'Yes,' " says Elizabeth, " 'And in the meantime you keep it knocked out with the sleeping pill of corruption.' " She then describes a chain of corruption that goes from crook through cop to deputy and president. As in *The Death of Artemio Cruz,* everyone is either "chingado" or "chingador"—violated or violator: " 'Everything in Mexico forms a pyramid: politics, economics, love, culture. You have to step on the poor bastard beneath you and let the son of a bitch above you step on you' " (159).

The Revolution still lurks in the background here, an aborted possibility. But it remains so far in the background that these characters are nostalgic for the *post*revolutionary period, not the Revolution itself. They seem to regret lost style more than lost illusions. In the fifteen years that separate *A Change of Skin* from *The Death of Artemio Cruz,* Fuentes himself has moved farther away from the Revolution in his fiction. *A Change of Skin* reflects international as well as Mexican politics; its revolutionary spirit is revealed primarily through its language and narrative design. Manuel Durán has suggested that *A Change of Skin* represents "the novel as total subversion."[20] Fuentes there undermines the societies that produced massacres of Indians and Nazi camps through a narrative structure that undermines traditional notions of individual character, plot, and cultivated language. The novel thus illustrates his sense that "especially in our area, in our culture, the fact of writing is always a revolutionary fact. You are breaking mental structures, breaking mental habits, you are breaking through silence, which is an enormous fact in Latin America, in the whole Spanish-speaking world I think."[21]

Old and New Worlds:
Terra Nostra

PALACES, PYRAMIDS, AND POWER

In *Terra Nostra* Fuentes escalates the multiplication of
characters and events that comprise *A Change of Skin.*
The narrative voice "changes its skin" even more times
here than in the earlier novel. There it was possible
(though not easy) to recuperate the entire fiction as the
dream or the imagined fantasies of a lunatic. Here we are
not given that option; the different narrators continually
disappear behind each other. The "story" they communal-
ly tell forms a series of scenes that range from Roman
times until 1999, replaying a number of historical and
literary events.[1]

In a sense, *Terra Nostra* represents a recent counterpart to Fuentes's first novel, *Where the Air is Clear.* In
both cases, Fuentes attempts a synthetic vision, combining
several cultures and eras, using a large cast of characters.
In *Where the Air is Clear,* the indigenous past shows
through the often rather shabby present where the action
of the novel is securely anchored. Here, the future is
glimpsed through a collage of events anchored in a decadent past. *Where the Air is Clear* recognizes native ancestral presences in Mexico, whereas *Terra Nostra*
investigates its Spanish heritage.

The novel opens amidst chaotic scenes in Paris: fla-
gellants converge on the church of Saint Germain des Près
and hundreds of women give birth along the banks of the
Seine. A man called Pollo Phoibee meets a girl with gray
eyes and tattooed lips called Celestina, who wants him to
explain to her all the things in Paris that she doesn't
understand:[2]

What do the lights without fire mean? The carts without oxen? The women's painted faces? The voices without mouths? The Books of Hours pasted to the walls? The pictures that move? The empty clotheslines hanging from house to house? The cages that rise and descend with no birds inside them? The smoke in the streets rising from Hell? The food warmed without fire, and snow stored in boxes?[3]

Immediately we see our world through ancient and yet innocent eyes. The chapter ends with Celestina repeating a reversible set of sentences: " 'I want you to hear my story. Listen. Listen. Netsil. Netsil. Yrots ym raeh ot uoy tnaw I. Yrots ym si siht' " (31). This sentence represents another version of the chiastic structure (ABBA) I have noted throughout Fuentes's work. The reversed pattern stands as a linguistic emblem, a sign over the door of the narrative, warning readers who enter there to abandon all hope of traditional linear time.[4]

In this first chapter, Pollo slips and falls into the river Seine. Fuentes's description of Pollo's disappearance prepares us for a shift in time and place. The description echoes the sixteenth-century Dutch artist Pieter Brueghel's painting "The Fall of Icarus." Symbolically, then, by means of this description, Pollo, and the reader with him, fall into the temporal realm of art. There, historical events are not abolished, but they may be shifted out of their traditional sequence and combined with fantastical events. As Pollo falls, the sandwich boards which he has been carrying to advertise a certain café "seemed like the wings of Icarus," and he sees "the flaming Paris sky." Before he goes down, his "white, emblematic" hand "was visible above the water" (30). In Brueghel's painting the sun is about to set, and all we see of Icarus are his pale legs about to disappear into the water. This pictorial time continues into the next chapter, and Pollo, now nameless, has fallen back into sixteenth-century Spain. He is discovered on a beach and taken up to a palace by the queen of the land, La Señora. This is the first of many instances in the novel where water serves as a connecting medium between distant places and times; it is an analogue for the fluid narrative voice which I will discuss later on.

The first part of *Terra Nostra,* called "The Old World," concerns the activities of La Señora's husband, El Señor, and his court. El Señor is an imaginary version of Philip II of Spain (1556–98), who built the elaborate palace of the Escorial, primarily as a royal mausoleum. He is obsessed by this task and by the prospect of his own death. By sacrificing his life to building the magnificent monument, with statues of his ancestors, he hopes to arrest time, to attain eternal life. He is opposed to all change. During one hallucinatory scene, El Señor sees the figure of Christ in a painting drip blood from a red cross on his back. El Señor screams, and begins to whip himself, muttering, "I do not want the world to change. I do not want my body to die, to disintegrate, to be transformed and reborn in animal form. . . . I want the world to stop and to release my resurrected body in the eternity of Paradise, by the side of God" (155). Fuentes has said that *Terra Nostra, Yo el supremo (I Above All,* 1974) by Augusto Roa Bastos, *Reasons of State* (1974) by Alejo Carpentier, and *The Autumn of the Patriarch* (1975) by Gabriel García Márquez, form a kind of imaginary Hispanic museum of dictators. In dealing with a Spanish rather than a Latin American despot, Fuentes claims he was investigating the origins of the tradition.[5]

El Señor's religious passion causes him to neglect and mistreat his queen. She recounts a bizarre scene where she falls on her back in the palace courtyard, and cannot get up by herself because of her heavy iron hoopskirts. Everyone abandons her to the elements for days because only the king is allowed to touch her. Mold grows on her, her skin burns and peels, and she is so lonely she learns to welcome the mouse that crawls under her skirts, and nestles in "places even my own husband does not know." Perhaps it represents the secret desire and passion that normally remain hidden, for "everyone knows that there is never any love between a husband and wife" (162). When El Señor finally appears and has a mirror held before her, La Señora screams at seeing her now unrecognizable face. She surmises that El Señor has caused her to fall and to rot, so that their appearances would be "equally decadent when again we met." El Señor leaves her in a medicinal bath, telling her: "I have loved you so devotedly that I shall never be able to touch you; . . . I was educated in this . . . ideal of the true Christian gentleman, and to it I must be faithful until death" (164). It is not the Devil, La Señora realizes, but his extreme Christian fervor which has motivated her husband's cruelty. She decides then that she will choose the Devil to combat him, and henceforth will follow her own desires of the flesh. She welcomes the pilgrim from the beach to her bed.

Besides El Señor and La Señora, the other principal inhabitant of the palace is El Señor's mother, the Mad Lady (historically his grandmother "Juana la Loca," Juana the Mad). She is pushed around the palace in a small cart by her lascivious old serving maid. In a scene which forms the precedent for the unwilling penance of La Señora, El Señor's mother lies down in the palace courtyard after her own husband's death, claiming that "a true Señora would not allow herself to be touched by anyone except her husband" (182). She creates a macabre erotic cult around her husband's body, rejoicing that "now he is mine, mine, alone, forever," and travels around the country with him in a kind of permanent funeral cortège. She finally retires to a niche in the wall of the Escorial's crypt with a double of La Señora's pilgrim lover to keep her company. Again, sexual oppression—and consequent repression of sexual energies—leads to bizarre behavior.

This first part—"The Old World"—ends with a third pilgrim who has been the companion of Celestina beginning to tell a tale to El Señor, the tale that constitutes his adventures in "The New World"—the second, and the

shortest part of *Terra Nostra.* At first the visions of the
new world are idyllic. In a scene that seems to echo *The
Tempest,* the pilgrim and his companion, an old man
called Pedro, survive a "whirlpool of the night"—"more
than a tempest, it was the end of all tempests, the frontier
of hurricanes, the sepulcher of storms"—and are cast up
on a beach covered with pearls: "Pearls black as jet, tawny
pearls, pearls yellow and scintillating as gold, thick and
clustered, bluish pearls, . . . glowing minute baroques"
(368). The pilgrim believes he has died and that this is the
"beach of the Beyond," "the coast of the Paradise that
God reserves for the blessed." Pedro stakes out a claim,
and is killed defending it from the natives. The pilgrim
exchanges gifts with these natives and presently hears the
reason for Pedro's death from their ancient sage, who lives
curled up in a palm basket filled with pearls, at the heart
of a pyramid. Pedro had not been expected, as the pilgrim
apparently has: " 'Furthermore, he defied us. He raised a
temple for himself alone. He wished to make himself
owner of a piece of the earth. But the earth is divine and
cannot be possessed by any man. It is she who possesses
us' " (388). Pedro has been destroyed by his adherence to
the ideal of private property in a society that seems to
practice a kind of cosmic socialism. He has violated the
native utopian tradition that Fuentes (in his essays) hopes
may one day resurface in Mexico.

The society's anticipation and acceptance of the pilgrim as one of their original princes naturally recalls the
Aztecs' belief that the arrival of Cortés constituted the
long-awaited reappearance of the plumed serpent god
Quetzalcóatl. In each case, the conquest of the new world
by the old is facilitated by the incorporation of an old
world explorer into the new world religion. The new world
might have done better to kill the intruder. The Spaniards
killed the Indians with guns; here the pilgrim offers them
a mirror as a gift, but it is no less fatal. The ancient views
himself and dies of terror. The people then acclaim the

pilgrim as their "young chieftan . . . youthful founder
. . . first man" (397). He has renewed the blood of the
dynasty for a while with his youth, as back in Spain, one
of his doubles inhabits magically for a while the dead body
of the first El Señor, husband of the Mad Lady. But his
rule cannot last forever. He finally sees his aged reflection
in a mirror, as the original ancient had done. He stabs at
the double, "ripping the face that was my face," conclud-
ing that he has killed both the "one called the Plumed
Serpent" and "the one called Smoking Mirror." The
image of the mirror continues here the disturbing function
it began in reminding Artemio Cruz of his age. In between, Claudia's mirror in *Holy Place* expands into her
movies, extending her reflection across the land; near the
end of the novel, Guillermo claws fiercely at that mirror,
accessory to her power and his enslavement. In *A Change
of Skin,* Elizabeth smashes the mirror in her hotel room
in despair over her and Javier's unhappiness; but it continues to reflect the tension between them. In becoming a
fearful deity in *Terra Nostra* (as it was in Aztec times), the
mirror achieves a kind of apotheosis. "Smoking Mirror,"
in addition to representing a war god (the Aztec deity
Tezcatlipoca), might also suggest a variety of external or
internal conflicts—between two cultures, two people, two
parts of the self.

Finally, before returning to the old world, the pilgrim
meets again the original ancient who explains to him that
he has killed his own hostile brother, "he who struggles
within you." (In Aztec mythology, Quetzalcóatl and Tezcatlipoca were enemy brothers representing the two halves
of a divine duality in continual opposition.) The ancient
says that this continual struggle between opposing forces
is necessary for life:

Your destiny is to be pursued. To struggle. To be defeated. To
be reborn from your defeat. To return. To speak. To remind men
of what they have forgotten. To reign for an instant. To be

defeated again by the forces of the world. To flee. To return. To remember. An endless labor. The most painful of all labors. Freedom is the name of your task. (475)

This life cycle is just what El Señor is trying so desperately to avoid by his plan for eternal fixity within the Escorial.

And this is why, at the beginning of the third part of *Terra Nostra,* El Señor resists the discovery of the new world. This third part is called "The Next World"—a title that may prefigure the end of the novel, where a synthetic vision of love and harmony is achieved. Meanwhile, however, we are back in Spain at the Escorial, and the title strikes us as a wish rather than a reality. Earlier, before hearing the story, El Señor has said he "would go mad if the world extended one inch beyond the confines we know" (319). After hearing the pilgrim's story, El Señor forbids anyone to write about it, and says, "weighing each word: 'We hereby decree . . . that a . . . new . . . world . . . does not . . . exist. . . .' " (491; ellipses in the original text).

But El Señor is unsuccessful, and "the rumor: 'There is a new world beyond the sea' " starts circulating, countered frantically by El Señor: "nonononono, Spain is Spain, not an inch of land exists outside of Spain, it's all here, all here contained within my palace, oh, help me, my Lord . . ." (493). For the next few pages, words from the sentence about the new world are inserted between monologues by El Señor, La Señora, and other members of the court. They form persistent intrusions in the monolithic prose as the rumors of novelty and freedom infiltrate El Señor's massive fortress.

El Señor is stunned by the knowledge of the new world, and also, of course by the philosophy of the ancient, who proclaims that the essence of life is change.[6] He wishes to keep these things from his people so that they will not envision a system other than the one by which he rules them. But most of all he fears the pilgrim himself, whose task is to achieve freedom. He and his two doubles reappear throughout the novel, always in contrast to El Señor, who, unlike the ancient, cannot accept the cycles of birth, death, and rebirth. This explains El Señor's increased frenzy when he perceives the red cross on the back of the Christ in the picture: the three pilgrims also have red crosses on their backs, and the emblem's appearance on the figure of "his" Lord seems to sanctify the antagonistic forces of change and freedom.[7]

Near the end of the novel, presumably after El Señor dies, he climbs a stairway in his palace, where "on each step the world offered the temptation to choose anew . . . but always in the same, if transfigured place: this land, land of Vespers, Spain, Terra Nostra" (756). We recall Artemio Cruz's desire to "choose anew" on his deathbed; and again here we wonder whether such a choice is possible. Terra Nostra is the known world on old maps, and El Señor has remained there, never venturing to explore his new domains across the sea.

ECSTATIC UNION

The last chapter of the novel returns us to the opening scene in Paris, where Pollo and Celestina meet in a final transfiguring embrace. Their union is prefigured by that of Robles and Hortensia in *Where the Air is Clear,* Consuelo and Felipe in *Aura,* and especially by a moment in *Birthday,* where, for the narrator and Nuncia, "our [pubic] down was identical, joined, with no possibility of separation" (61). Pollo and Celestina are fused into one androgynous being that can possess itself continuously in an ecstasy of love. Power struggles are abolished because this act of love abolishes the difference between self and other. Their embrace is thus a hierogamy—a wedding of sky father and earth mother—that reverses time, for its single self-fertilizing being resembles the figure of Uroboros, the

undifferentiated wholeness imagined in many ancient
mythologies to precede mankind's division into individual
creatures of different sexes.[8]

The contrast of this final vision with scenes of unsatisfied or perverted desire in El Señor's palace is striking.
But it is not clear just why Celestina and the pilgrim as
Pollo—and, indeed, the novel itself—are granted this joy-
fully apocalyptic end. Like the appearance of Quetzalcóatl
at the end of *All Cats are Gray,* it is a vision, not a confirmation, of paradise, and represents the hope that "the
next world" will succeed "our world." Love has the last
word here, but it cannot abolish the cruel cycles of history.[9] Just before his ecstatic union with Celestina, Pollo
expresses the conflicting view:

History has had its second chance, Spain's past was revived in
order to choose again, a few places changed, a few names, three
persons were fused into two, and two into one, but that was all:
differences in shading, unimportant distinctions, history repeated itself, history was the same, its axis the necropolis, its root
madness, its result crime, its salvation . . . a few beautiful buildings and a few elusive words. (774–75)

The weight of the novel really falls here, and the ending
rises magically, yet only temporarily, above it. In this, and
in its joyful eroticism, the ending of *Terra Nostra* is strikingly similar to the final pages of Joyce's *Ulysses.* There
Molly Bloom's vivid memory of her first lovemaking with
her future husband ends the novel. But again, though it is
an enthralling and buoyant vision, it is counterbalanced by
the more somber weight of the preceding text. In *Terra
Nostra,* then, as in *Ulysses,* the reader is left balanced
between two visions: unity vs. diversity; "ours" vs. "yours
or mine"; love vs. power; satisfaction vs. frustration.

A mystically powerful object appears just before
Pollo and Celestina's final embrace. This is the mask of
bright colored feathers said to be a map of the jungle as
well. The mask represents first of all a gorgeous object

from the new world, a native wonder unfamiliar to Europeans. It uses natural materials Europeans had not traditionally considered valuable, rather than the universally coveted gold and precious stones the explorers were so eager to find. Might the feather mask suggest a new kind of value, somehow purer, more "natural," than the "gold standard"? A hollow voice from behind Felipe's ancestral altar says that "Gold, Felipe, is the excrement of the gods" (712). We might well agree. Perhaps the ability to appreciate feathers rather than gold is a step in the right direction for those explorers who wish to reach "the next world."

In the last scene, as soon as Celestina and Pollo don identical feather masks, "the chamber begins to glow with warm luminosity, the color of new grass, a light like ground emeralds" (776). The vision of a new world Eden surges up: The "warm luminosity" resembles the waters on the pearly beach; emeralds come from the new world, too. Then, like Adam and Eve, Pollo and Celestina face one another naked. As they embrace, "the masks fall. But the light born of your masked gazes remains" (777). It is as if to wear the masks endows the two of them with a new and fulfilling vision, abolishing the previous history of the old world, just as the ending of *Terra Nostra* abolishes— for a moment—the text that precedes it. This is the significance of the mask's being also a map: it represents the new world. Fuentes has said that wearing the masks "is like putting the jungle on your face, the whole Amazon."[10] The brilliant view through these masks recalls the turquoise darts in Robles's eyes and Ixca's masklike face in *Where the Air is Clear*. There, too, Fuentes uses ancient art to suggest a vision that recognizes the past as it projects the future. To look literally through the shape of the new world, as Pollo and Celestina seem to do, is to look through new eyes and consequently to experience sexual love as it may have existed in Paradise, "without sin, and with pleasure."

The mask transforms Pollo's room into a sacred

space of love protected by ancestral presences; it contrasts with the Escorial's deadly space of power, guarded by ancestral corpses and ruled by El Señor. The transformation of the novel's space resembles Consuelo's construction of a house of love out of her ghostly mansion. Perhaps the mask also heralds the return of the benevolent Quetzalcóatl, for as he left Mexico he reportedly "put on his insignia of feathers and his green mask."[11] In the avowedly erotic nature of the description of Pollo and Celestina's embrace, we see that here "the moral of isolation, of decent and comfortable separation is destroyed by the freedom of extreme, dangerous, 'immoral' union" (*House with Two Doors,* 76). As Gloria Durán points out, in much of Fuentes's work the sexual act represents a ritual connection with the universe.[12]

Not only this final vision, but the very nature of the novel's grotesque imagery tends to counteract its somber events. In describing Rabelais, Mikhail Bakhtin argues that one must not reduce "the entire substance of the grotesque image" to pointed satire of social evils. This focus fails to explain the joyful—almost drunken—lavishness in Rabelais. The reader of *Terra Nostra* feels somewhat the same way. The sheer exuberance of the imagery with which Fuentes describes El Señor, La Señora, and the events at the Escorial, while it clearly denounces this system, nevertheless takes on an ebullient, almost an inebriated life of its own. Carnivalesque language joyously overflows its satirical confines. Bakhtin's contention that grotesque imagery stresses the ways "in which the life of one body is born from the death of the preceding one" seems to characterize the half-dead Señora's welcoming of the mouse as her lover, Barbarica's discovery of a lover in a tomb, and, especially, La Señora's attempts to conjure a man from the dead:[13]

La Señora, again transformed into a bat, flew several times from the crypts to her bedchamber, carrying each time in her mutilated phalanges a bone and an ear, a nose and an eye, a tongue and an arm, until from the parts stolen from the tombs she had formed upon the bed an entire figure of a man. (291)

Though they portray a futile quest for love in a deathly realm, the exuberance of the descriptions suits the energy of the women, and counteracts the morbid atmosphere of the palace, affirming the life that grows even out of death.[14]

NARRATIVE VOICES

In addition to evoking multiple times, places, and identities before its unified ending, *Terra Nostra* leads the reader on a chase after its narrative voice. As I have suggested briefly above, the chase is finally futile, for the narrators keep disappearing behind—or in front, or to the side of— each other.[15] At the beginning, Celestina says what follows is her story, yet for most of it she appears as a character in narrations by Father Julián or Father Toribio, or "the Chronicler." Near the end, Pollo suggests that all of the manuscripts—about Rome, Spain, and the rest—that we have presumably been reading with him, are in his Paris apartment, which he claims never to have left. But he does not mention the wondrous tales of the new world and he soon meets Celestina, who, like him, has appeared in many of the manuscripts. She presents him with an alternate interpretation: they have both lived all those events and the manuscripts simply confirm that. So we are lost again.

The reader would like to have enough control to know who is responsible for the various parts of the narrative, just as El Señor wishes to have absolute control over the narrative of history, over his realm, so he can annihilate the forces of change. In no case can a single mind— character's, narrator's, or reader's—exercise unquestioned control. After futile attempts to trace narrators, when we wonder, as we do in *A Change of Skin,* who has "really" narrated the novel, we end with the Borgesian answer of no one and everyone.

One of *Terra Nostra*'s narrators—the Chronicler—resembles Freddy Lambert in *A Change of Skin,* whose name, as I have already suggested in the preceding discussion, reflects this kind of composite literary voice. The Chronicler has lost a hand in the battle of Lepanto, is called Miguel, and has begun to write "the story of an hildalgo from La Mancha." We easily recognize the author of *Don Quixote.* [16] He is an unforgettable voice for any Spanish-speaking narrator, really the supreme novelist; and so his ubiquitous presence can serve to suggest all narrators.

In a similar merging of fictional and historical or literary figures, one of the pilgrims, who seduces women in El Señor's castle, collects allusions to Don Juan, a servant called Leporello, and an invitation to dine with his victim the Comendatore. Throughout Fuentes's work, Don Juan has a dual nature. As he defies traditional morality in favor of the freedom of desire, he is a revolutionary. But as he uses women and misuses the potentially unifying power of sexuality, he is tragic and oppressive. Fuentes prefigures his positive incarnation in *Terra Nostra* in his essay on "(His) Panic Time": Don Juan's victory is "to sow the seeds of secular love in palaces and convents, to pass like a strong wind over the sand castles of sexual hypocrisy. . . . Don Quixote and Don Juan were adventurers: creators of disorder" (*Mexican Time,* 50).

The principle of many voices, faces, personalities, that change continually, and therefore can never be fixed, is suggested in numerous smaller ways throughout *Terra Nostra.* Juan the pilgrim starts to look for his mask, and then says it is "the ultimate folly to mask myself, considering that I was already masked in my own flesh when I arrived here" (232). Early on, Pollo imagines that Celestina speaks out of two mouths (29). Again and again, pilgrims awake on sandy beaches, manuscripts are found in or out of bottles, are read or not read. Near the end of the novel, Father Julián says that he has listened through a hole in the wall to all that went on in El Señor's bedchamber, and consequently everyone who spoke or acted there "gave me their secret voices" (652).

In many ways, then, *Terra Nostra* illustrates Fuentes's theory of multivocal reading and writing in *Cervantes or the Critique of Reading*. At several places, the two works almost coincide, and Fuentes includes some of his theories from the essay in *Terra Nostra*. These ideas concern Don Quixote's desire to impose his chivalric ideas on reality. As we know from *Cervantes or the Critique of Reading,* "the knight will continue to live only in the book that recounts his story, . . . in the multiple readings life took from him in reality but granted him forever in the book . . . only in the book" (669).[17] Don Quixote forms a kind of benevolent counterpart to El Señor. Just as the knight wishes to impose his single-minded reading of novels of chivalry on a complex world, so El Señor wishes to have absolute power over the many disparate elements in his kingdom. Fuentes has made this parallel quite explicit, for El Señor often dictates to his henchman Guzmán, saying that a single, definitive text (the opposite of novels like *Don Quixote* or *Terra Nostra)* assures absolute power: "Power is founded upon the text. The only legitimacy is the reflection of one's possession of the unique text" (605). This is why "a strange invention recently brought from Germany, which is a very rabbit of books" (the printing press, of course), frightens him (604). The multiplication of books in the world resembles the multiplication of voices within a text; they both attack the absolute authority of the owner—of one text, or of one narrative voice, or one empire. El Señor wishes to monopolize them all.

As El Señor's control is threatened by the inevitable plurality of his empire, so the reader might prefer the orderly narration of a single voice to the multitude of disparate voices in *Terra Nostra.* When El Señor is instructing Guzmán to write, he has a sudden terrible thought:

Does a Devil never approach you and say, that . . . it could have happened that way but also in a thousand different ways, depending upon who is telling it; . . . imagine for an instant, Guzmán, what would happen if everyone offered their multiple and contradictory versions of what had happened . . . ? There would be too many truths. Kingdoms would be ungovernable. (188)

Exactly. The confusion El Señor fears parallels our own confusion as we read about him in the often "ungovernable" kingdom of *Terra Nostra.* But the horrible aspects of El Señor's absolute power—the torture, the lack of love, the fixation on death—persuade us to disavow temporarily his kind of reading, and to continue the "multiple and contradictory versions" of his story in *Terra Nostra.* Furthermore, we recall in this context Fuentes's earlier essays about the emergent voice of Latin American literature. Behind El Señor's statement that "unitary power" is founded on the "privileged possession of the unique written text, an unchanging norm that conquers, that imposes itself upon, the confused proliferation of custom," we might imagine early Latin American literature stifled by the importation of powerful Spanish texts.

The "ungovernable" nature of *Terra Nostra*'s narrative structure—the disappearance and reappearance of different voices—contributes to Fuentes's abandonment of traditional psychological depth in favor of a continual play of historical depths.[18] *Terra Nostra* belongs to the category of apsychological fiction, which centers primarily on the actions of a character, not on his personality or his psychological development.[19] Whereas the different voices in *The Death of Artemio Cruz* portray different layers of one personality, and the shifting from one voice to another often corresponds to conscious or unconscious needs of the central character, in *Terra Nostra* they correspond primarily to a principle of historical repetition. Characters represent archetypes rather than individuals.[20]

Terra Nostra reveals the same kind of comprehensive effort that Mario Vargas Llosa sees behind García Márquez's *One Hundred Years of Solitude*.[21] It attempts to be the total novel, to include all times, all places, all narrators. The large canvas of *Terra Nostra* with its many historical details confirms Fuentes's comprehensive and continuing interest in history, his desire to portray "what history has not said."[22] It might best be characterized as a historical fantasy. In this, *Terra Nostra* resembles the work of Alejo Carpentier. Even more significantly, Fuentes and Carpentier both investigate European history as an origin of Latin American culture. In both cases, the old world tries—with varying success—to incorporate the new world and its surprising unfamiliarities into an old world system of government or belief. That effort can be seen as a denial of the new world's newness and freedom. In a sense, these texts "win" the battle, at least temporarily, by exposing this strategy and assimilating Spanish history in their turn—imposing a new world interpretation on the history of the old world. They form part of the continuing dynamics of cultural colonialism and independence.

Together with *A Change of Skin*, *Terra Nostra* is the most problematic of Fuentes's novels. I fear that too many climactic moments weary the reader and weaken the structure of the novel, that theoretical exposition floats free from fictional character and narrative event as it did in *A Change of Skin*, and that the book's length and complexity are not sufficiently controlled by a rigorous design. Still, the intricacy of the conceptual patterns and historical meditations and the richness of many individual images make it one of the most significant of contemporary Latin American works of fiction.

As a final description of the novel, one could imagine a coat of arms done in black, red, and green. Black for death; red for passion; and green for the hope implicit in the discovery of a new world—an emerald-colored vision. In traditional blazons, as in *Terra Nostra,* events separated by hundreds of years are remembered in a single design. The colors might be embodied by a black castle, a green pyramid, and a red cross, all of which would then be worked into the form of an abstract mask. It would stand as a sign of the reader's voyage through *Terra Nostra,* and would represent the history not just of one particular family, but of all men.[23]

New Resources, Familiar Patterns:
The Hydra Head

The Hydra Head constitutes Fuentes's excursion into a distinctly popular genre—the spy thriller. Already ten years earlier, as we have noted, he claimed that his methods in *A Change of Skin* grew out of the desire to disrupt the sacrosanct "good taste" in Mexican letters. In *The Hydra Head* Fuentes reverses the habitual positions of popular and serious literature in many modern texts. Instead of imbedding the objects or languages of popular culture in an élite form, he adopts a popular genre and includes there references to Shakespeare and other consecrated masters. By switching cultural "sides," Fuentes temporarily becomes the intriguing double he describes in reference to *A Change of Skin:* "We are speaking of doubles: the novelist would like to be the twin of Luzbel, the curious, the tempter, the damned one."[1] He becomes a devil's advocate, of a sort, for a kind of literature that contrasts with his habitual domain. But as we shall see, within this form, Fuentes's perennial concerns emerge at every turn.[2] Less ambitious than Fuentes's major novels, the book is nevertheless an amusing, sometimes even an impassioned, narrative.

Fuentes has suggested that the thriller interests him from a theoretical point of view because "the characters are names and the actions are verbs. The verb and the action have a protagonistic quality in this genre. . . . So I tried to write this novel based on characters who are nothing but their names and actions which are nothing but verbs."[3] Fuentes does not, however, entirely conform to the genre of the murder mystery or spy thriller: he frustrates the reader who expects all mysteries to come clear at the end, for it is never certain who killed Sara Klein (though Felix's wife Ruth seems the most likely suspect).

In *The Hydra Head*, as in much of his writing, Fuentes is concerned with power, this time with the power struggle between Arabs and Israelis to obtain knowledge and control of Mexico's oil reserves. A man called the Director General, who heads the Ministry of Economic Development, sides with the Arabs, a Professor Bernstein with the Israelis. A third force, a man who calls himself Timon of Athens, wishes to keep the information for Mexico alone. He is an old friend of the central character, Felix Maldonado, and Timon has persuaded Felix to help him in this venture because Felix's father was a strong supporter of Cárdenas's nationalization of oil. He tells Felix to "call me a nationalistic conservative, if you want. I'd like to conserve *that*, keep the oil ours, and prevent outsiders from playing games with us."[4] Timon is an ambiguous figure, for while it is true that he is defending the national interest, he is also building up his own "petrochemical empire." Though confused, Felix himself seems genuinely to espouse these nationalistic ideals. (Fuentes has said that he designed Felix so that finally there would be a spy thriller whose hero wasn't a reactionary.)[5] Arabs, Israelis, and Timon are all after a stone in a ring; this stone is some kind of miraculous computer chip, which, when correctly

projected, shows the whole of Mexico's oil industry and
reserves:

Not a single place, not a single fact, not a single estimate, not a
single certainty, not a single control valve in the Mexican pe-
troleum complex had escaped the fluid stone gaze of Bernstein's
ring; whoever possessed it and deciphered it had all the necessary
information for utilizing, interrupting, or—depending on the
circumstances—appropriating the functioning of this machin-
ery, the fertile Hydra head the Director General had referred to,
which now was being projected on the wall like the shadows of
reality in Plato's cave. (239)

Within and around the intrigues involving this ring, symbolic details and elements of the plot evoke a number of
more general concerns. They fall into two basic categories:
modern man's lack of control over his life, and Mexican
character and culture.

Particularly at the start of the novel, as in many spy
stories, it is often unclear just who is working for whom,
and why. Though we find out near the end of the novel
that Felix is sympathetic to the idea of keeping Mexican
oil in Mexican hands, throughout much of the novel, he
appears to be completely at sea, to have been drawn into
a network of hostilities entirely alien to him. Our initial
impression turns out to be symbolically correct, for the
three opposing forces work through and disrupt Felix's
life. The Director General has ostensibly had Felix executed, and, after plastic surgery to alter his face, had him
resurrected as one Diego Velásquez. Velásquez will be a
man without a past, so to speak, so that no one will be able
to trace the Director's failed attempt to frame him as the
president's assassin. The alteration of Felix's face, as
Lanin Gyurko has pointed out, is the most striking symbol
of modern society's disregard for individual identity, and
of Mexico's domination by foreign "conquerors" aided by
Mexicans themselves.[6]

The private citizen is not free; his life is invaded and

transfixed by conglomerates. When Felix thinks he will finally act for himself by killing the man whom he believed to have murdered his true love, Sara Klein, the Director General anticipates his action and subverts it. He waits for Felix outside the supermarket where Felix has shut the man in a huge icebox and informs him that he has had the man shot—instead of leaving him to freeze to death as Felix had arranged. Sara herself speaks eerily to Felix from beyond the tomb (by means of a recording she has made before her death) about the problem of the individual's lack of control over his life and about the evils of power in general: "Because power knows itself to be temporary, it is always cruel" (109). To stress her point, she compares Bernstein to Hitler:

All Bernstein could talk about was security; the territories were indispensible to our security. I recalled Hitler's first speeches. First the Rhineland, then Austria, then the Sudentenland and the Polish Corridor. Finally, the world. (104)

From the beginning of the novel, haunting details lend an existential tone and a strong symbolic resonance to events. As a prelude to his plastic surgery, Felix is repeatedly denied an identity by people who themselves seem to be strangely incomplete. His secretary is behaving in an unusual way, so Felix asks her, "Who am I, Malena?" and she answers, "The chief, sir. . . ." Felix persists, and the dialogue continues thus:

"No, I mean, what is my name?"
"Uh . . . Licenciado . . ."
"Licenciado who?"
"Uh . . . just Licenciado . . . like all the others . . ." (16).

Similarly, although Felix forces the elevator operator to look in his direction, he cannot elicit any sign of recognition from him. The ministry's cashier refuses to cash Felix's check because he does not recognize him. When Felix returns to the office, one of the Director's henchmen

claims they've all been looking for "a man who . . . usually
. . . works in this office . . .—Felix Maldonado." Felix says,
"*I* am Felix Maldonado," to which the henchman replies,
"Well, that's not to your advantage, believe me." Felix
then asks incredulously, "It's not to my advantage to be
myself?" (23).

In the progressive destruction of Felix's individuality,
we recognize a terrifyingly literal application of Fuentes's
own theories of multiple identities in *Cervantes or the
Critique of Reading,* and a frightening analogue for the
narrative techniques of multiple voices in his fiction, for
the Director will soon arrange to have Felix's skin
changed for him without his permission. At one point
Felix tells the Director General, " 'Sir, I don't understand
a single word of what you're telling me. It's as if you were
talking to another person.' 'The fact is that you *are* another person [the Director replies.] Don't complain, man.
You have many personalities. Discard one of them and
keep the rest. What harm is there in that?' " (32). Just
before this the Director tells Felix that he is not being
judged because he's already been found guilty. Felix's experiences of disorientation, exploitation, and lack of identity recall Kafka's *The Trial* or *The Castle.* But in contrast
to Kafka's novel, the serious treatment of absurdity in *The
Hydra Head* is preceded by a round of slapstick comedy.

At the beginning of the novel, Felix hails a one peso
cab, which then proceeds to pick up, apparently at random, a number of people who will play parts in the story
that follows. One woman with a huge basketful of chicks
gets in, and "dozens of peeping yellow chicks erupted
from the basket, swarming around Felix's feet and climbing on his shoulders. Felix was afraid he was going to
crush them." When "two giggling nuns" get *out* of the
crowded taxi, Felix sees that "one of them raised her skirts
and whirled her leg as if dancing the cancan" (11). By this
time the fat woman is screaming that Felix has killed all
her chicks, for "there were dead chicks on the floor and

on the seats, and a few crushed against the taxi windows"
(12). Thus the narrative world in *The Hydra Head* starts
off as a riotous mixture of Kafka, the Marx Brothers, and
Alfred Hitchcock, with the lurid sex of a pulp novel
thrown in for good measure.

These disturbing and amusing details, the novel's
serious allegory and its popular mode, are reflected in the
two controlling sets of allusions—to Shakespeare's trage-
dies and to the movies. As Timon of Athens remembers,
"Felix's passion for the movies was equaled only by mine
for Shakespeare" (217). Both *Timon of Athens* and *Casablanca* recall heroic ideals that are not fulfilled here.
(Fuentes dedicates *The Hydra Head* to the memory of
Casablanca's four supporting actors.) Shakespeare's
Timon perishes because of his trusting and generous nature; Fuentes's Timon survives and increases his wealth
through manipulation of others. The heroism of Victor
Lazlo, and finally, of Rick, finds no analogue in *The Hydra
Head,* for though Felix may struggle heroically, his ideals
are not well defined and the outcome of his struggle
uncertain.[7]

The "double-faced" nature of Timon, his tendency to
play several parts, is suggested by the novel's title. Before
he goes to bed, Timon pulls off his false moustache and
"the gum arabic pulled at the real moustache growing
beneath the false one" (248). The double is doubled again
when Timon describes himself, already a character, playing an actor instead of a role: he arrives in Houston "looking for a Roman senator and giving a passable imitation
of Claude Rains" (242). He adds that it is a mistake to
define passion with a single name, for "behind every label
there is some unnameable, obscure political or personal
reality . . . that . . . compels us to disguise as action what
is actually passion or suffering or desire" (244). The artificial layers on Timon's face and the surgically imposed
mask on Felix's are structurally similar to the cultural
layers Fuentes exposes in his short stories and in *Where*

the Air is Clear. Yet the willful deception and the heightened artificiality of their masks make them a fearful variation on the country's pattern—the last in a series of conquests and transformations of the face of Mexico. The single voice of passion that speaks through many mouths is a murderous version of the many masks of the narrator in *Terra Nostra.* Layers of masks or multiple incarnations disguise but do not weaken the passionate will to power: "Cut off one head" of this hydra, "and a thousand will grow in its place" (244).

Fuentes extends this idea to encompass the politics of empire, and claims that the double-headed eagle controls "our"—Mexican, or third world—passions: "At times it is the beak of the Washington eagle that cuts off our head and eats it; at times, it is the beak of Moscow" (294). The image contrasts with the emblem of Mexico that the Indian elevator operator admires on a peso at the start of the novel: an eagle perched on a cactus devouring a serpent—presumably in control of its own land.

The hydra head is also an image for oil—"reborn, multiplied, from a single severed head"—the oil that itself is only one head of the larger hydra of passion and power that motivates this particular plot. Like passion, oil underlies power, is highly flammable, and exposes its owner to manipulation. Fuentes's poetic epilogue to *The Hydra Head* praises Mexico's natural resources and fears the dangers they attract. The epilogue celebrates the land itself as opposed to the powers that have tried to appropriate it, just as the poetic images of the land counterbalance the language of power and violence in *The Death of Artemio Cruz.* With Octavio Paz—and Emiliano Zapata—Fuentes has often suggested that the Mexican land represents a primary and positive wealth, a legitimate source of power for the people. (Recall Robles's regenerative return to the land in *Where the Air is Clear.*) It is as if the discovery of oil beneath that land makes this vague, almost mystical belief come literally true: "Beneath the land of the Malinche lie riches greater than all of Moctezuma's gold. . . . Dark semen in a land of hopes and betrayals, oil fecundates the realms of the Malinche beneath the mute voices of the stars and their nocturnal portents" (292). Malinche, "born under an evil sign," is the "voice that revealed to the Spaniards the hidden weaknesses of the Aztec empire and permitted fifteen hundred gold-hungry adventurers to conquer a nation five times larger than Spain" (292). Oil represents Mexico's second chance, as it were, to gain control of its own destiny.[8] In *The Hydra Head,* Fuentes implies that this material wealth from the Mexican soil, like the ancient cosmic forces, while it holds great promise, still seems to require sacrificial victims.

"Proustitution"??
Distant Relations

In *Distant Relations,* Fuentes continues to explore dynamics of colonialism and independence, concentrating this time on the transatlantic connections between Mexico and France. If *The Hydra Head* was a "real" mystery story, this is a magical mystery story, containing a net of mysteriously connected lives. The tone of *Distant Relations* seems to absorb the mellow, gently haunting atmosphere of autumnal Paris, where the story begins; it projects a softly poetic mood. As in all of Fuentes's recent fiction, the multiplication of narrative voices, scenes, and figures disrupts the reader's attempts to construct a logical story line. This disruption emphasizes the fictional status of the events narrated, the multiple origins of all fiction, and the necessity for the reader to participate in the creation of the text. Indeed, on one level, the novel might be considered a parable for the continuity of narrative itself: Fuentes suggests this idea by giving the narrator his own name, and by doing so only near the end of the book. The text is self-reflexive yet not sterile; Fuentes embodies his recent theoretical concerns with narrative voices and political structures in a well-articulated fiction.

The story begins as Fuentes the narrator meets his friend, the old French Count Branly, in their club overlooking the Place de la Concorde in Paris. For most of the novel, Branly tells Fuentes about his strange encounters with the Mexican archaeologist, Hugo Heredia, and Hugo's son Victor, together with Hugo's family history. When Hugo comes to Paris for an archaeology congress, he brings Victor, and they stay with Branly. Father and son continue there a strange game they've been playing for some time. It consists of calling up and sometimes visiting men with the name of Victor or Hugo Heredia.

Branly accompanies Victor on one such visit to a French Victor Heredia who lives at Le Clos des Renards, an old house surrounded by a park on the outskirts of Paris. An accident detains them there for several days and various mysterious events take place. The French Victor Heredia recounts the confusing story of his own ancestry, insinuating that Branly's father may have made love to a French woman living in Cuba whom he claims as his mother. Branly also relives scenes from his own past. And the young Mexican Victor plays with the French Heredia's son André and achieves some mystical kind of union with him. He remains at the Clos des Renards and never reappears. As Branly finally drives away, he sees a woman at the window of the chateau who resembles a portrait of the old French Heredia's mother, and also a description of Hugo's French wife, Lucie. When he returns home, Branly finds Hugo Heredia already gone, having made up a story that his son had been drowned. Branly traces him to Mexico, and there hears the story of his life. It includes three appearances of the strange and diabolical figure of Victor Heredia. After telling this story, which Hugo Heredia had begged him not to do, as Hugo's life depended on it, Branly nearly drowns in the club pool. A few days later Fuentes visits with him at home, where he appears close to death. In one room of Branly's mansion, he meets what seems to be the ghost of Hugo Heredia's wife. We gather that she leads a life that parallels Branly's in some way, for Fuentes says that she will live when he dies. At the end of the novel Fuentes himself has acquired a similar ghostly figure whose voice pursues him through the autumn air.

Here we might recall a statement by Siger de Brabante to George: "For Nuncia, you don't exist. You're my ghost" (50). Fuentes has said that the figure of Siger in *Birthday* hungers for analogy, yearns for knowledge of his ghostly incarnations or parallel lives.[1] In *Distant Relations* this desire is actualized, and it is frightening; a ghost pursues the narrator at the end of the story just as Lucie Heredia waits for Branly to die. Fuentes has indicated in several interviews that *Aura, Birthday,* and *Distant Relations* form a trilogy; all of them, it seems, develop this notion of parallel lives or reincarnations. They are, in a sense, Fuentes's modern version of the gothic novels and ghost stories which intrigued him as a child.

The narrative framework of *Distant Relations* establishes a set of connections between the members of a far-flung "family" spread between France and Latin America. The title of the book (in Spanish *Una familia lejana)* refers most specifically to Lucie's family, who from her Mexican husband and children's point of view always "lived in remote French indifference" (in Spanish "la indiferente lejanía francesca"—"the indifferent French distance").[2] The concept of "distant relations" extends by implication to all Europe—the forefather of Latin American civilization. But it can be expanded still further symbolically to encompass distant relationships of all kinds—among people, times, realms, and stories.

Fuentes plays on the notion of distance throughout the novel. The vista over the Place de la Concorde that

stretches out behind Branly as he talks and other views of
Paris during an Indian summer suggest the idea of time
that stretches back into the past. And the distance between Paris and Mexico is kept constantly before us. Besides these spatiotemporal distances, the narrative
structure itself reveals a distancing mechanism. The reader perceives the past events of Branly's story through
Fuentes's avowedly "wavering comprehension"; the stories of Hugo and the elder shadowy Victor Heredia are
filtered through both Branly and Fuentes; and some of the
most distant events involving old Heredia's ancestors have
been related to him years earlier by his mother's old nurse.
That makes a set of four narrators whose stories fit one
inside the other.

To return to the idea of "relations" in the title, all
figures in the tale are related in some way. But the tenu-
ousness of the connection between, for example, Branly
and the whole Heredia clan, serves rather to suggest that
all men and all stories are connected to each other—if only
by the acts of talking and listening. This is Fuentes's case,
of course. He inherits the burden of the Heredia story
from Branly, just as Branly has inherited it from Hugo.
The very name of Heredia suggests this process. It resembles the Spanish words for inheritance ("*herencia*") and
inheritor ("*heredero*").[3] But Fuentes does not want such
a legacy. He hints that it—and by implication the family
of stories any writer inherits from his precedessors—is a
kind of curse. This notion resembles John Barth's concept
of a "literature of exhaustion," where modern texts feel
crushed by the burden of the literary past. And Fuentes
solves the problem in the way Barth suggests—by making
the problem the subject of his fiction.[4]

After Branly tells Fuentes of Hugo's intention to pass
the story on to him, Fuentes violates his customarily re-
spectful treatment of Branly. He shakes him by the shoulders, demanding confirmation of Hugo's words. He
explains that

my action was motivated by sudden terror. I didn't want to be the one who knew, the last to know, the one who receives the devil's gift and then cannot rid himself of it . . . I didn't want to be the one who receives and then must spend the rest of his life seeking another victim to whom to give the gift, the knowing. I did not want to be the narrator. (199)

The life spent looking for a victim—a reading public—is the life of an author, condemned "to wander like a blind beggar [singing "songs of the blind," perhaps?] pleading for the few verbal coins I must have to finish the story I inherited" (214). This is why Fuentes wants to demand every detail before Branly dies, "as if exhausting all the possibilities of the narrative might mean the end of this story I never wanted to hear, and the resulting release from the responsibility of telling it to someone else" (213). But finally, in the words that conclude the novel, "no one remembers the whole story" (225).

With these words—if not before—the reader shudders as Fuentes did earlier, when Branly finished *his* story. He has just inherited an incomplete narrative, one whose resources have not been exhausted, and is thus condemned to the role of narrator himself. The many loose ends in the novel, its fantastical events and unanswered questions of time, place, and identity, like those in *A Change of Skin,* force the reader to construct his own interpretation—his own narrative. Did Branly's father "really" sleep with old Heredia's mother in a Cuban whorehouse? Just what kind of magical figure *is* this old Heredia? Is Lucie Heredia Branly's resident ghost? Is Branly perhaps Fuentes's? Has the young Mexican Victor found a replacement for his dead brother in his friend André? Does their union constitute the creation of an "angel," as old Heredia suggests? And so on and so forth. The life blood of narrative continues to flow as it is passed on; the story is not dead. Branly himself says several times that "I shall not understand this story until I have finished telling it" (144). No story is truly known until it is told in a particular way by a particular narrator and interpreted by a particular reader.

With this story as with the eternally open-ended series of stories that comprise the literary heritage of all writers and readers, "the generations are infinite; we are all fathers of our fathers and sons of our sons" (143). (Fuentes's version of a literary geneology in *Cervantes or the Critique of Reading* reiterates this point: "Cervantes, author of Borges; Borges, author of Pierre Menard; Pierre Menard, author of the Quixote" (95).) In a sense, any author or narrator is "possessed" by others, as words are possessed by them all and possess them all. The ghostly Heredia tells Branly that he's using Branly's "lips to speak" (116). As Branly himself says, "every novel is in a way incomplete, but, as well contiguous with another story"—just like a family tree (215).

The interaction of Branly and Fuentes suggests an intriguing speculation, a resonance of this text in the realm of Latin American literary history. The figure of Branly might be seen to represent the older generation of Latin American writers which preceded Fuentes's generation and which is now symbolically passing on the narrative torch, so to speak. Branly's advanced age, his presence in Paris, and his connections with the Caribbean through the Heredias, who in turn have French ancestors, all suggest Carpentier. (He, like Fuentes, served as ambassador to Paris, and he was half French.[5]) The magical mode of *Distant Relations* resembles Carpentier's work; its Parisian setting recalls Carpentier's *Reasons of State* (1974) and parts of *La consagración de la primavera (Rite of Spring,* 1978). In addition, Branly's statements about the inheritance of stories and especially his notion of infinite generations also recall Borges, whom Fuentes has already invoked in *Birthday.* Perhaps even more than Carpentier, Borges is the archetypal aging Latin American narrator, the "father" of the recent explosion of fantastical stories—including *Distant Relations*—in the new world. Like Carpentier, he will soon bequeath his role as leader of continued innovation in Latin American fiction to his inheritors. The tersely poignant ending of *Distant Relations,* Fuentes's use of himself as narrator, and his play with the facts of his own life within the story, all resemble Borges's fiction.

Buñuel is another possible element of this composite ancestor figure; he passes on his surrealistic imagination to Fuentes. Fuentes's dedication of the novel to Buñuel for his eightieth birthday emphasizes the succession of generations. Fuentes will be about fifty as Buñuel is eighty—a difference of thirty years, or approximately one generation. Fuentes must now assume the same role with regard to younger writers that these older artists played in his own development.

Still another possible literary ancestor of this story is Proust. Fuentes has written that "he who reads Proust Proustitutes himself," indicating Proust's particular strength as a possessor of his narrative successors.[6] In the spring of 1978, while he was beginning work on *Distant Relations,* Fuentes agreed that reading Proust was addictive: "It becomes your world. Once into it, you can't get out again until you've finished. It becomes obsessive. ... Rereading Proust after fifteen years was a crisis for me. It was not what I thought it was."[7] Perhaps *Distant Relations* represents the resolution of that crisis. Like Branly, Fuentes achieves understanding of his story by telling it.

The similarities with Proust's work are striking at the start of *Distant Relations.* Meditations on the passage of time, the nostalgic mood of autumnal Paris, vistas of the city and its parks, friendships between the young and the old, and a number of long sentences that seem to postpone their endings all recall *Remembrance of Things Past.* Most specifically, Branly's evocation of games in the Parc Monceau parallels Marcel's memories of playing in the Champs Elysées gardens; both Branly and Marcel share the notion of involuntary memory—the sense that a certain object or sensation can abolish present contingencies and transport one back suddenly to childhood, but only if it appears unexpectedly. Fuentes here, like Proust before him, focuses on the nature of memory itself and the narrator's confrontation with the past.

Three remembered figures evoke a common feeling of regret for past neglect of another person. The woman Branly sees at the Clos suggests old Heredia's "mother," reportedly abandoned by her husband to die on a heap of garbage; Hugo Heredia regrets not having spent more time with his wife before she died; and Branly is haunted by the memory of a child with whom he had refused to shake hands, shutting him out of his friends' games in the park. This trio, plus Fuentes's observation that as Branly told him his story, Branly was "inviting the heat [my] acceptance of his words would incur," points to the role of friendship in the novel (161). Fraternal relations form the basis of society and of narrative.

Early on, Fuentes establishes a firm, warm, and apparently long-standing relationship between his Fuentes/narrator and Branly; during the latter's narrative, we return again and again to the situation of the two friends at lunch. This solid base of human affection serves as an anchor point for the often fantastical events of the novel. Near the end of the book, when the club swimming pool becomes so agitated that Branly almost drowns, the commotion stops when Fuentes comes to rescue him. He stretches out the hand that Branly had denied the lonely child in the park. Fuentes asks if perhaps he and Hugo Heredia were each others' missing childhood friends. Branly himself likes to think he has corrected his refusal to shake hands by bringing Victor to join André Heredia, who now "will never be alone." These two versions of a "second chance" are achieved through the narrative imagination; they recall Artemio Cruz, and *his* desire for a second choice in imaginative recreations of the past. So does

Branly's contact with Victor, which represents an old man's encounter with his anterior and possible selves.

This idea of friendship connects the notion of a narrative lineage to the image of dead twins joined Siamese fashion at the end of the novel. As he walks back into the club after visiting Branly's house, Fuentes sees what we might presume to be old Heredia's "angel"—the mysterious fusion of young Victor and André—floating dead in the club pool. This "angel" figure is puzzling. One could regard the fusion as an attempt to achieve some kind of original plenitude, a union that—like Pollo and Celestina's—abolishes solitude. The conflation of Victor's dark with André's light body may also affirm the connection between Latin America and Europe. The strange shiny object whose halves fuse in their common grasp, might be the same artifact of which Victor had earlier found half in a Mexican ruin; it might also serve as a sign of narrative unity with the past. But not necessarily. For even earlier, Victor himself had broken what may be the same object because "he felt an irresistible hatred for that perfect object that could owe nothing to him, or to any man" (182). The dead fetuses may indicate that Victor is correct to hate a self-sufficient artifact. Perfect union between men cannot exist in life, but only in death, just as narrative can never be complete—"no one remembers the whole story." A hand that reaches out in friendship responds to a need —which implies an imperfect, incomplete, a "human, all too human," being. In the same way, a narrative must be incomplete in order to provide a point of entry, a handle, to attract a new narrator, and continue fictional life.

In discussing this image, Fuentes himself recognizes the tension it suggests. He says that

Heredia is trying to form an angel and he can't ever finish it; he devours little boys to make his angel complete. . . . The dead figure in the pool is the result—a being that is rapidly becoming seed, nothing. . . . The original plenitude is being fetus, it is being

sperm, that is the origin. . . . Once [Victor and André] have been
reunited they go back to the origin; . . . the origin is sperm. [But]
death is the price of recovering [this] image [of unity.] The origin
is death. . . . There is a tension there, between the perfection of
death at the origin, the unity, and the narration, which wants to
go forward and tell its story.[8]

Through an extension of these ideas, Fuentes links
narrative lineages to social justice. Hugo Heredia's exces-
sive devotion to the stones of the past, and his ideal of a
true, disciplined aristocracy causes Victor to adopt a
haughty manner. The fraternal nature of narrative memory contrasts with this aristocratic isolation. The latter
resembles Branly's childhood refusal to extend his hand.
It indicates a desire to forget human links in favor of
aesthetic perfection. In this context old Heredia becomes
a rather diabolical creator figure because he wants both
perfect unity and complete control. This is impossible, and
so his unified creation dies. The "two fetuses curled upon
themselves" float "with a placidity that repudiates all past,
all history, all repentance"—for Fuentes an impossible, a
deathly stance (225). We must remain aware of the past,
and perhaps even the dead, not through perfect union with
them or complete archaeological devotion to them, but
through the sense of our own incompleteness.

This is the same kind of incompleteness that keeps
the different texts that constitute our literary heritage
open to each other. Because they are always incomplete,
stories can always use more voices. Here, as elsewhere,
Fuentes modulates between a number of different narrators, who pass the story from one to the other. Each of
them is "one more river in this hydrograph we have been
tracing . . . this watershed whose true source we still do
not know, as we do not know the multiplicity of its tribu-
taries or the final destiny toward which it flows" (163).

The conflation of identities throughout *Distant Relations* suggests that separate events and characters may
constitute essentially one story, a story of the quest for a

meaningful relationship to the past and for a renewal of energy. Branly looks to the young Mexican as a source of rejuvenation, and the narration in the old world repeatedly leads to events in America. Perhaps aged Europe is looking toward the new world for new life. This idea in turn suggests an alternative to my theory regarding a historical analogue for Branly. He may represent a purely European narrator, symbolic of European literature, rather than a partly European Latin American writer. Europe passes the role of narrative innovator on to Latin America.

Besides the events in the novel that shift us from Latin America to France, comparisons between the new and old worlds abound. Old Heredia says that "the Creole revolutions weren't fought for *liberté, egalité, fraternité,* but to acquire a Napoleon" (100). Fuentes records a number of instances where the new world triumphs over the old. Old Heredia says that his nurse knew that the new world had changed Europe forever, and Fuentes the narrator notes as he and Branly talk that "the exhilaration of the Antillean world was subconsciously beginning to dominate me" (126). Fuentes has noted with reference to *Distant Relations* that "when the caravelles come from the Caribbean, they bring storms with them into the manicured gardens of France."[9] Here, as in *Terra Nostra,* the new world disturbs the old. A combination of new and old worlds is finally implied by a whole list of French writers who were born in the new world, but made their mark in the old, and by this narrative itself, which achieves a similar synthesis.[10]

It is interesting to speculate whether Fuentes's looking so consistently toward the past in *Terra Nostra* and *Distant Relations* indicates that Mexican society may be nearing a point in its development that parallels his own description of early twentieth-century Europe: "When, for the first time, a bourgeois novelist—Marcel Proust—looks backwards, it is because his society no longer looks forward" *(House with Two Doors,* 58). But perhaps, as

Fuentes has implied elsewhere, Latin America's future, its utopian possibilities, lie in responsible memories of its own past rather than in imported dreams of future progress, often already discredited at their points of origin. So that looking back is also looking forward. Though generally rather a negative figure, old Heredia suggests the fruitful combination of French and Spanish American literary traditions through an image of his grounds at the Clos: "French is like my garden, elegant. . . . Spanish is like my woods, indomitable" (46).

5

Conclusion: The Multivocal Text

For many years the French anthropologist Marcel Griaule studied the Dogon people of Mali and brought to light their sophisticated cosmology. After his death he was given a moving funeral ceremony by the subjects of his research. During the Dogon funeral rites the principal tool of a man's earthly labors is broken, then placed on a ceremonial pile with other relics. Normally a man leaves his hoe, a woman her shuttle. But for Griaule, his friends chose "the tool that they had always seen in the hand of he who had listened to their elders, a pencil."[1] And so they marked their appreciation of his sensitivity to their voices.

Carlos Fuentes might one day merit a similar ceremony, for his writings show a remarkable capacity to transmit the voices of Mexico. His pencil too is a sensitive recording instrument. Griaule listened for the complex but finally harmonious story of Dogon mythology; Fuentes has set himself the more difficult task of capturing the cacophony of modern Mexico. The pages of his fiction are often traversed by multiple narrative voices, which express a "plurality of meanings."[2] Though certain of his works reflect the pervasive influence of surrealism on Latin American writing (Fuentes himself remembers that "Breton called Mexico the preferred land of surrealism"[3]), Fuentes's pencil cannot be said to practice any simple kind of automatic writing. It is rather as if an "alternating current" (to use Octavio Paz's phrase) of different voices flows through it as it transforms them. The different voices contribute to Fuentes' dialectical mode, to his oppositions and shifts of perspective.[4]

It is appropriate to conclude a discussion of Fuentes's work by referring to an anthropologist, for Fuentes's writing often approaches a kind of literary anthropology, a portrait of the patterns of interaction that compose Mexican society. His most successful novel, *The Death of Artemio Cruz,* locates typical patterns of behavior in the society at large yet projects them through an individual, in this case a fictional character. But unlike a traditional anthropologist, Fuentes hopes that his work will lead the community it describes toward a greater self-awareness. This, in fact, explains Fuentes's insistence that the anthropologist Oscar Lewis's often unfavorable portraits of Mexican life must be read in Mexico.[5]

As we have seen, the most striking "multivocal" feature of Fuentes's fiction is the formal shift of narrative stance in many of his works. The device often reveals multiple perspectives even in the treatment of one character, like Artemio Cruz, allowing the reader different views of him, and, through him, of the class he represents. As Cruz is a victim, a product of history and society and the neuroses they engender, we identify and temporarily pardon; as he is an executioner, a powerful manipulator who chooses to dominate at any cost, we distance ourselves and condemn.[6] The narrative voice in *A Change of Skin* undergoes a different set of changes, shifting both the receiver and the time frame of its discourse frequently. Third-person narration dominates *Where the Air is Clear,* but as we have seen, in the last section of the novel first- and second-person stances compose a kind of universal song, and varied monologues reveal multiple inner voices in Mexico City throughout the text. *Terra Nostra* contains the most extensive shifts in narrative voice; there we move between third, second, and first persons, and even hear narration by a painting.

Throughout Fuentes's work, different voices may represent different times in the life of an individual or of a civilization. The three kinds of time that Fuentes discerns in Mexico—utopian, epic, and mythic, often exist simultaneously in his work.[7] As a complement to this synchronic use of superimposed layers of time, each with its own "voice," Fuentes recognizes the diachronic movement of change through time, and its effect on the processes of writing and reading: "the world that the work reads is a changing world; the work wishes to be fixed. Fortunately, it doesn't succeed. The changing world also multiplies its readings of the work."[8]

Fuentes's shifts of narrative voice parallel a variety of other multivocal elements in his work. They all attest to the basically cumulative nature of his technique; as he says, he is a *"puter-inner,* not a taker-outer."[9] First of all, characters often undergo an imaginative doubling or tripling in the text. This process of multiplication may also include condensation and metamorphosis. Artemio Cruz on his deathbed imagines himself in the place of his son; earlier he has usurped the place of Gonzalo Bernal. In *Holy Place,* Guillermo eternally renews the image of his mother—doubles it, triples it, quadruples it—in the series of film clips he projects. Elizabeth's multiple names in *A Change of Skin* expand her identity to include all women in their battle with men. In *Terra Nostra,* Agrippa Posthumus is multiplied by three, and perhaps even more, as Tiberius's slave suggests. Like the mirrors and masks in Fuentes's texts, these personal multiplications and transformations suggest national and individual quests for identity.[10]

A third type of multivocality in Fuentes's work appears when one text echoes another. The echo may exist on the surface of the text in the form of a name or an allusion, or it may be hidden "above or below the normal

sound"—a kind of "cry under the water" (*Holy Place*, 13).
Fuentes himself explains his extensive use of intertextual
allusion as a desire "to recapture a past that seems dead
but is really very much alive."[11] Just as one character may
recapitulate several, so one narrative is often traversed by
others. This idea of voices that come and go in a text is
suggested by a pile of sea-polished stones Elizabeth has
just gathered on the beach in *A Change of Skin:* "You sort
your pebbles out. You know that each of them will change
color as the sun moves. Noon's yellow becomes orange as
the afternoon lengthens, it is red at twilight, beneath the
moon violet, a fusion of red and blue" (*A Change of Skin*,
143). As we have seen, the earlier narratives we glimpse
behind the story we are reading often are Aztec or, less
frequently, classical myths. Ixca and Teódula reactivate
the myth of Huizilopochtli and Coatlicue, the narrator of
A Change of Skin that of Xipe Totec; Claudia reinterprets
the triple role of the goddess Tlazolzéotl and those of
Penelope and Circe as well. The chiastic designs I have
traced throughout Fuentes's works often structure the
returns of these voices from the past.

As I have suggested earlier, these mythic ancestral
presences in Fuentes's work project the message that they
are present and that they are not to be played with carelessly. Guillermo is held in thrall by the devouring goddess
Claudia, who in turn has destroyed much of her own
personal happiness in acquiring celluloid divinity. The
characters in *A Change of Skin* are trapped inside an
ancient pyramid after having wandered there in a frivo-
lously touristic mood. The clearest warning of this kind
emerges from the short story "Chac Mool," when Filiberto realizes that the old deity has begun to assert its power:
"My original idea was entirely different: I would dominate
the Chac Mool as one dominates a toy; it was, perhaps, an
extension of my childhood security."[12] His "toying" with
the spiritual powers of the past eventually results in his
death.

The textual voices that cross Fuentes's work are not always myths. Intertextual allusions encompass other art forms, or other kinds of narrative.[13] References to familiar paintings can instantly evoke a particular tone and style; such is the case when a triptych by Hieronymous Bosch appears near the end of *Terra Nostra*. Many of that novel's characters come directly from earlier literary texts—Celestina, Don Juan, the Knight of the Sorrowful Countenance—or from history, another grand text; the novel also contains lengthy quotations from the gospels, as well as shorter fragments of other books—including Fuentes's own *Cervantes or the Critique of Reading*. Popular songs resonate throughout *Where the Air is Clear* and *A Change of Skin,* whose narrator is a composite of earlier literary voices. In *The Hydra Head,* quotes from Shakespeare and film images proliferate. Fuentes's use of film is especially striking. Just as paintings do, films can evoke a particular mood, an era, a style, which has shaped a character like Elizabeth in *A Change of Skin* or Felix in *The Hydra Head.* The predominantly American titles of many of the films in Fuentes's works represent an intrusion of a foreign voice in the cultural language—acknowledged, often enjoyed, yet also disturbing, even resented. Furthermore, as we have seen, the persistent intertextual intrusions also suggest that literature is, to a large extent, made out of other literature.

Characters who take their identities from other texts, whether mythic, literary, or popular, imply a "multivocal" concept of literary character itself. People in Fuentes's novels are not so much observed in their individualities as composed of different parts. The many voices of history, art, film, even the tape recording of his own voice that Cruz plays over and over on his deathbed, present the individual invaded by his environment.

With regard to social problems as well, Fuentes's texts often speak with more than one voice. His thought is dualistic in nature, alternating between a tragic and a

reforming spirit. Fuentes's early novels, in particular, reveal a strong impetus toward social reform, though they
propose no concrete plans for its implementation. This
potentially constructive social criticism coexists with a
tragic view of life. Sacrifices continue, yet conditions do
not improve. The answer, as Fuentes himself has suggested, is that even though it may seem hopeless, one must
continue to work for reforms. The two tendencies represent two poles of his thought; he has said that his anar-
chistic subconscious believes—with Bakunin and Buñuel
—that there is no good government, but that his conscious
life leads him to fight for his government to be less bad.[14]

Finally, Fuentes's sensitivity to the many voices within a text extends to his essays on literature. In *Cervantes
or the Critique of Reading,* Fuentes reencounters a Spanish
literary voice in order to exorcize the "panic" out of the
"hispanic time" ("tiempo is pánico") that used to dominate his part of the new world, achieving a kind of
reconquest, or conquest in reverse. Thus the idea of "de-I-
ification," which Fuentes explicitly develops in this essay
and in his later fiction, is anticipated by the unusual recep-
tivity of his early fiction to the different voices of Mexico
and by the narrative strategies he develops to accommo-
date them.[15]

Fuentes shows individual voices dying into, strength-
ening a communal literary voice. The process is certainly
less brutal than the ritual sacrifice of victims to keep the
sun alive.[16] Yet it continues the utopian ideal of commitment to a community that Fuentes cherishes for the new
world. He locates this multivocal imperative in Mexico's
cultural tradition: "Rejected, the polyvalent, sculptural
space of our indigenous past persists beyond the univocal,
frontal space of the rationalist project through which
Mexico has tried to suppress the unfinished histories that
line the far shore of its destiny."[17] Fuentes's creation of
many voices allows him to explore these "unfinished histories," this variety of times, places, theories, and images in

the world and in the imagination in his texts. In doing this, he approaches what is for him the great truth of literature, that "all the imaginary becomes possible and all the possible becomes universal."[18]

Notes

BIOGRAPHICAL INTRODUCTION

1. Luis Harss and Barbara Dohmann, *Into the Mainstream: Conversations with Latin American Writers* (New York: Harper and Row, 1967), p. 281.
2. Volume I of Fuentes's *Complete Works (Obras completas* [Madrid: Aguilar, 1974]) contains the most comprehensive biographical information about him. I am indebted to that compilation for many of the facts I present here and in the preceding chronology.
3. Reprinted in Emmanuel Carballo, *Diecinueve protagonistas de la literatura mexicana del siglo XX* (Mexico City: Empresas Editoriales, 1965), p. 432.
4. See the interviews by Regina Janes, " 'No More Interviews': A Conversation with Carlos Fuentes," *Salmagundi,* 43 (Winter, 1979), 95; and Bill Moyers, "The Many Worlds of Carlos Fuentes," *Bill Moyers' Journal,* Shows #520 and 522 (June–July, 1980), Part I, p. 7.
5. See Carballo, p. 442, and Harss, p. 288.
6. See Moyers, Part I, p. 7.
7. Harss, p. 281.
8. Harss, p. 284.
9. See his discussion in Emir Rodríguez Monegal, *El arte de narrar: Diálogos* (Caracas: Monte Avila, 1968), p. 145.
10. Carlos Fuentes, "El otro K," *Vuelta* 28 (March 1979), 24.
11. In Herman Doezma, "An Interview with Carlos Fuentes," *Modern Fiction Studies* 18 (1972), 500–501.
12. Doezma, p. 501.
13. The Cuban writer Alejo Carpentier wrote what is generally

considered the first real "manifesto" of Latin American magical realism—which he called the "marvelous real" ("lo real maravilloso"). It appeared as the preface to his novel *The Kingdom of this World* (1949).

14. Monegal, *El arte de narrar,* p. 121.

15. The script of *Time to Die* was published in the *Revista de Bellas Artes* 9 (May–June 1966), 21–59.

16. Monegal, *El arte de narrar,* p. 120.

17. *Ibid.,* pp. 117–18.

18. *Los narradores ante el público,* First series (Mexico City: Joaquín Mortiz, 1966), p. 151.

19. The catalogue contains a face to face English translation of Fuentes's essay.

20. See the letter "Cinco intelectuales explican por qué han dejado de escribir en *Política*" ("Five intellectuals explain why they have ceased to write for *Política*) published first in *Siempre* August 5, 1964.

21. President Echeverría was elected in 1970 in the aftermath of the violent suppression of student uprisings in 1968.

22. Moyers, Part 2, p. 13.

23. Janes, " 'No More Interviews,' " p. 87.

24. Moyers, Part I, p. 3.

25. *Ibid.,* p. 13.

26. Carballo, p. 429. John Brushwood distinguishes two tendencies in Fuentes's work: a representational mode in *Artemio Cruz, The Good Conscience,* and *Hydra Head,* and a conceptual mode in *Aura, Birthday, Distant Relations,* and *Holy Place. A Change of Skin, Terra Nostra* and *Where the Air is Clear* combine the two tendencies, thus illustrating, perhaps, Fuentes's own idea of a "symbolic realism"; "Sobre el referente y la transfromación narrativa en las novelas de Carlos Fuentes y Gustavo Sainz," *Revista Iberoamericana* 116–17 (July–December 1981), 51–52.

27. Richard Reeve, "Carlos Fuentes," in *Narrativa y crítica de nuestra américa,* ed. Joaquín Roy (Madrid: Castalia, 1978), p. 314.

28. Carballo, p. 429.

29. Octavio Paz, "Presentación de Carlos Fuentes, en su conferencia inaugural en el Colegio Nacional el martes 17 de

octubre de 1972," *Memoria del Colegio Nacional* 7, iii (1972), 225.

1. EARLY NOVELS: ANCESTRAL PRESENCES, MODERN QUESTS

1. Carballo, p. 429.
2. Fuentes in *Los narradores ante el público*, p. 138
3. Octavio Paz, *El arco y la lira* (Mexico City: Fondo de Cultura Económica, 1970), p. 62.
4. Emir Rodríguez Monegal, *Narradores de esta américa* (Buenos Aires: Alfa, 1974) II, 15.
5. Lanin Gyurko maintains that gods in Fuentes's texts can be relentless and vengeful or they can represent the social conscience of a people; "Structure and Theme in Fuentes' *La muerte de Artemio Cruz,*" *Symposium* 34 (Spring 1980), 194.
6. Lanin Gyurko, "Social Satire and the Ancient Mexican Gods in the Narrative of Carlos Fuentes," *IberoAmerikanisches Archiv* 1, ii (1975), 138.

THE DEVELOPMENT OF A COLLECTIVE VOICE: *WHERE THE AIR IS CLEAR*

1. Alejo Carpentier, "Problemática de la actual novela latinoamericana," in Juan Loveluck, ed., *La novela hispanoamericana* (Santiago: Editorial Universitaria, 1969), p. 145.
2. Monegal, *Narradores de esta américa,* II, 15.
3. Fuentes acknowledges *The Edge of the Storm* as "the great moment of structural renovation in Mexican narration"; in James R. Fortson, *Perspectivas mexicanas desde París: Un diálogo con Carlos Fuentes* (Mexico City: Corporación Editorial, S. A.., 1973), supplement to *El,* p. 70.
4. Joseph Frank argues that major twentieth century novelists such as Joyce and Proust articulated a kind of "spatial form" in literature. They did this by disrupting traditional linear chronology, and placing different elements beside

each other somewhat in the manner of a collage; "Spatial Form in Modern Literature," *The Widening Gyre: Crisis and Mastery in Modern Literature* (Bloomington and London: Indiana University Press, 1963), pp. 3–62.

5. Carlos Fuentes, *Where the Air Is Clear*, trans. Sam Hileman, 6th printing (1960; New York: Farrar, Straus and Giroux, 1979), p. 283. Further references are given in the text.

6. Manuel Durán, "Carlos Fuentes," in his *Tríptico Mexicano: Juan Rulfo, Carlos Fuentes, Salvador Elizondo* (Mexico City: Secretaria de Educación Pública, 1973), p. 62. Shirley Williams points out that by starting rumors leading to Robles's financial ruin, Ixca obtains in Robles both a sacrificial victim and a consequent rebirth, the ancient objectives of sacrifices to the sun; "The Search for the Past: The Role of Aztec Mythology in *La región más transparente*," *Estudos Ibero-Americanos* 2, ii (1976), 25–30.

7. María Salgado makes this point in her article on "Supervivencia del mito azteca en el Méjico contemporáneo de *La región más transparente*," *Kentucky Romance Quarterly* 16 (1967), 127.

8. It is interesting to note that Fuentes first conceived of the novel in social terms, as the portrait of a class. In his application for a fellowship to work on the book, he says he will investigate "the construction, for the first time in Mexico, of a middle class and an upper bourgeoisie"; letter of application, on file at the Centro Mexicano de Escritores, Mexico City.

9. Fuentes has said that in having these different groups speak in distinct styles, he is following Joyce's example of creating different speech patterns for Stephen, Bloom, and Molly in *Ulysses;* in Carballo, p. 435.

10. For a discussion of Paz's ideas throughout *Where the Air is Clear*, see Joseph Sommers, *After the Storm: Landmarks in the Modern Mexican Novel* (Albuquerque: University of New Mexico Press, 1963), pp. 132–43.

11. Ixca's vision recently came to life when workers digging tunnels for a new subway near the Zócalo discovered an ancient Aztec temple.

12. See Alfonso Reyes, *Visión de Anáhuac* (1915).

13. Fuentes in Monegal, *El arte de narrar,* p. 118.

14. See Sommers's discussion of this point in *After the Storm,* pp. 128–32.

15. Fuentes discusses Teódula in an unidentified interview cited by Gloria Durán, and in a letter to Durán that is included in her study, *La magia y las brujas en la obra de Carlos Fuentes* (Mexico City: UNAM, 1976), pp. 73–76.

16. M. Kasey Hellerman traces the mythic paradigm of the violated earth goddess Coatlicue and her son Huizlopochtli in a number of Fuentes's works; "The Coatlicue-Malinche Conflict: A Mother and Son Identity Crisis in the Writings of Carlos Fuentes," *Hispania* 57 (1974), 868–75.

17. These discussions recall those in an earlier urban novel, *Adán Buenosayres* (1948) by the Argentine novelist Leopoldo Marechal. For more information about the cultural history behind this section, see the article by Richard Reeve, "Octavio Paz and Hiperion in *La región más transparente:* Plagiarism, Caricature, or . . . ?" *Chasqui* 3, iii (1974), 13–25.

18. Fortson, p. 91.

19. See Fuentes's comments in the article by Joseph Sommers, "The Present Moment in the Mexican Novel," *Books Abroad* 40 (Summer 1966), 261–66.

20. Moyers, I, p. 3.

21. Fuentes makes this distinction in his response to "Tres interrogaciones sobre el presente y futuro de México," *Cuadernos Americanos* 102 (1959), 50. Fuentes says there that "we would be wrong not to distinguish between this active head of the financial bourgeoisie and the bourgeoisie that carries on production, especially in the countryside. The productive bourgeoisie, right now, constitutes a force that supports Mexico's progress." Lanin Gyurko correctly points out that Robles goes from the extreme of the desire for domination to disengagement—an abandonment of his earlier ideals. "He does gain a personal transcendence, yet his moral victory does not imply a national redemption, because he chooses to drop out of the system rather than struggling to reform it"; "Abortive Idealism and the Mask in Fuentes' *La región más transparente,*" *Revue des Langues Vivantes,* 42 (1976), 295. I would argue that Ro-

bles's return to the land, combined with his affirmation of his mestizo origins, does indicate a redemptive direction for Mexico's remaining Robleses, a decentralization of wealth and power.

22. Daniel de Guzmán points out that Fuentes's attention to the mestizo corresponds to a significant increase in that component of Mexico's population. De Guzmán maintains that in 1910 mestizos constituted only 40 percent of the population and that by 1970 they had increased to at least 70 percent; *Carlos Fuentes* (New York: Twayne, 1972), p. 27.

23. G. Durán also recognizes the importance of this dichotomy in Fuentes's work: "Throughout Fuentes' work we find a conflict between the visual daylit impressions and the deeper knowledge imparted by the subconscious in the world of darkness"; *The Archetypes of Carlos Fuentes: From Witch to Androgyne* (Hamden, Connecticut: The Shoe String Press, 1980), p. 180.

24. Rodríguez Monegal and Mario Benedetti both agree that Fuentes has been particularly successful in combining literary excellence and social criticism; Monegal, *Narradores de esta américa,* II, 248; Benedetti, "Carlos Fuentes: Del signo barroco al espejismo," in Helmy F. Giacoman, *Homenaje a Carlos Fuentes* (New York: Las Américas, 1971), p. 94.

25. Fuentes has said that during the time he wrote *Where the Air is Clear* "Dos Passos was my literary bible"; Carballo, p. 434.

26. Sommers, *After the Storm,* p. 126. Sommers sees this subordination of individual to community as an ancient Aztec value.

27. Liliana Befumo Boschi and Elisa Calabrese maintain that in the mythic domain of primordial chaotic time evoked by various fiesta scenes in Fuentes's work, linguistic as well as personal and social barriers break down; *Nostalgia del futuro en la obra de Carlos Fuentes* (Buenos Aires: Cambeiro, 1974), p. 34.

28. Again, the technique is generally traced to Dos Passos.

TRADITION, REPRESSION, AND INDEPENDENCE: *THE GOOD CONSCIENCE*

1. Fuentes has said that "if *Where the Air is Clear* is a novel of extension, *The Good Conscience* is a novel of depth"; Carballo, p. 440.
2. Ibid., p. 433; and in Monegal, p. 136. The book was to have been the start of a tetralogy which Fuentes decided not to finish. As it stands, the novel is much less significant than *Where the Air is Clear* and *The Death of Artemio Cruz.*
3. Carlos Fuentes, *The Good Conscience,* trans. Sam Hileman (New York: Farrar, Straus, and Giroux, 1961; reprinted 1979), p. 4. Further references are given in the text. The English translation differs markedly from the Spanish original, particularly in the ordering of scenes.
4. As Manuel Echeverría has pointed out, Jaime's orphan status, his sense of injustice done to his mother, is at the base of his attempted rebellion; prologue to *Las buenas conciencias* in Fuentes, *Obras completas,* p. 638.
5. Carballo, p. 440.

FRAGMENTING FORCES IN THE REVOLUTION AND THE SELF: *THE DEATH OF ARTEMIO CRUZ*

1. Critical reactions to *The Death of Artemio Cruz* have generally been favorable. For a survey, see Isabel Siracusa, "Las novelas y su repercusión," *Nueva Crítica* 2 (1970), 148–55.
2. Hernán Vidal sees naturalistic determinism and moral vision meet in Fuentes's portrait of Artemio Cruz, and associates the observation with Fuentes's declaration that Marx and Nietzsche divide each man; "El modo narrativo en *La muerte de Artemio Cruz* de Carlos Fuentes," *Thesaurus: Boletín del Instituto Caro y Cuervo* 31 (1976), 322.
3. In his excellent article on "Self, Double, and Mask in Fuentes' La *muerte de Artemio Cruz,*" *Texas Studies in Language and Literature* 16 (1974), 363–84, Lanin Gyurko points to a number of characters who can be identified as doubles of Artemio Cruz. These doubles serve "first of all to dramatize the complexity of Cruz's character, which is

a fusion of opposites." Gyurko divides the figures into two groups. "Compensatory doubles" represent Cruz's positive potential (Regina, Bernal, Lorenzo, Laura). "Antagonistic doubles" seem at first to be the opposites of Cruz, but he finally comes to resemble them, as the compensatory figures are sacrificed (Gamaliel Bernal, Father Paez, Catalina). This concept of character doubling resembles the tripling of Artemio Cruz's narrative voice, which I will discuss later.

4. Carlos Fuentes, *The Death of Artemio Cruz*, trans. Sam Hileman (New York: Farrar, Straus and Company, 1964), p. 11. Further references are given in the text.

5. René Jara Cuadro makes the point that Doña Ludivinia hides in her memories against old age and death just as Artemio Cruz does in his house in Coyoacán, but that the "sacred spaces" they construct enclose those very dangers; "El mito y la nueva novela hispanoamericana: A propósito de *La muerte de Artemio Cruz,*" in Giacoman, p. 190.

6. Juan Loveluck considers that the ideological basis of *The Death of Artemio Cruz* is formed around three major related concerns: Mexico and what is Mexican, Mexico and the United States, and Mexico and its revolution; "Intención y forma en *La muerte de Artemio Cruz,*" *Nueva Narrativa Latinoamericana* I, i (1971), 114.

7. Fuentes dedicates the novel to the radical sociologist C. Wright Mills, "true voice of North America," because Mills has consistently criticized the economic domination of Latin America by the U.S. in cooperation with the native oligarchies. See the conversation between Mills and a number of Mexican intellectuals, including Fuentes: "Izquierda, subdesarollo y guerra fría—Un coloquio sobre cuestiones fundamentales," *Cuadernos Americanos* 19 (1960), 53–69. M. Durán imagines Artemio Cruz as a supporter of President Mateo Alemán. His term, from 1946–52, saw the most concessions to North American business in Mexico; p. 63.

8. Carlos Fuentes, *El mundo de José Luis Cuevas* (Mexico City: Galería de Arte Misrachi, 1969), p. 9.

9. Fuentes speaks of his own writing as power, but a constructive sort of power: when you write, "you're there in a

prodigious act of truth, of affirmation of power—of power that doesn't corrupt"; Fortson, p. 18.

10. For detailed discussions of the arrangement of Cruz's monologue, see the study by Nelson Osorio, which plots the social and moral rises and falls of Cruz's career; "Un aspecto de la estructura de *La muerte de Artemio Cruz,*" in Giacoman, pp. 125–46.

11. For M. Durán, Cruz's repeated sentence about crossing the river reminds us that the river is an ancient symbol for human life, and that the novel is thus "a journey back upstream from the point where [the river] is already spilling into the sea of death to its birth in infancy," p. 68.

12. Alberto Díaz-Lastra defines these voices in the following way: "the I is an old man in his present surroundings; the you is an authorial conscience that condemns more than it remembers; the he is a more impersonal voice"; "Carlos Fuentes y la revolución traicionada," in Giacoman, p. 349.

13. Carballo, pp. 440–41.

14. Lorenzo crosses the water Artemio Cruz continually dreams of to go fight in Spain, while Cruz remains forever on this side of the cleansing element. Boschi and Calabresi associate Lorenzo with the benevolent God Quetzalcóatl who departed by water, never to retrun, and Artemio Cruz with the destructive God Tezcatlipoca, the smoking mirror who adopts various appearances to trick Quetzalcóatl, p. 64.

15. Boschi and Calabresi maintain that "Artemio Cruz will be able to assume unchosen options and travel freely only when death permits the enrichment of his symbolic world" and his entrance into "the temporal zone of the mythic"; p. 55. They may be correct in associating this idea with Aztec beliefs that "life and death were two aspects of the same thing." But in wishing to follow Artemio Cruz through this mythic pattern, they seem to forget that the novel ends when Cruz dies. The nearness of death motivates his mental journeys, but death itself finally annihilates them. A mythic view of Fuentes's works, while establishing many fascinating connections with ancient culture, tends to be too optimistic; it underestimates their existential ele-

ments, and softens Fuentes's portrayal of the finality of death—particularly in the case of Artemio Cruz.

16. Lanin Gyurko notes that this self-condemnation suggests that Fuentes blames Mexico itself rather than other nations for its problems; "Structure and Theme," p. 32.

17. Carballo, p. 441.

18. Octavio Paz, *The Labyrinth of Solitude: Life and Thought in Mexico*, trans. Lysander Kemp (New York: Grove Press, 1961), pp. 76–77.

19. Rodríguez Monegal argues that fratricide is central to several of Fuentes's works; with it Fuentes suggests that Mexico goes on requiring human sacrifices in modern times; *Narradores de esta américa*, II, 259.

2. SHORT FICTION AND THEATER: MAGICAL REALISM, SYMBOLIC ACTION

1. Carballo, pp. 427–28. For a concise discussion of this aspect of Fuentes's work (in *Aura, Holy Place,* and *Birthday*), see Margaret Sayers Peden, "The World of the Second Reality in Three Novels by Carlos Fuentes," in *Otros mundos, otros fuegos,* ed D. A. Yates (East Lansing: Michigan State University Press, 1975), pp. 83–86.

2. Fortson, p. 100.

3. Similarly, Fuentes says "Chac Mool" was inspired by a news story about the terrible rains that accompanied the statue of the Chac Mool on his visit to a European museum; Carballo, p. 428.

4. Carlos Fuentes, *Tiempo mexicano* (Mexico City: Joaquín Mortiz, 1971), p. 19.

5. See the introduction to Carpentier's novel *The Kingdom of this World.*

6. Fuentes cited in Antonio J. Ciccone, "La reencarnación sobrenatural en *Los días enmascarados* de Carlos Fuentes," in *Otros mundos, otros fuegos,* p. 114.

7. Fuentes, "El otro K," p. 27.

8. Tzvetan Todorov, *The Fantastic: A Structural Approach to a Literary Genre,* trans. Richard Howard (Ithaca: Cornell University Press, 1974), p. 41.

THE WITCHES OF DESIRE: *AURA*

1. For a complete discussion of this aspect of Fuentes's work, see G. Durán, *La magia y las brujas,* recently enlarged and updated to include Fuentes's later works and translated as *The Archetypes of Carlos Fuentes; From Witch to Androgyne* (New York: Shoe String Press, 1980). Durán traces the appearance in Fuentes's work of witches as unavoidable evil or destiny that chains man to his remote past. These witches are Jungian anima figures and thus elicit a combination of fascination and disgust from Fuentes. According to Durán, this "Nietzschean" or "Dionysian" side of Fuentes often overpowers his Marxism, particularly in *A Change of Skin,* where the witch figures increase dramatically. With this increase in numbers, Fuentes suggests that "the subconscious instincts of humanity are gaining in power." The force of the witch, the anima, the subconscious, as man's destiny, is affirmed at the end of mythical works. Durán believes that as Fuentes submitted himself more and more completely to this anima, the fruitful tension in his earlier works like *Where the Air is Clear* and *Aura,* in which he, and with him, his characters, resisted it, has disappeared; pp. 202–203.

2. Critical reaction to *Aura* has been very favorable. For a summary, see Richard Reeve, "An Annotated Bibliography on Carlos Fuentes: 1949–69," *Hispania* 53 (1970), 605–606. I believe *Aura* is so successful because the novella achieves an accessible elegance through a relatively simple yet powerful story. Fuentes sustains the tension of a well-articulated progression toward a dénouement that is continually suggested yet not entirely revealed until the end.

3. Carlos Fuentes, *Aura,* trans. Lysander Kemp, bilingual edition (New York: Farrar, Straus and Giroux, 1975), p. 3. Further references are given in the text.

4. Richard Reeve studies Fuentes's use of the second person in an article on "Carlos Fuentes y el desarollo del narrador en segundo persona: Un ensayo exploratorio," in Giacoman, pp. 75–87. Reeves surveys previous uses of the technique, the most recent and sustained appearing in *La Modification (A Change of Heart)* by Michel Butor, with

whose writings Reeves feels sure Fuentes was familiar when he wrote *Aura*. G. Durán associates the second person future narration with the doctrine of reincarnation, which will become even more important in *Birthday*. The narrator is then imagined as an older Felipe who knows what he will do since he has done it before; *La magia y las brujas,* pp. 68–69.

5. Santiago Rojas proposes the interesting theory that the speaker in Aura is not Felipe but Consuelo, who conjures up both him as her husband and her younger self in Aura. Felipe's apparent autonomy is essential to her recreation of the past, though she still controls his movements; "Modalidad narrativa en *Aura:* Realidad y enajenación," *Revista Iberoamericana* 56: 112–13 (July–December 1980), 487–97.

6. G. Durán maintains that Felipe's encounter with Aura/Consuelo causes him to lose his individual identity in the comforting figure of the great mother, from whom he is finally unable to rescue the youthful anima figure of Aura; *The Archetypes of Carlos Fuentes,* p. 62.

7. Salvador Reyes Nevares, "Una obra maestra," *La Cultura en México,* No. 127 (22 July 1964), 19.

8. Rodríguez Monegal, *Narradores de esta américa,* II, 258.

9. M. Durán, p. 103.

10. See the article by Ana María Albán de Viqueira, "Estudio de las fuentes de *Aura* de Carlos Fuentes," *Comunidad,* 28 (August 1967), 396–402. Besides discussing *The Aspern Papers,* Albán de Viqueira records a number of other sources, including books on black magic. See also Djelal Kadir, "Another Sense of the Past: Henry James's *The Aspern Papers* and Carlos Fuentes' *Aura,*" *Revue de Littérature Comparée* 50 (1976), 448–54.

11. Lois Parkinson Zamora, of the University of Houston, drew my attention to Hawthorne's story as a possible source of inspiration for *Aura*.

12. Fuentes himself claims that he had a number of other precedents in mind in writing *Aura:* Circe, *The Metamorphoses* of Apuleius, Miss Havisham in *Great Expectations,* and that the immediate inspiration for the story in 1961 was

the Japanese film, *Ugetsu Monogatari,* directed by Kenji Misoguchi; Interview with WBF, September, 1980.

"MANY RETURNS OF THE DAY": *BIRTHDAY*

1. Carlos Fuentes, *Cumpleaños* (Mexico City: Joaquín Mortiz, 1969), pp. 23, 26, 91. Further references are given in the text. My translations.

2. José L. Mas suggests that *Birthday* might be imagined as a series of scenes in the theater of memory that Fuentes describes in *Terra Nostra;* "Historia y mito en *Cumpleaños* de Carlos Fuentes," *La Semana de Bellas Artes,* No. 98 (Oct. 17, 1979), 4.

3. George McMurray interprets the events in this way in an article on "*Cumpleaños* y 'La nueva novela,' " in Giacoman, pp. 385–98.

4. Interview with WBF, September, 1980.

5. Fuentes also pointed out the Borgesian ubiquity of the central figure: "this Borges/Georgie is present at the crucifixion of Christ; . . . he travels with Marco Polo," and appears at all sorts of places and times; Interview with WBF, September, 1980.

6. Adriana García de Aldridge notes that the architecture of the octagonal castle of Capodimonte—one source of this imaginary palace—is often thought to represent eternal life. The narrator suggests this when he asks if the house he explores "was, is, or will be" (30); "La dialéctica contemporánea: 'tiempo propio-tiempo total' en *Cumpleaños,*" *Revista Iberoamericana* 108–109 (Jul-Dec 1979), 532. G. Durán imagines the labyrinthine house in *Birthday* as a womb, source of incarnations—and, I might add, of stories; *The Archetypes of Carlos Fuentes,* p. 141.

7. Borges proposes this idea in his essay on "Kafka and his Precursors," in *Labyrinths: Selected Stories and Other Writings,* ed. Donald A. Yates and James E. Irby (New York: New Directions, 1964), pp. 199–201.

8. See William L. Siemens, "Maniqueismo e inmortalidad en *Cumpleaños,*" *Explicación de Textos Literarios,* 2, ii (1974), 129–30. Siemens notes the importance in the novella of

Eastern religions such as Taoism with its union of opposites. G. Durán maintains that Nuncia serves as a Jungian anima figure, who changes from nurturing mother to mistress to nurse as Siger passes from youth through maturity to old age in the novella; "Carlos Fuentes, *Cumpleaños (Birthday):* A Mythological Interpretation of an Ambiguous Novel," *Latin American Literary Review,* 2, iv (1974), 75–86.

9. García de Aldridge emphasizes the way reincarnation motivates the treatment of time in *Birthday:* the novella shows us neither cyclical time nor linear time, but "the encounter of a time that is unique and total at once"; pp. 513–535.

10. It is tempting to note that in comparison to Fuentes's other works, the novella, like Siger, has been "condemned" to relative obscurity.

The Bedroom and the Public Square: *The One-Eyed Man is King* and *All Cats are Gray*

1. Since *All Cats are Gray* is the better known of the two plays and develops historical themes that pervade Fuentes's work, I will discuss it in greater detail than *The One-Eyed Man is King.* The title of *All Cats are Gray* comes from the saying "at night, all cats are gray."

2. Carlos Fuentes, *El tuerto es rey* (Mexico City: Joaquín Mortiz, 1970), p. 10. Further references are given in the text. My translations.

3. Fuentes notes in his introduction to *All Cats are Gray* that the American playwright Arthur Miller provided the point of departure for the play by saying that he had always been fascinated by the "dramatic encounter of a man who had everything—Moctezuma—and a man who had nothing—Cortez"; *Todos los gatos son pardos* (1970; Mexico City: Siglo Veintiuno Editores, 1980), p. 5. Further references are given in the text. My translations. Miller himself has also written a play, *The Golden Years,* where he investigates the topic. In an interesting article, María Sten compares a number of plays that portray Moctezuma, among them

those by Miller and Fuentes. Sten concludes that in all of the plays Moctezuma is basically pessimistic and defeated primarily by his own inner struggles; "Los múltiples rostros de Moctezuma Xocoyotzín en el teatro," *La Palabra y el Hombre* 26 (April-June 1978), 40–49.

4. Fuentes makes this point in his introduction to *All Cats are Gray*, p. 8.

5. For a discussion of Fuentes's use of ritual to externalize psychological conflicts in this play, see John Skirius, "Mexican Introspection in the Theater: Carlos Fuentes," *Revista de Estudios Hispánicos* 12, i (1978), 25–40.

6. See Lanin Gyurko, "Fuentes and the Ancient Aztec Past: The Role of Moctezuma in *Todos los gatos son pardos,*" in Juan Loveluck and Isaac Levy, eds. *Simposio Carlos Fuentes: Actas* (Columbia, South Carolina: University of South Carolina, Department of Foreign Languages and Literatures, 1980), p. 209.

7. Gyurko compares Fuentes's portrait of Moctezuma to several other versions. According to Gyurko, Fuentes's view of him accords with that recorded by Fray Sahagún in the 16th century; Sahagún's informers apparently characterized Moctezuma as "a weak and cowardly king." Bernal Díaz, on the other hand, whose account is more widely known in Mexico, evokes a respected ruler, dignified even in defeat; "The Role of Moctezuma," p. 197.

8. For a full discussion of La Malinche in Fuentes's play, see the excellent article by Lanin Gyurko, "The Vindication of La Malinche in Fuentes' *Todos los gatos son pardos,*" *Ibero-Amerikanisches Archiv* 3, iii (1977), 233–66.

9. From the introduction to *All Cats are Gray*, p. 6.

10. James Stais suggests a further resonance for the title: the killing of Moctezuma shows that, finally, all men are the same, and puts an end to the distinction between gods and men: "*Todos los gatos son pardos:* Un acto de rebelión en nueve escenas," in Giacoman, p. 471.

11. "Diálogo con Carlos Fuentes," in Levy and Loveluck, eds., *Simposio Carlos Fuentes.*

SCENES FROM THE CITY: SHORT STORIES

1. In discussing Fuentes's short stories, I have concentrated on those he has included in *Burnt Water,* since it is the most readily available source in English.

2. The book by Laurette Séjourné, *Burning Water: Thought and Religion in Ancient Mexico,* trans. Irene Nicholson (1957; reprinted Berkeley: Shambhala Publications, 1976), may have suggested the title to Fuentes, who is familiar with Séjourné's work, having dedicated his essay on *París, la revolución de mayo* to her.

3. Harss, p. 294.

4. Paz, *The Labyrinth of Solitude,* p. 11.

5. Lanin Gyurko argues that "the final victory belongs neither to the overambitious Filiberto nor to the atrocious Chac Mool but to time and to the tremendous power of twentieth century materialism, which even the gods cannot resist"; "Social Satire and the Gods," p. 120. For a detailed discussion of this story, see Shirley A. Williams, "Prisoners of the Past: Three Fuentes Short Stories from *Los días enmascarados,*" *Journal of Spanish Studies, Twentieth Century* 6, i (1978), 39–52.

6. The four other stories in *Los días enmascarados* are similarly fantastic, perhaps even more allegorical, but the magical intrusions in them come less specifically from the past. The intrusions disturb characters who fail to deal with them, and thus constitute an implicit criticism of societies with limited imaginative powers. For information about four early *uncollected* short stories by Fuentes, see Richard Reeve, "An Annotated Bibliography on Carlos Fuentes," p. 626. Reeve maintains that the theme of the inescapable past unites the stories in *Los días enmascarados;* "Carlos Fuentes and The New Short Story in Mexico," *Studies in Short Fiction* 8 (1971), 169–79.

7. See Julio Cortázar, *End of the Game and Other Stories,* trans. Paul Blackburn (New York: Harper and Row, 1978).

8. Two stories in *Cantar de ciegos* do not appear in *Burnt Water:* "A la víbora de la mar" ("Into the Sea Serpent") and "Fortuna lo que ha querido" (the latter recently translated by Margaret Sayers Peden as "Man Proposes

. . ." and published in the *Denver Quarterly* 14, i (Spring 1979), 15–26.

9. Luis Harss proposes another interpretation, focusing on the narrative vision rather than the characters in the stories. For him, the title alludes to the old belief that the blind can see into men's hearts and reveal their secret crimes; p. 303.

10. Mario Benedetti maintains that all the stories in *Cantar de ciegos* portray characters who succumb to a mirage; p. 104.

11. M. Durán, pp. 75–76.

3. POETICS AND POLITICS: THE ESSAYS

1. Juan Loveluck notes the interdependence of fiction and essay in modern Latin American literature in his "Crísis y renovación de la novela hispanoamericana," the introduction to *La novela hispanoamericana,* ed. Loveluck (Santiago: Editorial Universitaria, 1969). Rodríguez Monegal also discusses the common concerns of essayists and writers of fiction in *Narradores de esta américa,* I.

2. Carlos Fuentes, *Tiempo mexicano,* 7th ed. (1971; Mexico City: Joaquín Mortiz, 1978), pp. 56–92. Further references are given in the text. My translations.

3. Fuentes's articles originally appeared in a wide variety of journals throughout the world. The essays on Austen and Melville form prologues to Mexican editions of *Pride and Prejudice* and *Moby Dick.* The studies on Adami and Cuevas originally appeared as exhibition catalogues (see bibliography). Immediately preceding his two volumes of essays, Fuentes published a short book about the 1968 Paris student riots, *París, la revolución de mayo,* illustrated with photographs of the events. The piece starts and ends in gestures of solidarity with the French students, with the idea that finally, "this revolution is ours too."

4. In *The Labyrinth of Solitude,* Paz discusses the Revolution as a fiesta—an explosive moment when people let their daily masks fall momentarily; p. 149

5. Fuentes, "Opciones críticas en el verano de nuestro descontento," *Plural* (August 1972), p. 4.

6. In a recent article called "Tomás y Nicolás hablan de políti-

ca," Fuentes satirizes a whole list of imaginary dangers from which the continued monopoly of the PRI saves Mexico: takeovers by emperors or communists, the election of "Cantinflas" as president, a Texas invasion, a restoration of the reactionary triumvirate—the clergy, the landowners, and the military. Amusingly enough, Tomás and Nicolás finally despair of agreeing on a democratic form of government and send a telegram inviting Solzhenitzyn to come and explain his authoritarian ideas in Mexico; *Vuelta,* No. 21 (August 1978), 29–32.

7. Fuentes, "El otro K," p. 29.

8. In reviewing John Womack's book on *Zapata and the Mexican Revolution,* Fuentes celebrates the temporary fulfillment of utopian community ideals in Zapata's state of Morelos in 1914–15; *Tiempo mexicano,* 141.

9. Fuentes, "Opciones críticas," p. 6.

10. See Fuentes's discussion of these questions in Janes, " 'No More Interviews,' " pp. 92–93.

11. Fuentes makes these points in "Opciones críticas." Gastón García Cantú has criticized Fuentes's position. He claims that because the constitution of Mexico accords the president so much power, a strong state simply means a strong executive, and there you are again, with a paternalistic structure; "El desafío y la marea," *Plural,* No. 57 (June 1976), 51–53.

12. See Janes, " 'No More Interviews,' " p. 92.

13. For a defense of Echeverría, see Fuentes, "Opciones críticas," p. 6.

14. Fortson, p. 14.

15. Interview with WBF, September, 1980.

16. Fuentes, "Opciones críticas," p. 4.

17. Commentators often stress the importance of linguistic innovation in recent Latin American narrative. Julio Ortega, for example, speaks of the "Latin American desire for a reality that is questioned by the breakup of language"; Preface, *La contemplación y la fiesta: Ensayos sobre la nueva novela latinoamericana* (Lima: Editorial Universitaria, 1968). Rodríguez Monegal locates Fuentes in a generation of writers who were particularly sensitive to language; *Narradores de esta américa,* I, 26.

18. This idea sets *The New Hispanic American Novel* in the same general category as the Cuban writer Roberto Fernández Retámar's well-known essay, *Caliban,* which discusses literary colonialism and independence in Latin America—though Retámar objects specifically to Fuentes's concentration on technique and his application of European linguistic analysis to Latin American texts. For a polemical comparison of Fuentes and Retámar, see Marta E. Sanchez, "Caliban: The New Latin American Protagonist of *The Tempest,*" *Diacritics* 6, i (1976), 54–61.

19. Carlos Fuentes, *La nueva novela hispanoamericana* (Mexico City: Joaquín Mortiz, 1969), p. 9. Further references are given in the text. My translations.

20. Fuentes puts it well in the appendix to his essay on Faulkner in *House with Two Doors:* "The writer, like Faulkner's idiots and old women, is the diachronic agitator of structures, the malevolent angel that takes temporary possession of language only because previously he has been possessed by language"; *Casa con dos puertas* (Mexico City: Joaquín Mortiz, 1970), p. 80. Further references are given in the text. My translations.

21. The Mexican painter José Luis Cuevas creates strange, often grotesque and partially deformed figures. Their contorted postures suggest that they have undergone mental or physical torture. They are monumental in shape and proportion—sometimes resembling Picasso's monolithic figures—but delicately drawn. Marta Traba proposes affinities with the work of Bacon, Cuevas, Dubuffet, and de Kooning; *Los Quatro Monstruos Cardinales: Bacon, Cuevas, Dubuffet, de Kooning* (Mexico City: Ediciones Era, 1965).

22. Fuentes, *El mundo de José Luis Cuevas,* pp. 7–8.

23. *Ibid.,* p. 10

24. *Ibid.,* p. 23.

25. The heroine of *An Obscure Object of Desire,* according to Fuentes, looks for desire alone, not for property; her desire is therefore surrealistic, revolutionary; "El límpido deseo de Luis Buñuel," *Vuelta,* no. 14 (January 1978), 32.

26. Fuentes, *El mundo de José Luis Cuevas,* p. 6.

27. Carlos Fuentes, *Cervantes o la crítica de la lectura* (Mexico

City: Joaquín Mortiz, 1976), pp. 15, 35. Further references
are given in the text. My translations. The title *Cervantes
or the Critique of Reading* refers to the Spanish version of
Fuentes's essay; there is an earlier English one, *Don Quixote or the Critique of Reading* (Austin: University of Texas
Press, The Hackett Memorial Lecture, 1975). I have used
the later version because it includes the final chapter on
Joyce and recent French criticism that does not appear in
the earlier version.

28. Fuentes applies the notion of multivocal reading to pre-
Columbian Mexican art; the ensemble of buildings at
Uxmal or an Olmec statue, for example, "demand several
readings" because "they exist at different levels": historical,
social, religious, psychological, esthetic, symbolic, physical, and metaphysical, real and "suprareal"; *Tiempo mexicano,* 18.

29. Hélène Cixous, "Joyce, la ruse de l'écriture," *Poétique* 1, iv
(1970), 419–20. The piece appears in a slightly revised form
as part of the "ensemble Joyce" in Cixous's *Prénoms de
personne* (Paris: Seuil, 1974).

30. Borges, "The Argentine Writer and Tradition," in *Labyrinths,* p. 181.

4.   LATER NOVELS, PSYCHOLOGY, POP, AND THE PAST

1. Fuentes constantly combats what he considers intellectual
complacency. It is not enough that Mexicans recognize the
value of the indigenous past; they must not become too
comfortable in that recognition, but rather question their
own position and look out for the dangers inherent in it.
Mexican muralism, according to Fuentes, while initially a
valuable contribution to national consciousness, "in following the trends of bourgeois nationalism, ended up by contributing to its strength: in a certain way, the Mexican
banker or bureaucrat who passes in front of the murals of
Rivera at the National Palace serves his conscience by
reasoning that he is the owner of a past and that he himself
represents the future. We are the fatherland"; *El mundo de
José Luis Cuevas,* p. 19. Perhaps this partially explains why

Fuentes himself has shifted some of his attention away from indigenous myth to history—in order not to become the writer who has comfortably appropriated his nation's past.

2. Fuentes's recent novels resemble his description of Buñuel's films, where open endings place responsibility on "the conscience and the imagination of each spectator"; *House with Two Doors,* p. 213.

3. M. Durán, pp. 125–26.

4. Paul Valéry, *Oeuvres,* II (Paris: La Pléiade, 1960), 477.

A MODERN IDOL: *HOLY PLACE*

1. Carlos Fuentes, "La Cultura en México," *Siempre!,* 470 (June 1962), vi.

2. M. Durán contrasts the destruction of Guillermo's will by his love to the triumph of Consuelo's will in creating Aura, who symbolizes the power of love over death; p. 112.

3. It is an open secret that Fuentes's model for Claudia was the well-known Mexican film star María Félix.

4. Carlos Fuentes, *Holy Place,* trans. Suzanne Jill Levine, in *Triple Cross* (New York: E. P. Dutton, 1972), p. 118. Further references are given in the text.

5. Carlos Fuentes, "Situación del escritor en América Latina," *Mundo Nuevo* 1 (July 1966), 15. G. Durán recognizes that underneath this Ulysses myth, Fuentes reveals what is perhaps the more basic myth of Oedipus; *La magia y las brujas,* p. 94.

6. Lanin Gyurko provides an excellent discussion of the classical models that underlie Guillermo's situation. Gyurko maintains that Guillermo "oscillates among the roles of Telemachus, Oedipus, and Orestes, as he varies between adoration of his mother and a vindictive desire to destroy her"; "The Myths of Ulysses in Fuentes' *Zona Sagrada,*" *Modern Language Review* 69 (1974), 320.

7. Cf. Fuentes: "Movie stars are the ghosts of gods"; Fortson, p. 85.

8. The ability to undergo metamorphoses is also a quality often attributed to witches. G. Durán argues convincingly that Claudia is at once witch and goddess, and that such

witch figures are not always old and ugly; "La bruja de
Carlos Fuentes," in Giacoman, p. 241.

9. Severo Sarduy, in an excellent article on "Un fetiche de
cachemira gris perla," in *Escrito sobre un cuerpo: Ensayos
de crítica* (Buenos Aires: Sudamericana, 1969), pp. 29–35,
maintains that Claudia is generally idolized as a face, and
that this presentation corresponds to a particular cinematic
technique: "Claudia Nervo belongs to the imaginary realm
of the close-up, her sign is a face that is static in its iconic
authority, immobile like a mask, reproduced a thousand
times, copied, imitated, distorted, broken down and put
back together at every point, obsessive, multiplying her
penetrating look, a butterfly printed with pupils, a totem."
She is a concept rather than a woman. According to Sarduy, this kind of face belongs to the "age of terror" in the
movies. Later on, we had the age of "charm," of individual-
ized faces.

10. See Salgado, "Supervivencia del mito azteca," p. 130.

11. G. Durán also notes that Claudia is the antithesis of the
"chingada"—the violated woman—incarnating instead the
"chingadora"—the violator; *La magia y las brujas,* p. 106.

12. Daniel de Guzmán lists "home base," "safety," and "sanctuary" as additional meanings of the Spanish "zona sagrada"; *Carlos Fuentes,* p. 125.

13. Severo Sarduy discusses how Guillermo transforms a gray
sweater of Claudia's into a veritable fetish—a sacred symbol of the Mother; "Un fetiche de cachemira," pp. 36–38.

14. Recall that as her reward for dancing in front of Herod,
Salome demanded the head of John the Baptist, who had
earlier refused her offers of love.

15. Boschi and Calabresi make the point that Fuentes's characters need mythic spaces and that if they cannot find them
they will invent them; this may explain the artificial nature
of Guillermo's room in *Holy Place;* p. 44.

16. Todorov, *The Fantastic,* p. 114. Todorov gives two similar
examples. Instead of a person just "cavorting like a monkey" or "eating like a lion," he is turned into a monkey or
a lion.

Breaking Mental Habits: *A Change of Skin*

1. Carlos Fuentes, *A Change of Skin,* trans. Sam Hileman (New York: Farrar, Straus and Giroux, 1968), p. 278. Further references are given in the text.
2. Monegal, *El arte de narrar,* p. 124.
3. John M. Lipski makes a similar point in his discussion of "La estructura holográfica de *Cambio de piel,*" Levy and Loveluck, eds., *Simposio Carlos Fuentes,* p. 130.
4. Lanin Gyurko offers another interpretation. He maintains that the shifting identities in the novel represent a desire not a reality. Elizabeth, Javier, and Franz are all searching for a "change of skin" that would "mean rejuvenation or redemption," but they do not achieve it; "El yo y su imagen en *Cambio de piel* de Carlos Fuentes," *Revista Iberoamericana* 37 (1971), 693. Perhaps only the narrator —and perhaps he is crazy—can achieve changes of skin through his fiction. Jaime Giordano discusses the novel's denial of saving inventions, like music and love, and its possibly dangerous affirmation of the power of invention itself; "Preguntas a propósito de *Cambio de piel,* o de como un narrador podría desacreditar a su autor," Levy and Loveluck, eds., *Simposio Carlos Fuentes,* pp. 143–50.
5. Mircea Eliade, *Le mythe de l'éternel retour: archétypes et répétition* (Paris: Gallimard, 1969), p. 30.
6. Boschi and Calabrese stress the sacrificial nature of Franz's death, complete with a knife covered in sacred blood to nourish the Aztec gods. Franz is judged by the younger generation, for the mythic pattern dictates that the old must die and the new arrive. Thus here, as in the Aztec world, death serves to nourish life; pp. 54–55. I believe this mythic interpretation is more fitting here than in the case of Artemio Cruz. Even so, it tends to overlook the negative components of genocide and retribution implicit in a more historical perspective.
7. Julio Ortega sees the third part of the novel with the scenes in the pyramid and the brothel and the trial of Franz as a narrative conflagration, a synthesis of time and space, which abolishes and recuperates the characters—a fearful fiesta or breaking of barriers; "Carlos Fuentes: *Cambio de*

piel," in Giacoman, pp. 121–22. Boschi and Calabrese make a similar point, p. 30

8. Lipski, "La estructura holográfica," p. 134–35.

9. Monegal, *El arte de narrar,* p. 123.

10. Lanin Gyurko affirms the multivocal nature of *A Change of Skin* by focusing on the multiple selves it presents: "The self becomes an image. It is conjured, multiplied, divided, fused with movies, sculpture, painting, and music. . . . The unity and continuity of the self disappear and are replaced by alienation and disintegration. . . . *A Change of Skin* is a narrative of the plural self"; "El yo y su imagen," p. 709.

11. Doezma, p. 497.

12. Fuentes also explains that the character of Louis Lambert prefigures that of Nietzsche; his mind ran too fast for ordinary man, who consequently considered him crazy. This, he says, is how we might regard Freddy Lambert. He knows the story too well and therefore he tells it so fast that we have to fill in the gaps he leaves; Doezma, p. 497.

13. Gyurko discusses *A Change of Skin* as a story of various failed artists in "The Artist Manqué in Fuentes' *Cambio de piel,"* *Symposium* 31 (1977), 126–50.

14. Doezma, p. 495.

15. Gyurko discusses the many similarities between *The Cabinet of Dr. Caligari*—one of the films in Freddy Lambert's trunk—and *A Change of Skin.* Gyurko also argues that Elizabeth first gains freedom through her identification with heroines in movies, but that she finally becomes trapped in these fantasy images of herself; "The Artist Manqué," pp. 146–47. Richard Reeve notes that in *A Change of Skin* Buenos Aires is seen through Argentine films of the thirties, Europe as if in old postcards; "Carlos Fuentes," p. 128.

16. Monegal, *El arte de narrar,* p. 131.

17. *Ibid.,* p. 124.

18. Ortega, "Carlos Fuentes: *Cambio de piel,"* in Giacoman, p. 118.

19. Edith Grossman documents several instances of specific idenfication between the pyramids at Cholula and the Nazi camp at Theresienstadt, both unified by the theme of madness; "Myth and Madness in Carlos Fuentes' *A Change of*

Skin," *Latin American Literary Review* 3, v (1974), 100–102.

20. M. Durán, p. 112.
21. Doezma, p. 499.

OLD AND NEW WORLDS: *TERRA NOSTRA*

1. Juan Goytisolo maintains that the dreamlike sequences in the novel cause us to reflect on actual history, which "serves Fuentes as his basic point of reference." And in addition to being a rewriting of history to include what history hasn't said, the novel is also a rewriting of other books—particularly, as Goytisolo has said, "a deliberate exploration of the literary space opened up by Cervantes"; "Our Old New World," *Review* 19 (1976), 13, 19.

2. Note that Pollo's name is a modernized version of the name for the Greek god Phoebus Apollo—the god of the sun and of poetry. This particular version comes from Ezra Pound (as Michael Wood points out in his review, "The New World and the Old Novel," *INTI* 5–6 [1977], 110).

3. Carlos Fuentes, *Terra Nostra,* trans. Margaret Sayers Peden (New York: Farrar, Straus and Giroux, 1976), p. 29. Further references are given in the text.

4. José Miguel Oviedo considers the sentence central. For him it suggests the mobility of events, their rapid transformations into others often opposite to themselves. All of this (as we shall see) rests "on a system of multiple narrators that cede to each others' voices in an uninterrupted chain that tends toward circularity"; "Sinfonía del nuevo mundo," *Hispamérica* 6, no. 16 (1977), 27.

5. Interview with WBF, September, 1980.

6. In one of several schemas for the novel, Fuentes notes that El Señor conquers America because there he can freeze Spain—or so he thinks. In a section of manuscript notes entitled "consequences new world" Fuentes writes: "the marvelous mystery of the American myth destroys, makes dust of, El Señor's complicated theories"; Carlos Fuentes Papers, Firestone Library, Princeton University; special collections.

7. In Fuentes's working papers for *Terra Nostra* are quantities of notes concerning the number three. One of them that Fuentes seems to have marked specially, and which appears in *Terra Nostra,* states that three "stands for the ultimate and the action of the agencies of time—past, present, and future" (from Walter Gibson, *The Sciences of Numerology*); Fuentes Papers, Princeton. Fuentes has also said that the figures in *Terra Nostra* yearn for the number three, but can never reach it; Interview with WBF, September, 1980. William Siemens argues that the division of the pilgrims into three abolishes the fratricidal conflict that might ensue were they two. It thus permits them to constitute a unity representing life that does battle with El Señor, who represents death; "El héroe y el juego de opuestos en *Terra nostra,*" Lévy and Loveluck, eds., *Simposio Carlos Fuentes,* p. 156.

8. See, for example, Erich Neumann's discussion in his book *The Origins and History of Consciousness* (New York: Pantheon, 1954).

9. Regina Janes agrees that the ending of *Terra Nostra* contrasts with the rest of the novel: "The return to androgyny fulfills the promise of unity even as it denies the promise of multiplicity. But the book itself is an enactment of multiplicity, a statement that defies its own resolution"; *"Terra Nostra:* Charting the Terrain," *The Literary Review* 23, ii (1980), 266.

10. Interview with WBF, September, 1980.

11. From the Annals of Cuauhtitlán, quoted in Séjourné, *Burning Water,* p. 58, a book, with which, as we have noted, Fuentes is familiar.

12. G. Durán, *The Archetypes of Carlos Fuentes,* p. 37.

13. Mikhail Bakhtin, *Rabelais and His World,* trans. Helen Iswolsky (Cambridge: MIT Press, 1968), p. 318.

14. In his manuscript notes Fuentes sets down "the paradox of La Señora's vampirism: instead of taking life away, she gives it, confers it"; Fuentes Papers, Princeton.

15. There have been a number of discussions about who might be imagined as the "original" narrator of *Terra Nostra,* the one who sits over all the others; see, for example, Juan Goytisolo, "Our Old New World," pp. 3, 48–50; and

Roberto González Echevarría, *"Terra nostra* and *Cervantes o la crítica de la lectura,"* World Literature Today, 52, i (1978), 84. I would agree with Lucille Kerr that the continual shifts in perspective make it impossible to establish a primary narrator; "The Paradox of Power and Mystery: Carlos Fuentes' *Terra nostra,"* PMLA 95, i (1980), 95.

16. Walter L. Reed ends his book, *An Exemplary History of the Novel: The Quixotic versus the Picaresque* (Chicago: University of Chicago Press, 1981), with a brief discussion of *Terra Nostra* because it illustrates the continuing vitality of the picaresque and Quixotic traditions as well as the interaction of history and fiction. María Teresa Fernández Muñoz sees Fuentes's extensive use of earlier works and historical figures as a reappropriation of literary contexts, a break with the language of conquest; "El lenguaje profanado: *Terra Nostra* de Carlos Fuentes," *Cuadernos Hispanoamericanos* 359 (1980), 419–28.

17. This passage virtually duplicates part of *Cervantes or the Critique of Reading,* p. 81.

18. Milan Kundera claims that *Terra Nostra* epitomizes the contemporary novel's capacity "to become that privileged space [a "holy place" perhaps] where humanity's distant past can fraternize with the present"; "Esch est Luther," *La Quinzaine Littéraire* 16 (16–30 March 1981), 7.

19. See Tzvetan Todorov's formulations in "Narrative—Men," *The Poetics of Prose,* trans. Richard Howard (Ithaca: Cornell University Press, 1977), p. 66.

20. Pere Gimferrer believes the novel evokes a collective Hispanic persona called "I" or "History" or "The Spains"; "El mapa y la máscara," *Plural* 5, no. 10 (July 1976), 58. For Zunilda Gertel, "The identity of the narrators masks itself in a protean I-you-he (we) that covers and discovers the absence of all individuality"; "Semiótica, historia y ficción en *Terra Nostra,"* Revista Iberoamericana 116–17 (July-December 1981), 65.

21. See Mario Vargas Llosa's discussion of *One Hundred Years of Solitude* in his *García Márquez: Historia de un deicidio* (Barcelona: Barral, 1971).

22. Fortson, 136. Lilvia Soto-Duggan maintains that history remembered (as it is in *Terra Nostra),* an act of imagina-

tion, is history's second chance, and provides access to a
primordial reality; *"Terra nostra:* memoria e imaginación,"
Levy and Loveluck, eds., *Simposio Carlos Fuentes,* p. 167.

23. The novel has received a mixed critical response. Partisans
stress the richness of its historico-fictional world and its
symbolic force; detractors complain of overcrowding and
too much theoretical exposition.

NEW RESOURCES, FAMILIAR PATTERNS: *THE HYDRA HEAD*

1. Monegal, *El arte de narrar,* p. 131.
2. As Lanin Gyurko has pointed out, *The Hydra Head* continues Fuentes's earliest preoccupations with national identity; "Individual and National Identity in Fuentes' *La cabeza
de la hidra,*" in Rose S. Minc., ed., *Latin American Fiction
Today* (Tacoma Park, Maryland: *Hispamérica,* 1980), pp.
33–47.
3. Interview with Fuentes by Jonathan Tittler, *Diacritics* 10,
iii (September 1980), 54.
4. Carlos Fuentes, *The Hydra Head,* trans. Margaret Sayers
Peden (New York: Farrar, Straus and Giroux, 1978), p.
226. Further references are given in the text.
5. Levy and Loveluck, eds., *Simposio Carlos Fuentes,* p. 217.
6. As usual, I recommend Professor Gyurko's article on *The
Hydra Head.* He argues "that Felix's birth on the occasion
of nationalization situates him at the point of a new beginning, but that his subsequent fate represents Fuentes' warning about the dangers of Reconquest"; "Individual and
National Identity," p. 33.
7. Gyurko has noted the parallel between the collaboration-
ists in Casablanca and Vichy France and the subversion
from within that the Director General and others like him
represent for Mexico. In both cases, foreign interests dominate without bloodshed through a nation's own leaders; "El
tema del doble en *La cabeza de la hidra,*" paper presented
at the XXth Congress of the Instituto Internacional de
Literatura Iberoamericana, Austin, Texas; March, 1981.
8. Lucrezio Pérez Blanco argues that the circular structure of
The Hydra Head challenges Mexicans to change the de-

structive repetitions of history; *"La cabeza de la hidra* de Carlos Fuentes: Novela-ensayo de estructura circular," *Cuadernos Americanos* 221, (1978), 222.

"PROUSTITUTION"?? *DISTANT RELATIONS*

1. Fuentes pointed out to me that Mrs. Heredia "has already installed herself in [Branly's] house; she's already there with all her candlesticks, waiting for Branly to die. Then Branly will become the ghost and she will become the reality"; Interview with WBF, September, 1980.
2. Carlos Fuentes, *Distant Relations,* trans. Margaret Sayers Peden (New York: Farrar, Straus and Giroux, 1981), p. 172. Further references are given in the text.
3. Fuentes has confirmed that these resonances were intentional; Interview with WBF, September, 1980.
4. See John Barth, "The Literature of Exhaustion," *Atlantic Monthly* 220, ii (August 1967), 29–34.
5. Strangely enough, Carpentier died in the Spring of 1980 at about the time *Una familia lejana* was published in the original Spanish.
6. Fuentes wrote this in a letter to Gloria Durán on December 8, 1968. The letter is reprinted in *La magia y las brujas,* pp. 209–210 and in *The Archetypes of Carlos Fuentes,* pp. 204–5.
7. Janes, " 'No More Interviews,' " p. 92.
8. Interview with WBF, September, 1980.
9. *Ibid.*
10. Fuentes maintains that *Distant Relations* is in one sense a narrative reading of the poem "La Chambre voisine" ("The Neighboring Room") by Jules Supervielle (who was born in Uruguay but wrote in French). He says that "the very concentrated images of that poem become vast vistas of Paris in the novel"; *ibid.* Fuentes has made the poem an epigraph to the English translation of the novel.

5. CONCLUSION: THE MULTIVOCAL TEXT

1. From the forward by Geneviève Calame-Griaule to Marcel Griaule, *Dieu d'eau: Entretiens avec Ogotemmeli* (Paris: Fayard, 1975).

2. Fuentes, *La nueva novela hispanoamericana,* p. 31.

3. Monegal, *El arte de narrar,* p. 117.

4. Fuentes praises the contemporary Mexican artist José Luis Cuevas for leading viewers toward the perception of multiple identities in his work. He contrasts this with the univocal nature of Mexican mural art, which presents only one social message. Fuentes's words confirm the trajectory of his own work, for, even though *Where the Air Is Clear* is multivocal in nature and *Terra Nostra* implies a political stance, *Where the Air is Clear* resembles the earlier murals in its clear social message, while *Terra Nostra*—and even more, *Distant Relations*—approach the multiple identities Fuentes sees in Cuevas's work, moving away from the social commentary in the earlier "muralistic" mode.

5. See the conversation by Oscar Lewis, K. S. Karol, and Carlos Fuentes, "Diálogo: Pobreza, burguesía y revolución," *Mundo Nuevo* 11 (May 1967), 5–18; and a report in *The New York Times:* "Mexicans Debate Book on Poverty: *Children of Sanchez* Stirs Anger of the Nationalists" (February 21, 1963) 28:1.

6. Fuentes has recently suggested the presence of a collective voice even in Artemio Cruz's monologues: he wonders whether the *you* sections are "perhaps the Mexican people —the collective voice—speaking to Artemio Cruz"; "Diálogo con Fuentes," in Levy and Loveluck, eds. *Simposio Carlos Fuentes,* p. 225.

7. According to Fuentes, America was discovered and invented as a utopia; that was immediately denied by the concrete necessities of history and the land was forced to enter the epic mode under whose sign it has lived during most of its existence. The only way out of this worn-out epic mode is a mythic possibility of reactivating the past and reducing it to human proportions; Monegal, *El arte de narrar,* p. 133.

8. Fuentes, *Tiempo mexicano,* p. 43.

9. Monegal, *El arte de narrar,* p. 128.

10. For a brief discussion of the importance of masks in Fuentes's work, see Octavio Paz, "Mask and Transparency," in *Alternating Current,* pp. 40–45.

11. "Diálogo con Carlos Fuentes," in Levy and Loveluck, eds., *Simposio Carlos Fuentes,* p. 222.

12. Fuentes, *Burnt Water,* p. 12.

13. M. Durán describes the intertextual nature of Fuentes's works by maintaining that often in penetrating a novel by Fuentes we "traverse various layers of literature," both outside and inside the characters; p. 56.

14. Fuentes, "Opciones críticas," p. 9.

15. M. Durán suggests that Fuentes's later works propose "oriental" or "primitive" notions of "the transmigration of souls, doubles, and the recurrence of types, faces, attitudes." In this, they go beyond individual experience. They also connect early and contemporary times, both characterized by communal forms of life—tribe or corporation; pp. 125–26.

16. Julio Ortega explores another kind of "voice" Fuentes and other contemporary Latin American novelists include in their texts; this is the self-reflexive voice of criticism: "The critique installed in the operation of writing itself stems from the fragmentation and from the various implied speakers: the narrative persona, the complex *I* of the neighboring *he,* deny univocality because they deny classical development. Thus, the different faces are different moments in a geometry whose potential for order derives from transmutation: deaths and rebirths compromise the whole shape of these verbal worlds"; *La contemplación y la fiesta,* p. 13.

17. Fuentes, *El mundo de José Luis Cuevas,* p. 9.

18. Fortson, p. 152.

Bibliography

WORKS BY CARLOS FUENTES

Los días enmascarados. Mexico City: Los Presentes, 1954.

La región más transparente. Mexico City: Fondo de Cultura Económica, 1958.

Las buenas conciencias. Mexico City: Fondo de Cultura Económica, 1959.

La muerte de Artemio Cruz. Mexico City: Fondo de Cultura Económica, 1962.

Aura. Mexico City: Ediciones Era, 1962.

Cantar de ciegos. Mexico City: Joaquín Mortiz, 1964.

Cambio de piel. Mexico City: Joaquín Mortiz, 1967.

Zona sagrada. Mexico City: Siglo XXI Editores, 1967.

París, la revolución de mayo. Mexico City: Ediciones Era, 1968.

Righe per Adami. Venice: Alpieri, 1968.

Cumpleaños. Mexico City: Joaquín Mortiz, 1969.

El mundo de José Luis Cuevas. Bilingual Edition, trans. Consuelo de Aerenlund. Mexico City: Galería de Arte Misrachi, 1969.

La nueva novela hispanoamericana. Mexico City: Joaquín Mortiz, 1969.

Casa con dos puertas. Mexico City: Joaquín Mortiz, 1970.

Todos los gatos son pardos. Mexico City: Siglo XXI Editores, 1970.

El tuerto es rey. Mexico City: Joaquín Mortiz, 1970.

Tiempo mexicano. Mexico City: Joaquín Mortiz, 1970.

Terra Nostra. Barcelona: Seix Barral, 1975.

Don Quixote or the Critique of Reading. Austin: Institute of

Latin American Studies, University of Texas at Austin, 1976.

Cervantes o la crítica de la lectura. Mexico City: Joaquín Mortiz, 1976.

La cabeza de la hidra. Barcelona: Argos, 1978.

Una familia lejana. Mexico City: Ediciones Era, 1980.

Agua quemada. Mexico City: Fondo de Cultura Económica, 1981.

TRANSLATIONS

La región más transparente: Where the Air is Clear, trans. Sam Hileman. New York: Ivan Obolensky, 1960.

Las buenas conciencias: The Good Conscience, trans. Sam Hileman. New York: Ivan Obolensky, 1961.

La muerte de Artemio Cruz: The Death of Artemio Cruz, trans. Sam Hileman. New York: Ivan Obolensky, 1964.

Aura: Aura, trans. Lysander Kemp. Bilingual Edition. New York: Farrar, Straus and Giroux, 1968.

Cambio de piel: A Change of Skin, trans. Sam Hileman. New York: Farrar, Straus and Giroux, 1968.

Zona sagrada: Holy Place, trans Suzanne Jill Levine, in *Triple Cross.* New York: E. P. Dutton, 1972.

Terra Nostra: Terra Nostra, trans. Margaret Sayers Peden. New York: Farrar, Straus and Giroux, 1976.

La cabeza de la hidra: The Hydra Head, trans. Margaret Sayers Peden. New York: Farrar, Straus and Giroux, 1978.

Agua quemada: Burnt Water, trans. Margaret Sayers Peden. New York: Farrar, Straus and Giroux, 1980.

Una familia lejana: Distant Relations, trans. Margaret Sayers Peden. New York: Farrar, Straus and Giroux, 1982.

Note: I have not included here the hundreds of articles Fuentes has published in periodicals in Mexico and throughout the world. For a comprehensive list of Fuentes's articles and for a complete annotated bibliography of works on Fuentes, see Richard Reeve, "An Annotated Bibliography on Carlos Fuentes," *Hispania,* 53

(1970), 597–652. Professor Reeve is preparing an updated bibliography, which should appear in 1983.

WORKS ON CARLOS FUENTES

BOOKS

Befumo Boschi, Liliana, and Calabresi, Elisa. *Nostalgia del futuro en la obra de Carlos Fuentes.* Buenos Aires: Fernando García Cambeiro, 1974.

Brody, Robert, and Rossman, Charles, eds. *Carlos Fuentes: A Critical View.* Austin: University of Texas Press, 1982 (forthcoming).

Carranza, Luján. *Aproximación a la literatura del mexicano Carlos Fuentes.* Santa Fé, Argentina: Colmegna, 1974.

Durán, Gloria. *La magia y las brujas en la obra de Carlos Fuentes.* Mexico City: Universidad Nacional Autónoma de México, 1976. English version (enlarged and revised): *The Archetypes of Carlos Fuentes: From Witch to Androgyne.* Hamden, Connecticut: The Shoe String Press, 1980.

García Gutiérrez, Georgina. *Los disfraces: La obra mestiza de Carlos Fuentes.* Mexico City: El Colegio de México, 1981.

Giacoman, Helmy F., ed.. *Homenaje a Carlos Fuentes: Variaciones en torno a su obra.* New York: Las Américas, 1971.

Guzmán, Daniel de. *Carlos Fuentes.* New York: Twayne, 1972.

Loveluck, Juan, and Levy, Isaac, eds. *Simposio Carlos Fuentes: Actas.* University of South Carolina, Department of Foreign Languages and Literatures: Hispanic Studies Number 2, 1980.

Ortega Martínez, Fidel. *Carlos Fuentes y la realidad de México.* Mexico City: published by the author, 1969.

Sánchez Reyes, Carmen. *Carlos Fuentes y La región más transparente.* UPREX Estudios Literarios Number 45. San Juan, Puerto Rico: University of Puerto Rico, 1975.

INTERVIEWS

Carballo, Emmanuel. "Carlos Fuentes." *Diecinueve protagonistas de la literatura mexicana del siglo XX.* Mexico City: Empresas Editoriales, 1965, pp. 427–448.

Coddou, Marcelo. "Terra Nostra o la crítica de los cielos. Entrevista a Carlos Fuentes." *American Hispanist* 3, no. 24 (1978), 8–10.

Doezma, Herman P. "An Interview with Carlos Fuentes." *Modern Fiction Studies* 18, iv (Winter 1972–73), 491–503.

Fortson, James R. *Perspectivas mexicanas desde París: Un diálogo con Carlos Fuentes.* Pamphlet, supplement to the magazine *El.* Mexico City: Corporación Editorial, 1973.

Fuentes, Carlos. Autobiographical statement in *Los narradores ante el público.* Mexico City: Joaquín Mortiz, 1966, First Series, pp. 137–55.

Fuentes, Carlos, Lewis, Oscar, and Karol, K. S. "Diálogo: Pobreza, burguesía, y revolución." *Mundo Nuevo,* 11 (May 1967), 5–18.

Fuentes, Carlos *et al.* "Izquierda, subdesarollo y guerra fría: Un coloquio sobre cuestiones fundamentales." *Cuadernos Americanos,* 19 (May–June 1960), 53–69.

Janes, Regina. " 'No More Interviews:' A Conversation with Carlos Fuentes." *Salmagundi,* 43 (Winter 1979), 87–95.

MacAdam, Alfred, and Coleman, Alexander. "An Interview with Carlos Fuentes." *Book Forum* 4 (1978–79), 672–85.

Mc Shane, Frank. "A Talk with Carlos Fuentes." *New York Times Book Review,* 7 (Nov. 1976), 50.

Monegal, Emir Rodríguez. "Carlos Fuentes." *El arte de narrar: Diálogos.* Caracas: Monte Avila, 1968), pp. 113–46.

Moyers, Bill. "The Many Worlds of Carlos Fuentes," 2 parts. Transcripts of television interviews on *Bill Moyers' Journal,* WNET/Thirteen, Library No. M-46, Show No. 520 and Library No. M-48, Show No. 522, 1980.

Tittler, Jonathan. "Interview: Carlos Fuentes." *Diacritics* 10, iii (Sept 1980), 46–56.

Torres Fiero, Danubio. "Carlos Fuentes: Miradas al mundo actual." *Vuelta* 43 (1980), 41–44.

ARTICLES

Avellaneda, Andrés O. "Mito y negación de la historia en *Zona sagrada* de Carlos Fuentes." *Cuadernos Americanos*, 175 (1971), 239–248.

Bland, Carole C. "Carlos Fuentes' *Cambio de piel:* The Quest for Rebirth." *Journal of Spanish Studies* 4, ii (Fall 1976), 77–88.

Brushwood, John S. "Sobre el referente y la transformación narrativa en las novelas de Carlos Fuentes y Gustavo Sainz." *Revista Iberoamericana*, 116–17 (Jul-Dec 1981), 49–54.

Ciccone, Antonio J. "La reencarnación sobrenatural como elemento fantástico en *Los días enmascarados* de Carlos Fuentes." *Otros mundos, otros fuegos: Fantasía y realismo mágico en Iberoamérica. Memoria del XVI Congreso Internacional de Literatura Iberoamericana.* Donald A. Yates, ed. East Lansing: Michigan State University, Latin American Studies Center, 1975, 113–16.

————. "The Supernatural Persistence of the Past in *Los días enmascarados* by Carlos Fuentes." *Latin American Literary Review*, 3, vi (1975), 37–58.

Durán, Gloria. "Carlos Fuentes, *Cumpleaños:* A Mythological Interpretation of an Ambiguous Novel." *Latin American Literary Review*, 2, iv (Spring–Summer, 1974), 75–86.

Durán, Manuel. "Carlos Fuentes." *Tríptico mexicano: Juan Rulfo, Carlos Fuentes, Salvador Elizondo.* Mexico City: Secretaria de Educación Pública, 1973.

Eyzaguirre, Luis B. "Carlos Fuentes y el héroe malogrado." *El héroe en la novela hispanoamericana del siglo XX.* Santiago: Editorial Universitaria, 1973, pp. 293–312.

Faris, Wendy B. "*Ulysses* in Mexico: Carlos Fuentes." *Comparative Literature Studies,* 19, ii (1982), 236–53.

Fernández Muñoz, María Teresa. "El lenguaje profanado: *Terra Nostra* de Carlos Fuentes." *Cuadernos Hispanoamericanos* 359 (1980), 419–428.

Fogelquist, James D. "Tiempo y mito en *Cambio de piel.*" *Cuadernos Americanos* 231 (1980), 96–107.

Foster, David W. "*La región más transparente* and the Limits of Prophetic Art." *Hispania* 56 (1973), 35–42.

García de Aldridge, Adriana. "La dialéctica contemporánea: 'tiempo propio-tiempo total' en *Cumpleaños.*" *Revista Iberoamericana* 108–109 (Jul-Dec 1979), 513–36.

Gertel, Zunilda. "Semiótica, historia y ficción en *Terra nostra.*" *Revista Iberoamericana* 116–17 (July–December 1981), 63–72.

González, Eduardo. "Fuentes' *Terra Nostra.*" *Salmagundi,* 41 (1978), 148–52.

González Echevarría, Roberto. *"Terra Nostra:* Teoría y práctica."* *Revista Iberoamericana* 116–17 (July–December 1981), 289–98.

Goytisolo, Juan. "Our Old New World." *Review* (Center for Inter-American Relations) 19 (1976), 5–24.

Grossman, Edith. "Myth and Madness in Carlos Fuentes' *A Change of Skin.*" *Latin American Literary Review* 3, v (1974), 97–110.

Gyurko, Lanin A. "Abortive Idealism and the Mask in Fuentes' *La región más transparente.*" *Revue des Langues Vivantes,* 42 (1976), 278–96.

———. "The Artist Manqué in Fuentes' *Cambio de piel.*" *Symposium* 31 (Summer 1977), 126–50.

———. "Individual and National Identity in Fuentes' *La cabeza de la hidra.*" *Latin American Fiction Today,* Rose S. Minc, ed. Montclair, New Jersey: Ediciones Hispamérica, 1980, pp. 33–48.

———. "The Myths of Ulysses in Fuentes' *Zona sagrada.*" *Modern Language Review,* 69 (1974).

———. "Social Satire and the Ancient Mexican Gods in the Narratives of Fuentes." *Ibero-Amerikanisches Archiv,* I, ii (1975), 113–50.

———. "Structure and Theme in Fuentes' *La muerte de Artemio Cruz.*" *Symposium,* 34 (Spring 1980), 29–41.

———. "The Vindication of La Malinche in Fuentes' *Todos los gatos son pardos.*" *Ibero-Americanisches Archiv,* 3, iii (1977), 233–66.

———. "El yo y su imagen en *Cambio de piel* de Carlos Fuentes." *Revista Iberoamericana* 76–77 (July–December 1971), 689–709.

Hall, Linda B. "The Cipactli Monster: Woman as Destroyer in Carlos Fuentes." *Southwest Review* 60 (1975), 246–55.

Harss, Luis, and Dohmann, Barbara, "Carlos Fuentes, or the New Heresy." *Into the Mainstream: Conversations with Latin American Writers.* New York: Harper and Row, 1967, pp. 276–309.

Hellerman, M. Kasey. "The Coatlicue-Malinche Conflict: A Mother and Son Identity Crisis in the Writings of Carlos Fuentes." *Hispania* 57 (1974), 868–75.

Janes, Regina. *"Terra Nostra:* Charting the Terrain." *The Literary Review* 23, ii (Winter 1980), 261–71.

Jansen, André. *"Todos los gatos son pardos,* o la defensa de la mexicanidad en la obra de Carlos Fuentes." *Explicación de Textos Literarios* 11, ii (1974), 83–94.

Kerr, Lucille. "The Paradox of Power and Mystery: Carlos Fuentes' *Terra Nostra."* *PMLA* 95, i (1980), 91–102.

Knight, Thomas J. and Werner, Flora M. " 'Timeliness' in Carlos Fuentes' *Cambio de piel."* *Latin American Literary Review* 4, vii (Fall–Winter 1975), 23–30.

Kundera, Milan. "Esch est Luther." *Quinzaine Littéraire* 16 (16–31 March 1981), 5–8.

Lemaître, Monique. "Enajenación y revolución en *Todos los gatos son pardos* de Carlos Fuentes." *Revista Iberoamericana* 112–23 (Jul-Dec 1980), 553–62.

McMurray, George R. *"Cambio de piel:* An Existential Novel of Protest." *Hispania,* 70 (1969), 150–54.

Rodríguez Monegal, Emir. "El México alucinado de Carlos Fuentes." *Narradores de esta américa,* II. Buenos Aires: Alfa, 1974, pp. 247–264.

Moody, Michael. "Existentialism, Mexico and Artemio Cruz." *Romance Notes* 10 (1968), 27–31.

Oviedo, José Miguel. "Fuentes: Sinfonía del nuevo mundo: *Hispamérica* 6, no. 16 (1977), 19–32.

Paz, Octavio. "Presentación de Carlos Fuentes en su conferencia inaugural en el Colegio Nacional el Martes 17 de octubre de 1972." *Memoria de El Colegio Nacional* 7, iii (1972), 223–26.

––––––. "Mask and Transparency." *Alternating Current,* trans. Helen R. Lane. New York: Viking, 1973, pp. 40–45.

Peden, Margaret S. "The World of the Second Reality in Three Novels by Carlos Fuentes." *Otros mundos, otros fuegos,* Yates ed., pp. 83–87.

Peñuela Canizal, Eduardo. "Myth and Language in a Play by Carlos Fuentes." *Latin American Theater Review,* 13, i (1979), 15–27.

Pérez Blanco, Lucrezio. "*La cabeza de la hidra* de Carlos Fuentes: Novelaensayo de estructura circular." *Cuadernos Americanos* 221 (1978), 205–22.

Reeve, Richard. "Los cuentos de Carlos Fuentes: De la fantasía al neorealismo." *El cuento hispanoamericano ante la crítica,* Enrique Pupo-Walker, ed. Madrid: Castalia, 1973, pp. 249–63.

———. "Carlos Fuentes and the New Short Story in Mexico." *Studies in Short Fiction* 8 (1971), 169–79.

———. "Octavio Paz and Hiperion in *La región más transparente:* Plagiarism, Caricature, or . . . ?" *Chasqui* 3, iii (1974), 13–25.

———. "Carlos Fuentes." *Narrativa y crítica de nuestra américa,* Joaquín Roy, ed. Madrid: Castalia, 1978, pp. 287–316.

———. "Un poco de luz sobre nueve años oscuros: Los cuentos desconocidos de Carlos Fuentes." *Revista Iberoamericana* 36 (1970), 473–80.

Rojas, Santiago. "Modalidad narrativa en *Aura:* Realidad y enajenación." *Revista Iberoamericana* 112–13 (July–December 1980), 487–98.

Sanchez, Marta E. "Caliban: The New Latin American Protagonist of 'The Tempest.' " *Diacritics* 6, i (Spring 1976), 54–61.

Seale-Vásquez, Mary. "Character and its Development in Fuentes' *A Change of Skin.*" *Latin American Literary Review* 6, no. 12 (1978), 68–85.

Shaw, Donald L. "Narrative Arrangement in *La muerte de Artemio Cruz.*" *Contemporary Latin American Fiction,* ed. Salvador Bacarisse. Edinburgh: Scottish Academic Press, 1980, pp. 34–47.

Skirius, John. "Mexican Introspection in the Theater: Carlos Fuentes." *Revista de Estudios Hispánicos* 12, i (1978), 25–40.

Siemens, William L. "Maniqueismo e inmortalidad en *Cumpleaños.*" *Explicación de Textos Literarios* I, ii (1974), 123–30.

Sommers, Joseph. "The Field of Choice: Carlos Fuentes." *After the Storm: Landmarks in the Modern Mexican Novel.* Al-

buquerque: University of New Mexico Press, 1968, pp. 133–
64.

Vidal, Hernán. "El modo narrativo en *La muerte de Artemio
Cruz.*" *Thesaurus: Boletín del Instituto Caro y Cuervo* 31
(1976), 300–326.

Williams, Shirley A. "Prisoners of the Past: Three Fuentes Short
Stories from *Los días enmascarados.*" *Journal of Spanish
Studies, Twentieth Century* 6, i (1978), 39–52.

————. "The Search for the Past: The Role of Aztec Mythology
in *La región más transparente.*" *Estudos Ibero-Americanos*
2, i (1976), 25–30.

Wood, Michael. "The New World and the Old Novel." *INTI*
5–6 (Spring–Fall 1977), 109–112.

Note: I have not listed separately the many excellent articles in the volumes edited by Giacoman and Loveluck and
Levy.

Index